Golden Numbers: A Book of Verse for Youth

by Smith and Wiggin

CONTENTS

INTRODUCTION
On the Reading of Poetry

There is no doubt, I fear, that certain people are born without, as certain other people are born with, a love of poetry. Any natural gift is a great advantage, of course, be it physical, mental, or spiritual. The dear old tales which suggest the presence of fairies at the cradle of the new-born child, dealing out, not very impartially, talents, charms, graces, are not so far from the real truth. You may have been given a straight nose, a rosy cheek, a courteous manner, a lively wit, a generous disposition; but perhaps the Fairy Fine-Ear, who hears the grass grow, and the leaf-buds throb, had a pressing engagement at somebody else's cradle-side when you most needed her benefactions. There is another elf too, a Dame o' Dreams; she is clad all in color-of-rose, and when she touches your eyelids you see visions forever after; beautiful haunting things hidden from duller eyes, visions made of stars and dew and magic. Never any great poet lived but these two fairies were present at his birth, and it may be that they stole a moment to visit you. If such was the case you love, need, crave poetry, to understand yourself, your neighbor, the world, God; and you will find that nothing else will satisfy you so completely as the years go on. If, on the other hand, these highly mythical but interesting personages were absent when the question of your natural endowment was being settled, do not take it too much to heart, but try to make good the deficiencies.

You must have liked the rhymes and jingles of your nursery-days:

Ride a Cock-horse To Banbury Cross!

or

Mistress Mary quite contrary How does your garden grow?

I am certain you remember what pleasure it gave you to make "contrary" rhyme with "Mary" instead of pronouncing it in the proper and prosy way.

"But" you answer, "I did indeed like that sort of verse, and am still fond of it when it dances and prances, or trips and patters and tinkles; it is what is termed "sublime" poetry that is dull and difficult to understand; the verb is always a long distance from its subject; the punctuation comes in the middle of the lines, so that it reads like prose in spite of one, and it is generally sprinkled with allusions to Calypso, Œdipus, Eurydice, Hesperus, Corydon, Arethusa, and the Acroceraunian Mountains; or at any rate with people and places which one has to look up in the atlas and dictionary."

Of course, all poems are not equally simple in sound and sense. It does not require much intelligence to read or chant Poe's Raven, and if one does not quite understand it, one is so taken captive by the weird, haunting music of the lines, the recurrence of phrases and repetition of words, that one does not think about its meaning:

"While I nodded, nearly napping, suddenly there came a tapping, As of some one gently rapping, rapping at my chamber door. ''Tis some visitor, I muttered, 'tapping at my chamber door— Only this, and nothing more.'"

The moment, however, that your eye falls upon the following lines from "Paradise Lost" you confess privately that if you were obliged to parse and analyze them the task would cause you a weary half-hour with Lindley Murray or Quackenbos.

"Adam the goodliest man of men since born His sons; the fairest of her daughters Eve. Under a tuft of shade that on a green Stood whispering soft, by a fresh fountain-side, They sat them down;"

Very well then, do not try to parse them; Paradise Lost was not written exclusively for the grammarians; content yourself with enjoying the picture; the frisking of the beasts of the earth, while Adam and Eve watched them from a fountain-side in Paradise.

No one need be ashamed of liking a good deal of rhyme and rhythm, swing and movement and melody in poetry; absolute perfection of form, though all too rarely attained, is one of the chief delights of the verse-lover. *The procession of beautiful sounds that is a poem,*" says Walter Raleigh. It is quite natural to love the music of verse before you catch the deeper thought, and you feel, in some of the greatest poetry, as if only the angels could have put the melodious words together. There is more in this music than meets the eye or ear; it is what differentiates prose from poetry, which, to quote Wordsworth, is the breath and finer spirit of all knowledge. Prose it is said can never be too truthful or too wise, but song is more than mere Truth and Wisdom, it is the "rose upon Truth's lips, the light in Wisdom's eyes." That is why the thought in it finds its way to the very heart of one and makes one glow and tremble, fills one with desire to do some splendid action, right some wrong, be something other than one is, more noble, more true, more patient, more courageous.

We who have selected the poems in this book have had to keep in mind the various kinds of young people who are to read it. The boys may wish that there were more story and battle poems, and verses ringing with spirited and war-like adventures; the girls may think that there are too many already; while both, perhaps, may miss certain old favorites like Horatius or The Ancient Mariner, omitted because of their great length. Some of you will yawn if the book flies open at Milton; some will be bored whenever they chance upon Pope; others will never read Wordsworth except on compulsion. Romantic little maids will turn away from "Tacking Ship off Shore," while their brothers will disdain "The Swan's Nest Among the Reeds"; but it was necessary to make the book for all sorts and conditions of readers, and such a volume must contain a taste of the best things, whether your special palate is ready for them or not. When you are twenty-one you may say, loftily, "I do not care for Pope and Dryden, I prefer Spenser and Tennyson, or Ben Jonson and Herrick," or whatever you really do prefer,—but now, although, of course, you have your personal likes and dislikes, you cannot be sure that they are based on anything real or that they will stand the test of time and experience.

So you will find between these covers we hope, a little of everything good, for we have searched the pages of the great English-speaking poets to find verses that you would either love at first sight, or that you would grow to care for as you learn

11

what is worthy to be loved. Where we found one beautiful verse, quite simple and wholly beautiful, we have given you that, if it held a complete thought or painted a picture perfect in itself, even although we omitted the very next one, which perhaps would have puzzled and wearied the younger ones with its involved construction or difficult phraseology.

Will you think, I wonder, that this very simple talk is too informal to be quite proper when one remembers that it is to serve as introduction to the greatest poets that ever lived? Informality is very charming in its place, no doubt (for so the thought might cross your mind), but one does not use it with kings and queens; still the least things, you know, may sometimes explain or interpret the greatest. The brook might say, "I am nothing in myself, I know, but I am showing you the way to the ocean; follow on if you wish to see something really vast and magnificent."

There are besides gracious courtesies to be observed on certain occasions. If a famous poet or author should chance to come to your village or city and appear before the people, someone would have to introduce the stranger and commend him to your attention; and if he did it modestly it would only be an act of kindliness; a wish to serve you and at the same time bespeak for him a gentle and a friendly hearing. Once introduced—Presto, change! If he is a great poet he is a great wizard; the words he uses, the method and manner in which he uses them, the cadence of his verse, the thoughts he calls to your mind, the way he brings the quick color to your cheek and the tear to your eye, all these savor of magic, nothing else. Who could be less than modest in his presence? Who could but wish to bring the whole world under his spell? You will readily be modest, too, when you confront these splendid poems, even although some of you may not wholly comprehend as yet their grandeur and their majesty; may not fully understand their claim to immortality. Where is there a girl who would not make a low curtsey to Shakespeare's Silvia, Milton's Sabrina, Wordsworth's Lucy, or Mrs. Browning's Elizabeth? And if there is a boy who could stand with his head covered before Horatius, Hervé Riel, Sir Launfal, or Motherwell's Cavalier he is not one of those we had in mind when we made this book. Neither is it altogether the personality of hero or heroine that fills us with reverence; it is the beauty and perfection of the poem itself that almost brings us to our knees in worship. A little later on you will have the same feeling of admiration and awe for Shelley's Skylark, Emerson's Snow Storm, Wordsworth's Daffodils, Keats's Daybreak, and for many another poem not included in this book, to which you must hope to grow. For it is a matter of growth after all, and growth, in mind and spirit, as in body, is largely a matter of will. It is all ours, the beauty in the world: your task is merely to enter into possession. Chaucer, Spenser, and Shakespeare are yours as much as another's. The great treasury of inspiring thoughts that has been heaped together as the ages went by, that "rich deposit of the centuries," is your heritage; if you wish to assert your heirship no one can say you nay; if you will to be a Crœsus in the things of the mind and spirit, no one can ever keep you poor.

We have brought you only English verse, so you must wait for the years to give you Homer, Virgil, Dante, Goethe, Schiller, Victor Hugo, and many another; and of English verse we have only given a hint of the treasures in store for you later on.

We have quoted you poems from the grand old masters, those "bards sublime,"

"Whose distant footsteps echo Through the corridors of Time,"

and many a verse:—

—"from some humbler poet Whose songs gushed from his heart As showers from the clouds of summer, Or tears from the eyelids start; Who through long days of labor, And nights devoid of ease, Still heard in his soul the music Of wonderful melodies."

Since you will not like everything in the book equally well, may we advise you how to use it? First find something you know and love, and read it over again. (Penitent, indeed, shall we be if it has been omitted!) The meeting will be like one with a dear playfellow and friend in a new and strange house, and the house will seem less strange after you have met and welcomed the friend.

Then search the pages until you see a verse that speaks to you instantly, catches your eye, begs you to read it, willy-nilly. There are dozens of such poems in this collection, as simple as if they had been written for six-year-olds instead of for the grown-up English-speaking world: little masterpieces like Tennyson's Brook, Kingsley's Clear and Cool, Shakespeare's Fairy Songs, Burns's Mountain Daisy, Emerson's Rhodora, Motherwell's Blithe Bird, Hogg's Skylark, Wordsworth's Pet Lamb, Scott's Ballads, and scores of others.

This so far is pure pleasure, but why not, as another step, find something difficult, something you instinctively draw back from? It will probably be Milton, Pope, Dryden, Browning, or Shelley. You cannot find any "story" in it; its rhymes do not run trippingly off the tongue; there are a few strange and unpronounceable words, the punctuation and phrasing puzzle you, and worse than all you are obliged to read it two or three times before you really understand its meaning. Very well, that is nothing to be ashamed of, and you surely do not want to be vanquished by a difficulty. You will realize some time or other that all learning, like all life, is a sort of obstacle race in which the strongest wins.

I once said to a dear old minister who was preaching to a very ignorant and unlearned congregation, "It must be very difficult, sir, for you to preach down to them"; for he was a man of rare scholarship and true wisdom;—"I try to be very simple a part of the time," he answered, "but not always; about once a month I fling the fodder so high in the rack that no man can catch at a single straw without stretching his neck!"

Now pray do not laugh at that illustration; smile if you will, but it serves the purpose. Just as we develop our muscles by exercising our bodies, so do we grow strong mentally and spiritually by this "stretching" process. You are not obliged to love an impersonal, remote, or complex poem intimately and passionately, but read it faithfully if you do not wish to be wholly blind and deaf to beauties of sense or sound that happier people see and hear. Joubert says most truly: "You will find poetry nowhere unless you bring some with you," but there are some splendid things in verse as in prose that you stand in too great awe of to love in any real, childlike way. It is never scenes from Paradise Lost that run through your mind when you are going to sleep. It is something with a lilt, like:

"Up the airy mountain, Down the rushy glen, We daren't go a-hunting For fear of little men;"

or a poem with a gallant action in it like Marco Bozzaris, or with a charming story like The Singing Leaves, or a mysterious and musical one, like Kubla Khan or The Bells, or something that when first you read it made you a little older and a little sadder, in an odd, unaccustomed way quite unlike that of real grief:

"A feeling of sadness and longing That is not akin to pain And resembles sorrow only As the mist resembles rain."

When you read that verse of Longfellow's afterwards you see that he has expressed your mood exactly. That is what it means to be a poet, and that is what poetry is always doing for us; revealing, translating thoughts we are capable of feeling, but not expressing.

Perhaps you will not for a long time see the beauty of certain famous reflective poems like Gray's Elegy, but we must include a few of such things whether they appeal to you very strongly or not, merely because it is necessary that you should have an acquaintance, if not a friendship, with lines that the world by common consent has agreed to call immortal. They show you, without your being conscious of it, show you by their lines "all gold and seven times refined,"—how beautiful the English language can be when it is used by a master of style. Young people do not think or talk very much about style, but they come under its spell unconsciously and respond to its influence quickly enough. To give a sort of definition: style is a way of saying or writing a thing so that people are *compelled to listen.* When you grow sensitive to beauty of language you become, in some small degree at least, capable of using it yourself. You could not, for instance, read daily these "honey-tongued" poets without gathering a little sweetness for your own unruly member.

There are certain spiritual lessons to be gained from many of these immortal poems, lessons which the oldest as well as the youngest might well learn. Turn to Milton's Ode on his Blindness. It is not easy reading, but you will begin to care for it when experience brings you the meaning of the line, "They also serve who only stand and wait." It is one of a class of poems that have been living forces from age to age; that have quickened aspiration, aroused energy, deepened conviction; that have infused a nobler ardor and loftier purpose into life wherever and whenever they were read.

Prefacing each of the divisions of this volume you will find a page or "interleaf" of comment on, and appreciation of, the poems that follow. These pages you may read or not as you are minded; they are only friendly or informal letters from an old traveller to a pilgrim who has just taken his staff in hand.

By and by you will add poem after poem to your list of favorites, and so, gradually, you will make your own volume of Golden Numbers, which will be far better than any book we can fashion for you. Perhaps you will copy single verses and whole poems in it and, later, learn them by heart. Such treasures of memory "will henceforth no longer be forgettable, detachable parts of your mind's furniture, but well-springs of instinct forever."

Kate Douglas Wiggin.

GOLDEN NUMBERS

INTERLEAVES
A Chanted Calendar

Here is the Year's Processional in verse; the story of her hours, her days, her seasons, told as only poets can, because they see and hear things not revealed to you and me, and are able by their magic to make us sharers in the revelation. Read the first six poems and ask yourself whether you have ever realized the glories of the common day; from the moment when morning from her orient chambers comes, and the lark at heaven's gate sings, to the hour when the moon, unveiling her peerless light, throws her silver mantle o'er the dark, and the firmament glows with living sapphires.

It is the task of poetry not only to say noble things, but to say them nobly; having beautiful fancies, to clothe them in beautiful phrases, and if you search these poems you will find some of the most wonderful word-pictures in the English language. How charming Drayton's description of the summer breeze:

"The wind had no more strength than this, That leisurely it blew, To make one leaf the next to kiss That closely by it grew."

If the day is dreary you need only read Lowell's "June Weather," and like the bird sitting at his door in the sun, atilt like a blossom among the leaves, your "illumined being" will overrun with the "deluge of summer it receives."

Then turn the page; the picture fades as you read Trowbridge's "Midwinter." The speckled sky is dim; the light flakes falter and fall slow; the chickadee sings cheerily; lo, the magic touch again and the house mates sit, as Emerson saw them,

"Around the radiant fireplace enclosed In a tumultuous privacy of storm."

I

A CHANTED CALENDAR

Daybreak

Day had awakened all things that be, The lark, and the thrush, and the swallow free, And the milkmaid's song, and the mower's scythe, And the matin bell and the mountain bee: Fireflies were quenched on the dewy corn, Glowworms went out, on the river's brim, Like lamps which a student forgets to trim: The beetle forgot to wind his horn, The crickets were still in the meadow and hill: Like a flock of rooks at a farmer's gun, Night's dreams and terrors, every one, Fled from the brains which are its prey, From the lamp's death to the morning ray.

Percy Bysshe Shelley.

Morning

Now morning from her orient chambers came, And her first footsteps touch'd a verdant hill: Crowning its lawny crest with amber flame, Silvering the untainted gushes of its rill, Which, pure from mossy beds of simple flowers By many streams a little lake did fill, Which round its marge reflected woven bowers, And, in its middle space, a sky that never lowers.

John Keats.

A Morning Song

Hark! hark! the lark at heaven's gate sings. And Phœbus 'gins arise, His steeds to water at those springs On chaliced flowers that lies; And winking Mary-buds begin To ope their golden eyes: With every thing that pretty bin, My lady sweet, arise: Arise, arise!

William Shakespeare.

From "Cymbeline."

Evening in Paradise

Now came still Evening on, and Twilight gray Had in her sober livery all things clad; Silence accompanied; for beast and bird— They to their grassy couch, these to their nests, Were slunk, all but the wakeful nightingale; She all night long her amorous descant sung; Silence was pleased: now glowed the firmament With living sapphires: Hesperus, that led The starry host, rode brightest, till the Moon, Rising in clouded majesty, at length Apparent queen, unveiled her peerless light, And o'er the dark her silver mantle threw.

John Milton.

From "Paradise Lost."

Evening Song

Shepherds all, and maidens fair, Fold your flocks up, for the air 'Gins to thicken, and the sun Already his great course hath run. See the dew-drops how they kiss Every little flower that is, Hanging on their velvet heads, Like a rope of crystal beads: See the heavy clouds low falling, And bright Hesperus down calling The dead Night from under ground; At whose rising, mists unsound, Damps and vapors fly apace, Hovering o'er the wanton face Of these pastures, where they come, Striking dead both bud and bloom: Therefore, from such danger lock Every one his lovèd flock; And let your dogs lie loose without, Lest the wolf come as a scout From the mountain, and, ere day, Bear a lamb or kid away; Or the crafty thievish fox Break upon your simple flocks. To secure yourselves from these, Be not too secure in ease; Let one eye his watches keep, Whilst the other eye doth sleep; So you shall good shepherds prove, And for ever hold the love Of our great god. Sweetest slumbers, And soft silence, fall in numbers On your eyelids! So, farewell! Thus I end my evening's knell.

John Fletcher.

Night

How beautiful is night! A dewy freshness fills the silent air; No mist obscures, nor cloud, nor speck, nor stain, Breaks the serene of heaven: In full-orb'd glory yonder Moon divine Rolls through the dark-blue depths. Beneath her steady ray The desert-circle spreads, Like the round ocean, girdled with the sky. How beautiful is night!

Robert Southey.

A Fine Day

Clear had the day been from the dawn, All chequer'd was the sky, Thin clouds like scarfs of cobweb lawn Veil'd heaven's most glorious eye. The wind had no more strength than this, That leisurely it blew, To make one leaf the next to kiss That closely by it grew.

Michael Drayton.

The Seasons

So forth issued the seasons of the year; First, lusty Spring, all dight in leaves of flowers That freshly budded, and new blooms did bear, In which a thousand birds had built their bowers.

Edmund Spenser.

From "The Faerie Queene."

The Eternal Spring

The birds their quire apply; airs, vernal airs, Breathing the smell of field and grove, attune The trembling leaves, while universal Pan, Knit with the Graces and the Hours in dance, Led on the eternal Spring.

John Milton.

March

The stormy March is come at last, With wind, and cloud, and changing skies; I hear the rushing of the blast That through the snowy valley flies.

Ah, passing few are they who speak, Wild, stormy month, in praise of thee; Yet though thy winds are loud and bleak, Thou art a welcome month to me.

For thou, to northern lands, again The glad and glorious sun dost bring; And thou hast joined the gentle train And wear'st the gentle name of Spring.

Then sing aloud the gushing rills In joy that they again are free, And, brightly leaping down the hills, Renew their journey to the sea.

Thou bring'st the hope of those calm skies, And that soft time of sunny showers, When the wide bloom, on earth that lies, Seems of a brighter world than ours.

William Cullen Bryant.

By courtesy of D. Appleton & Co., publishers of Bryant's Complete Poetical Works.

Spring

Now that the winter's gone, the earth hath lost Her snow-white robes; and now no more the frost Candies the grass or casts an icy cream Upon the silver lake or crystal stream: But the warm sun thaws the benumbèd earth, And makes it tender; gives a sacred birth To the dead swallow; wakes in hollow tree The drowsy cuckoo and the bumble-bee. Now do a choir of chirping minstrels bring In triumph to the world the youthful spring! The valleys, hills, and woods, in rich array, Welcome the coming of the longed-for May.

Thomas Carew.

Song to April

April, April, Laugh thy girlish laughter; Then, the moment after, Weep thy girlish tears! April, that mine ears Like a lover greetest, If I tell thee, sweetest, All my hopes and fears, April, April, Laugh thy golden laughter, But the moment after, Weep thy golden tears!

William Watson.

By courtesy of John Lane.

April in England

Oh, to be in England Now that April's there, And whoever wakes in England Sees, some morning, unaware, That the lowest boughs and the brushwood sheaf Round the elm-tree hole are in tiny leaf, While the chaffinch sings on the orchard bough In England—now!

And after April, when May follows, And the whitethroat builds, and all the swallows! Hark! where my blossomed pear-tree in the hedge Leans to the field, and scatters on the clover Blossoms and dewdrops,—at the bent spray's edge— That's the wise thrush; he sings each song twice over, Lest you should think he never could recapture The first fine careless rapture! And though the fields look rough with hoary dew, All will be gay when noontide wakes anew The buttercups, the little children's dower, —Far brighter than this gaudy melon flower.

Robert Browning.

April and May

April cold with dropping rain Willows and lilacs brings again, The whistle of returning birds, And trumpet-lowing of the herds; The scarlet maple-keys betray What potent blood hath modest May; What fiery force the earth renews, The wealth of forms, the flush of hues; What Joy in rosy waves outpoured, Flows from the heart of Love, the Lord.

Ralph Waldo Emerson.

From "May-Day."

May

Then came fair May, the fairest maid on ground, Deck'd all with dainties of her season's pride, And throwing flowers out of her lap around: Upon two brethren's shoulders she did ride; The twins of Leda, which on either side Supported her like to their sovereign queen. Lord! how all creatures laughed when her they spied, And leapt and danced as they had ravish'd been. And Cupid's self about her fluttered all in green.

Edmund Spenser.

Song on May Morning

Now the bright morning star, Day's harbinger, Comes dancing from the East, and leads with her The flowery May, who from her green lap throws The yellow cowslip and the pale primrose. Hail, bounteous May, that doth inspire Mirth, and youth, and warm desire; Woods and groves are of thy dressing, Hill and dale doth boast thy blessing. Thus we salute thee with our early song, And welcome thee, and wish thee long.

John Milton.

Summer

Then came jolly Summer, being dight In a thin silken cassock, colored green, That was unlined, all to be more light, And on his head a garland well beseene.

Edmund Spenser.

From "The Faerie Queene."

June Weather

For a cap and bells our lives we pay, Bubbles we earn with a whole soul's tasking; 'T is heaven alone that is given away, 'T is only God may be had for the asking; No price is set on the lavish summer; June may be had by the poorest comer. And what is so rare as a day in June? Then, if ever, come perfect days; Then Heaven tries the earth if it be in tune, And over it softly her warm ear lays: Whether we look, or whether we listen, We hear life murmur, or see it glisten; Every clod feels a stir of might, An instinct within it that reaches and towers, And, groping blindly above it for light, Climbs to a soul in grass and flowers; The flush of life may well be seen Thrilling back over hills and valleys; The cowslip startles in meadows green, The buttercup catches the sun in its chalice, And there's never a leaf nor a blade too mean To be some happy creature's palace; The little bird sits at his door in the sun, Atilt like a blossom among the leaves, And lets his illumined being o'errun With the deluge of summer it receives; His mate feels the eggs beneath her wings, And the heart in her dumb breast flutters and sings; He sings to the wide world, and she to her nest,— In the nice ear of Nature which song is the best?

Now is the high tide of the year, And whatever of life hath ebbed away Comes flooding back, with a ripply cheer, Into every bare inlet and creek and bay; Now the heart is so full that a drop overfills it, We are happy now because God wills it; No matter how barren the past may have been, 'T is enough for us now that the leaves are green; We sit in the warm shade and feel right well How the sap creeps up and the blossoms swell; We may shut our eyes, but we cannot help knowing That skies are clear and grass is growing; The breeze comes whispering in our ear, That dandelions are blossoming near, That maize has sprouted, that streams are flowing, That the river is bluer than the sky, That the robin is plastering his house hard by; And if the breeze kept the good news back, For other couriers we should not lack, We could guess it all by yon heifer's lowing,— And hark! how clear bold chanticleer, Warmed with the new wine of the year, Tells all in his lusty crowing!

James Russell Lowell.

From "The Vision of Sir Launfal."

July

When the scarlet cardinal tells Her dream to the dragon fly, And the lazy breeze makes a nest in the trees, And murmurs a lullaby, It is July.

When the tangled cobweb pulls The cornflower's cap awry, And the lilies tall lean over the wall To bow to the butterfly, It is July.

When the heat like a mist-veil floats, And poppies flame in the rye, And the silver note in the streamlet's throat Has softened almost to a sigh, It is July.

When the hours are so still that time Forgets them, and lets them lie 'Neath petals pink till the night stars wink At the sunset in the sky, It is July.

Susan Hartley Swett.

By courtesy of Dana Estes & Co.

August

The sixth was August, being rich arrayed In garment all of gold down to the ground; Yet rode he not, but led a lovely maid Forth by the lily hand, the which was crowned With ears of corn, and full her hand was found: That was the righteous Virgin, which of old Lived here on earth, and plenty made abound.

Edmund Spenser.

In August

All the long August afternoon, The little drowsy stream Whispers a melancholy tune, As if it dreamed of June, And whispered in its dream.

The thistles show beyond the brook Dust on their down and bloom, And out of many a weed-grown nook The aster flowers look With eyes of tender gloom.

The silent orchard aisles are sweet With smell of ripening fruit. Through the sere grass, in shy retreat Flutter, at coming feet, The robins strange and mute.

There is no wind to stir the leaves, The harsh leaves overhead; Only the querulous cricket grieves, And shrilling locust

16

weaves A song of summer dead. William Dean Howells.

Autumn

Then came the Autumn all in yellow clad, As though he joyèd in his plenteous store, Laden with fruits that made him laugh, full glad That he had banished hunger, which to-fore Had by the belly oft him pinchèd sore: Upon his head a wreath, that was enroll'd With ears of corn of every sort, he bore; And in his hand a sickle he did hold, To reap the ripen'd fruits the which the earth had yold.

Edmund Spenser.
From "The Faerie Queene."

Sweet September

O sweet September! thy first breezes bring The dry leafs rustle and the squirrel's laughter, The cool, fresh air, whence health and vigor spring, And promise of exceeding joy hereafter.

George Arnold.

Autumn's Processional

Then step by step walks Autumn, With steady eyes that show Nor grief nor fear, to the death of the year, While the equinoctials blow.

Dinah Maria Mulock.

October's Bright Blue Weather

O suns and skies and clouds of June, And flowers of June together, Ye cannot rival for one hour October's bright blue weather;

When loud the bumblebee makes haste, Belated, thriftless vagrant, And goldenrod is dying fast, And lanes with grapes are fragrant;

When gentians roll their fringes tight To save them for the morning, And chestnuts fall from satin burrs Without a sound of warning;

When on the ground red apples lie In piles like jewels shining, And redder still on old stone walls Are leaves of woodbine twining; When all the lovely wayside things Their white-winged seeds are sowing, And in the fields, still green and fair, Late aftermaths are growing;

When springs run low, and on the brooks, In idle golden freighting, Bright leaves sink noiseless in the hush Of woods, for winter waiting;

When comrades seek sweet country haunts, By twos and twos together, And count like misers, hour by hour, October's bright blue weather.

O sun and skies and flowers of June, Count all your boasts together, Love loveth best of all the year October's bright blue weather.

H. H.

Maple Leaves

October turned my maple's leaves to gold; The most are gone now; here and there one lingers: Soon these will slip from out the twigs' weak hold, Like coins between a dying miser's fingers.

Thomas Bailey Aldrich.

"Down to Sleep"

November woods are bare and still, November days are clear and bright, Each noon burns up the morning's chill, The morning's snow is gone by night, Each day my steps grow slow, grow light, As through the woods I reverent creep, Watching all things "lie down to sleep."

I never knew before what beds, Fragrant to smell and soft to touch, The forest sifts and shapes and spreads. I never knew before, how much Of human sound there is, in such Low tones as through the forest sweep, When all wild things "lie down to sleep."

Each day I find new coverlids Tucked in, and more sweet eyes shut tight. Sometimes the viewless mother bids Her ferns kneel down full in my sight, I hear their chorus of "good night," And half I smile and half I weep, Listening while they "lie down to sleep."

November woods are bare and still, November days are bright and good, Life's noon burns up life's morning chill, Life's night rests feet that long have stood, Some warm, soft bed in field or wood The mother will not fail to keep Where we can "lay us down to sleep."

H. H.

Winter

Lastly came Winter cloathèd all in frize, Chattering his teeth for cold that did him chill; Whilst on his hoary beard his breath did freeze, And the dull drops that from his purple bill As from a limbeck did adown distill; In his right hand a tippèd staff he held With which his feeble steps he stayèd still, For he was faint with cold and weak with eld, That scarce his loosèd limbs he able was to weld.

Edmund Spenser.

When Icicles Hang by the Wall

When icicles hang by the wall, And Dick the shepherd blows his nail, And Tom bears logs into the hall, And milk comes frozen home in pail, When blood is nipped, and ways be foul, Then nightly sings the staring owl, To-whit! To-who!—a merry note, While greasy Joan doth keel the pot.

When all aloud the wind doth blow, And coughing drowns the parson's saw, And birds sit brooding in the snow, And Marian's nose looks red and raw, When roasted crabs hiss in the bowl, Then nightly sings the staring owl, To-whit! To-who!—a merry note, While greasy Joan doth keel the pot.

William Shakespeare.

From "Love's Labor's Lost."

A Winter Morning

There was never a leaf on bush or tree, The bare boughs rattled shudderingly; The river was dumb and could not speak, For the weaver Winter its shroud had spun; A single crow on the tree-top bleak From his shining feathers shed off the cold sun; Again it was morning, but shrunk and cold, As if her veins were sapless and old, And she rose up decrepitly For a last dim look at earth and sea.

James Russell Lowell.

From "The Vision of Sir Launfal."

The Snow Storm

Announced by all the trumpets of the sky, Arrives the snow, and, driving o'er the fields, Seems nowhere to alight; the whited air Hides hills and woods, the river, and the heaven, And veils the farmhouse at the garden's end. The sled and traveler stopped, the courier's feet Delayed, all friends shut out, the housemates sit Around the radiant fireplace, inclosed In a tumultuous privacy of storm.

Come see the north-wind's masonry. Out of an unseen quarry evermore Furnished with tile, the fierce artificer Curves his white bastions with projected roof Round every windward stake, or tree, or door. Speeding, the myriad-handed, his wild work So fanciful, so savage, naught cares he For number or proportion. Mockingly, On coop or kennel he hangs Parian wreaths; A swan-like form invests the hidden thorn; Fills up the farmer's lane from wall to wall, Maugre the farmer's sighs; and, at the gate, A tapering turret overtops the work: And when his hours are numbered, and the world Is all his own, retiring, as he were not, Leaves, when the sun appears, astonished Art To mimic in slow structures, stone by stone, Built in an age, the mad wind's night-work, The frolic architecture of the snow.

Ralph Waldo Emerson.

Old Winter

Old Winter sad, in snow yclad, Is making a doleful din; But let him howl till he crack his jowl, We will not let him in.

Ay, let him lift from the billowy drift His hoary, hagged form, And scowling stand, with his wrinkled hand Outstretching to the storm.

And let his weird and sleety beard Stream loose upon the blast, And, rustling, chime to the tinkling rime From his bald head falling fast.

Let his baleful breath shed blight and death On herb and flower and tree; And brooks and ponds in crystal bonds Bind fast, but what care we?

Let him push at the door,—in the chimney roar, And rattle the window pane; Let him in at us spy with his icicle eye, But he shall not entrance gain.

Let him gnaw, forsooth, with his freezing tooth, On our roof-tiles, till he tire; But we care not a whit, as we jovial sit Before our blazing fire.

Come, lads, let's sing, till the rafters ring; Come, push the can about;— From our snug fire-side this Christmas-tide We'll keep old Winter out.

Thomas Noel.

Midwinter

The speckled sky is dim with snow, The light flakes falter and fall slow; Athwart the hill-top, rapt and pale, Silently drops a silvery veil; And all the valley is shut in By flickering curtains gray and thin.

But cheerily the chickadee Singeth to me on fence and tree; The snow sails round him as he sings, White as the down of angels' wings.

I watch the slow flakes as they fall On bank and brier and broken wall; Over the orchard, waste and brown, All noiselessly they settle down, Tipping the apple-boughs, and each Light quivering twig of plum and peach.

On turf and curb and bower-roof The snow-storm spreads its ivory woof; It paves with pearl the garden-walk; And lovingly round tattered stalk And shivering stem its magic weaves A mantle fair as lily-leaves.

The hooded beehive small and low, Stands like a maiden in the snow; And the old door-slab is half hid Under an alabaster lid.

All day it snows: the sheeted post Gleams in the dimness like a ghost; All day the blasted oak has stood A muffled wizard of the wood; Garland and airy cap adorn The sumach and the wayside thorn, And clustering spangles lodge and shine In the dark tresses of the pine.

The ragged bramble, dwarfed and old, Shrinks like a beggar in the cold; In surplice white the cedar stands, And blesses him with priestly hands.

Still cheerily the chickadee Singeth to me on fence and tree: But in my inmost ear is heard The music of a holier bird; And heavenly thoughts as soft and white As snow-flakes on my soul alight, Clothing with love my lonely heart, Healing with peace each bruised part, Till all my being seems to be Transfigured by their purity.

John Townsend Trowbridge.

Dirge for the Year
"Orphan Hours, the Year is dead! Come and sigh, come and weep!" "Merry Hours, smile instead, For the Year is but asleep; See, it smiles as it is sleeping, Mocking your untimely weeping."

Percy Bysshe Shelley.

INTERLEAVES
The World Beautiful
"Study Nature, not books," said that inspired teacher, Louis Agassiz.

The poets do not bring you the fruit of conscious study, perhaps, for they do not analyze or dissect Dame Nature's methods; with them genius begets a higher instinct, and it is by a sort of divination that they interpret for us the power and grandeur, romance and witchery, beauty and mystery of "God's great out-of-doors." The born poet, like the born naturalist, seems to have additional senses. Emerson says of his friend Thoreau that he saw as with microscope and heard as with ear-trumpet, while his memory was a photographic register of all he saw and heard; and Thoreau the naturalist might have said the same of Emerson the poet.

Glance at the succession of beautiful images in Shelley's "Cloud" or Aldrich's "Before the Rain", lend your ear to the tinkle of Tennyson's "Brook." Contrast them with the bracing lines of the "Northeast Wind," the rough metre of "Highland Cattle," the chill calm of "Snow Bound," the grand style of Milton's "Morning," the noble simplicity of Addison's "Hymn," and note how the great poet bends his language to the mood of Nature, grim or sunny, stormy or kind, strong or tender. There is a stanza in Pope's "Essay on Criticism" which conveys the idea perfectly:

"Soft is the strain when zephyr gently blows, And the smooth stream in smoother numbers flows; But when loud surges lash the sounding shore, The hoarse, rough verse should like the torrent roar. When Ajax strives some rock's vast weight to throw, The line too labors, and the words move slow: Not so when swift Camilla scours the plain, Flies o'er th' unbending corn, and skims along the main."

II
THE WORLD BEAUTIFUL
The World Beautiful
Sweet is the breath of Morn, her rising sweet With charm of earliest birds; pleasant the Sun When first on this delightful land he spreads His orient beams, on herb, tree, fruit, and flower, Glistening with dew; fragrant the fertile Earth After soft showers; and sweet the coming on Of grateful Evening mild; then silent Night With this her solemn bird, and this fair Moon, And these the gems of Heaven, her starry train.

John Milton.
From "Paradise Lost."

The Harvest Moon
It is the harvest moon! On gilded vanes And roofs of villages, on woodland crests And their aerial neighborhoods of nests Deserted, oh the curtained window-panes Of rooms where children sleep, on country lanes And harvest-fields, its mystic splendor rests! Gone are the birds that were our summer guests; With the last sheaves return the laboring wains!

Henry Wadsworth Longfellow.

The Cloud
I bring fresh showers for the thirsting flowers, From the seas and the streams; I bear light shade for the leaves when laid In their noonday dreams. From my wings are shaken the dews that waken The sweet buds every one, When rocked to rest

on their mother's breast, As she dances about the sun. I wield the flail of the lashing hail, And whiten the green plains under; And then again I dissolve it in rain, And laugh as I pass in thunder.

I sift the snow on the mountains below, And their great pines groan aghast; And all the night 'tis my pillow white, While I sleep in the arms of the blast. Sublime on the towers of my skyey bowers, Lightning my pilot sits; In a cavern under is fettered the thunder, It struggles and howls at fits; Over earth and ocean, with gentle motion, This pilot is guiding me, Lured by the love of the genii that move In the depths of the purple sea; Over the rills, and the crags, and the hills, Over the lakes and the plains, Wherever he dream, under mountain or stream, The Spirit he loves remains; And I all the while bask in heaven's blue smile, Whilst he is dissolving in rains.

The sanguine sunrise, with his meteor eyes, And his burning plumes outspread, Leaps on the back of my sailing rack When the morning-star shines dead, As on the jag of a mountain crag, Which an earthquake rocks and swings, An eagle alit one moment may sit In the light of its golden wings. And when Sunset may breathe, from the lit sea beneath Its ardors of rest and of love, And the crimson pall of eve may fall From the depth of heaven above, With wings folded I rest, on mine airy nest, As still as a brooding dove.

That orbèd maiden with white fire laden, Whom mortals call the moon, Glides glimmering o'er my fleece-like floor, By the midnight breezes strewn; And wherever the beat of her unseen feet, Which only the angels hear, May have broken the woof of my tent's thin roof, The stars peep behind her and peer; And I laugh to see them whirl and flee, Like a swarm of golden bees, When I widen the rent in my wind-built tent, Till the calm rivers, lakes, and seas, Like strips of the sky fallen through me on high, Are each paved with the moon and these.

I bind the sun's throne with a burning zone, And the moon's with a girdle of pearl; The volcanoes are dim, and the stars reel and swim, When the whirlwinds my banner unfurl. From cape to cape, with a bridge-like shape, Over a torrent sea, Sunbeam-proof, I hang like a roof, The mountains its columns be. The triumphal arch through which I march With hurricane, fire, and snow, When the powers of the air are chained to my chair, Is the million-colored bow; The sphere-fire above its soft colors wove, While the moist earth was laughing below. I am the daughter of earth and water, And the nursling of the sky: I pass through the pores of the ocean and shores; I change, but I cannot die. For after the rain when with never a stain, The pavilion of heaven is bare, And the winds and sunbeams with their convex gleams, Build up the blue dome of air, I silently laugh at my own cenotaph, And out of the caverns of rain, Like a child from the womb, like a ghost from the tomb, I arise and unbuild it again.

Percy Bysshe Shelley.

Before the Rain

We knew it would rain, for all the morn, A spirit on slender ropes of mist Was lowering its golden buckets down Into the vapory amethyst

Of marshes and swamps and dismal fens— Scooping the dew that lay in the flowers, Dipping the jewels out of the sea, To sprinkle them over the land in showers.

We knew it would rain, for the poplars showed The white of their leaves, the amber grain Shrunk in the wind—and the lightning now Is tangled in tremulous skeins of rain!

Thomas Bailey Aldrich.

Rain in Summer

How beautiful is the rain! After the dust and heat, In the broad and fiery street, In the narrow lane, How beautiful is the rain! How it clatters along the roofs Like the tramp of hoofs! How it gushes and struggles out From the throat of the overflowing spout!

Across the window-pane It pours and pours; And swift and wide, With a muddy tide, Like a river down the gutter roars The rain, the welcome rain!

The sick man from his chamber looks At the twisted brooks; He can feel the cool Breath of each little pool; His fevered brain Grows calm again, And he breathes a blessing on the rain.

From the neighboring school Come the boys, With more than their wonted noise And commotion; And down the wet streets Sail their mimic fleets, Till the treacherous pool Engulfs them in its whirling And turbulent ocean.

In the country on every side, Where, far and wide, Like a leopard's tawny and spotted hide, Stretches the plain, To the dry grass and the drier grain How welcome is the rain!

In the furrowed land The toilsome and patient oxen stand, Lifting the yoke-encumbered head, With their dilated nostrils spread, They silently inhale The clover-scented gale, And the vapors that arise From the well-watered and smoking soil. For this rest in the furrow after toil, Their large and lustrous eyes Seem to thank the Lord, More than man's spoken word.

Henry Wadsworth Longfellow.

Invocation to Rain in Summer

O gentle, gentle summer rain, Let not the silver lily pine, The drooping lily pine in vain To feel that dewy touch of thine—

To drink thy freshness once again, O gentle, gentle summer rain!

In heat the landscape quivering lies; The cattle pant beneath the tree; Through parching air and purple skies The earth looks up, in vain, for thee; For thee—for thee, it looks in vain, O gentle, gentle summer rain!

Come, thou, and brim the meadow streams, And soften all the hills with mist, O falling dew! from burning dreams By thee shall herb and flower be kissed; And Earth shall bless thee yet again, O gentle, gentle summer rain!

William C. Bennett.

The Latter Rain

The latter rain,—it falls in anxious haste Upon the sun-dried fields and branches bare, Loosening with searching drops the rigid waste As if it would each root's lost strength repair; But not a blade grows green as in the spring; No swelling twig puts forth its thickening leaves; The robins only 'mid the harvests sing, Pecking the grain that scatters from the sheaves; The rain falls still,—the fruit all ripened drops, It pierces chestnut-bur and walnut-shell; The furrowed fields disclose the yellow crops; Each bursting pod of talents used can tell; And all that once received the early rain Declare to man it was not sent in vain.

Jones Very.

The Wind

I saw you toss the kites on high And blow the birds about the sky; And all around I heard you pass, Like ladies' skirts across the grass— O wind, a-blowing all day long, O wind, that sings so loud a song!

I saw the different things you did, But always you yourself you hid, I felt you push, I heard you call, I could not see yourself at all— O wind, a-blowing all day long, O wind, that sings so loud a song!

O you that are so strong and cold, O blower, are you young or old? Are you a beast of field and tree Or just a stronger child than me? O wind, a-blowing all day long, O wind, that sings so loud a song!

Robert Louis Stevenson.

From "A Child's Garden of Verses." By courtesy of Charles Scribner's Sons.

Ode to the Northeast Wind

Welcome, wild Northeaster! Shame it is to see Odes to every zephyr; Ne'er a verse to thee. Welcome, black Northeaster! O'er the German foam; O'er the Danish moorlands, From thy frozen home. Tired we are of summer, Tired of gaudy glare, Showers soft and steaming, Hot and breathless air. Tired of listless dreaming, Through the lazy day; Jovial wind of winter Turn us out to play! Sweep the golden reed-beds; Crisp the lazy dyke; Hunger into madness Every plunging pike. Fill the lake with wild-fowl; Fill the marsh with snipe; While on dreary moorlands Lonely curlew pipe. Through the black fir forest Thunder harsh and dry, Shattering down the snowflakes Off the curdled sky. Hark! the brave Northeaster! Breast-high lies the scent, On by holt and headland, Over heath and bent. Chime, ye dappled darlings, Through the sleet and snow, Who can override you? Let the horses go! Chime, ye dappled darlings, Down the roaring blast; You shall see a fox die Ere an hour be past. Go! and rest to-morrow, Hunting in your dreams, While our skates are ringing O'er the frozen streams. Let the luscious South-wind Breathe in lovers' sighs, While the lazy gallants Bask in ladies' eyes. What does he but soften Heart alike and pen? 'Tis the hard gray weather Breeds hard English men. What's the soft Southwester? 'Tis the ladies' breeze, Bringing home their true loves Out of all the seas; But the black Northeaster, Through the snowstorm hurled, Drives our English hearts of oak, Seaward round the world! Come! as came our fathers, Heralded by thee, Conquering from the eastward, Lords by land and sea. Come! and strong within us Stir the Vikings' blood; Bracing brain and sinew; Blow, thou wind of God!

Charles Kingsley.

The Windy Night

Alow and aloof, Over the roof, How the midnight tempests howl! With a dreary voice, like the dismal tune Of wolves that bay at the desert moon;— Or whistle and shriek Through limbs that creak, "Tu-who! tu-whit!" They cry and flit, "Tu-whit! tu-who!" like the solemn owl!

Alow and aloof, Over the roof, Sweep the moaning winds amain, And wildly dash The elm and ash, Clattering on the window-sash, With a clatter and patter, Like hail and rain That well nigh shatter The dusky pane!

Alow and aloof, Over the roof, How the tempests swell and roar! Though no foot is astir, Though the cat and the cur Lie dozing along the kitchen floor, There are feet of air On every stair! Through every hall— Through each gusty door, There's a jostle and bustle, With a silken rustle, Like the meeting of guests at a festival!

Alow and aloof, Over the roof, How the stormy tempests swell! And make the vane On the spire complain— They heave at the steeple with might and main And burst and sweep Into the belfry, on the bell! They smite it so hard, and they smite it so well, That the sexton tosses his arms in sleep, And dreams he is ringing a funeral knell!

Thomas Buchanan Read.

By courtesy of J. B. Lippincott & Co.

The Brook

I come from haunts of coot and hern, I make a sudden sally, And sparkle out among the fern, To bicker down a valley.

By thirty hills I hurry down, Or slip between the ridges; By twenty thorps, a little town, And half a hundred bridges.

* * * *

I chatter over stony ways, In little sharps and trebles, I bubble into eddying bays, I babble on the pebbles.

With many a curve my banks I fret, By many a field and fallow, And many a fairy foreland set With willow-weed and mallow.

I chatter, chatter, as I flow To join the brimming river; For men may come and men may go, But I go on forever.

I wind about, and in and out, With here a blossom sailing, And here and there a lusty trout, And here and there a grayling, And here and there a foamy flake Upon me, as I travel, With many a silvery waterbreak Above the golden gravel.

* * * *

I steal by lawns and grassy plots, I slide by hazel covers; I move the sweet forget-me-nots That grow for happy lovers.

I slip, I slide, I gloom, I glance, Among my skimming swallows; I make the netted sunbeams dance Against my sandy shallows.

I murmur under moon and stars In brambly wildernesses; I linger by my shingly bars; I loiter round my cresses.

And out again I curve and flow To join the brimming river, For men may come and men may go, But I go on forever.

Alfred, Lord Tennyson.

The Brook in Winter

Down swept the chill wind from the mountain peak, From the snow five thousand summers old; On open wold and hill-top bleak It had gathered all the cold, And whirled it like sleet on the wanderer's cheek; It carried a shiver everywhere From the unleafed boughs and pastures bare; The little brook heard it and built a roof 'Neath which he could house him, winter-proof; All night by the white stars' frosty gleams He groined his arches and matched his beams; Slender and clear were his crystal spars As the lashes of light that trim the stars; He sculptured every summer delight In his halls and chambers out of sight; Sometimes his tinkling waters slipt Down through a frost-leaved forest crypt, Long, sparkling aisles of steel-stemmed trees Bending to counterfeit a breeze; Sometimes the roof no fretwork knew; But silvery mosses that downward grew; Sometimes it was carved in sharp relief With quaint arabesques of ice-fern leaf; Sometimes it was simply smooth and clear For the gladness of heaven to shine through, and here He had caught the nodding bulrush-tops And hung them thickly with diamond drops, That crystalled the beams of moon and sun, And made a star of every one: No mortal builder's most rare device Could match this winter-palace of ice; 'Twas as if every image that mirrored lay In his depths serene through the summer day, Each flitting shadow of earth and sky, Lest the happy model should be lost, Had been mimicked in fairy masonry By the elfin builders of the frost.

James Russell Lowell.

From "The Vision of Sir Launfal."

Clear and Cool

Clear and cool, clear and cool, By laughing shallow, and dreaming pool; Cool and clear, cool and clear, By shining shingle, and foaming wear; Under the crag where the ouzel sings, And the ivied wall where the church-bell rings, Undefiled, for the undefiled; Play by me, bathe in me, mother and child.

Dank and foul, dank and foul, By the smoky town in its murky cowl; Foul and dank, foul and dank, By wharf and sewer and slimy bank; Darker and darker the farther I go, Baser and baser the richer I grow; Who dare sport with the sin-defiled? Shrink from me, turn from me, mother and child. Strong and free, strong and free, The floodgates are open, away to the sea, Free and strong, free and strong, Cleansing my streams as I hurry along, To the golden sands, and the leaping bar, And the taintless tide that awaits me afar. As I lose myself in the infinite main, Like a soul that has sinned and is pardoned again. Undefiled, for the undefiled; Play by me, bathe in me, mother and child.

Charles Kingsley.

From "The Water-Babies."

Minnows

How silent comes the water round that bend; Not the minutest whisper does it send To the overhanging sallows; blades of grass Slowly across the chequer'd shadows pass,— Why, you might read two sonnets, ere they reach To where the hurrying freshnesses aye preach A natural sermon o'er their pebbly beds; Where swarms of minnows show their little heads, Staying their wavy bodies 'gainst the streams, To taste the luxury of sunny beams Tempered with coolness. How they ever wrestle With their own sweet delight, and ever nestle Their silver bellies on the pebbly sand. If you but scantily hold out the hand, That very instant not one will remain; But turn your eye, and they are there again. The ripples seem right glad to reach those cresses, And cool themselves among the em'rald tresses; The while they cool themselves, they freshness give, And moisture, that the bowery green may live.

John Keats.

Snow-Bound

(Extracts)

The sun that brief December day Rose cheerless over hills of gray, And, darkly circled, gave at noon A sadder light than waning moon. Slow tracing down the thickening sky Its mute and ominous prophecy, A portent seeming less than threat, It sank from sight before it set. A chill no coat, however stout, Of homespun stuff could quite shut out, A hard dull bitterness of cold, That checked, mid-vein, the circling race Of life-blood in the sharpened face, The coming of the snow-storm told. The wind blew east: we heard the roar Of ocean on his wintry shore, And felt the strong pulse throbbing there Beat with low rhythm our inland air.

* * * *

Unwarmed by any sunset light The gray day darkened into night, A night made hoary with the swarm And whirl-dance of the blinding storm, As zig-zag wavering to and fro Crossed and recrossed the wingéd snow: And ere the early bedtime came The white drift piled the window-frame, And through the glass the clothes-line posts Looked in like tall and sheeted ghosts.

* * * *

The old familiar sights of ours Took marvellous shapes; strange domes and towers Rose up where sty or corn-crib stood, Or garden wall, or belt of wood; A smooth white mound the brush-pile showed, A fenceless drift what once was road; The bridle-post an old man sat With loose-flung coat and high cocked hat; The well-curb had a Chinese roof; And even the long sweep, high aloof, In its slant splendor, seemed to tell Of Pisa's leaning miracle.

* * * *

All day the gusty north wind bore The loosening drift its breath before; Low circling round its southern zone, The sun through dazzling snow-mist shone. No church-bell lent its Christian tone To the savage air, no social smoke Curled over woods of snow-hung oak. A solitude made more intense By dreary-voicéd elements, The shrieking of the mindless wind, The moaning tree-boughs swaying blind, And on the glass the unmeaning beat Of ghostly finger-tips of sleet. Beyond the circle of our hearth No welcome sound of toil or mirth Unbound the spell, and testified Of human life and thought outside. We minded that the sharpest ear The buried brooklet could not hear, The music of whose liquid lip Had been to us companionship, And in our lonely life, had grown To have an almost human tone. As night drew on, and, from the crest Of wooded knolls that ridged the west, The sun, a snow-blown traveller, sank From sight beneath the smothering bank, We piled with care, our nightly stack Of wood against the chimney-back,— The oaken log, green, huge and thick, And on its top the stout back-stick; The knotty fore-stick laid apart, And filled between with curious art The ragged brush; then hovering near, We watched the first red blaze appear, Heard the sharp crackle, caught the gleam On whitewashed wall and sagging beam, Until the old rude-fashioned room Burst flower-like into rosy bloom; While radiant with a mimic flame Outside the sparkling drift became, And through the bare-boughed lilac tree Our own warm hearth seemed blazing free. The crane and pendent trammels showed, The Turks' heads on the andirons glowed; While childish fancy, prompt to tell The meaning of the miracle, Whispered the old rhyme: "*Under the tree, When fire outdoors burns merrily, There the witches are making tea.*"

* * * *

Shut in from all the world without, We sat the clean-winged hearth about, Content to let the north wind roar In baffled rage at pane and door, While the red logs before us beat The frost-line back with tropic heat; And ever, when a louder blast Shook beam and rafter as it passed, The merrier up its roaring draught The great throat of the chimney laughed, The house-dog on his paws outspread Laid to the fire his drowsy head, The cat's dark silhouette on the wall A couchant tiger's seemed to fall; And, for the winter fireside meet, Between the andirons' straddling feet, The mug of cider simmered slow, The apples sputtered in a row, And close at hand the basket stood With nuts from brown October's wood.

* * * *

John Greenleaf Whittier.

Highland Cattle

Down the wintry mountain Like a cloud they come, Not like a cloud in its silent shroud When the sky is leaden and the earth all dumb, But tramp, tramp, tramp, With a roar and a shock, And stamp, stamp, stamp, Down the hard granite rock, With the snow-flakes falling fair Like an army in the air Of white-winged angels leaving Their heavenly homes, half grieving, And half glad to drop down kindly upon earth so bare: With a snort and a bellow Tossing manes dun and yellow, Red and roan, black and gray, In their fierce merry play, Though the sky is all leaden and the earth all dumb— Down the noisy cattle come!

Throned on the mountain Winter sits at ease: Hidden under mist are those peaks of amethyst That rose like hills of heaven above the amber seas. While crash, crash, crash, Through the frozen heather brown, And dash, dash, dash, Where the ptarmigan drops down And the curlew stops her cry And the deer sinks, like to die— And the waterfall's loud noise Is the only living voice— With a plunge and a roar Like mad waves upon the shore, Or the wind through the pass Howling o'er the reedy grass— In a wild battalion pouring from the heights unto the plain, Down the cattle come again!

23

*   *   *   *

Dinah Maria Mulock.

A Scene in Paradise

Adam the goodliest man of men since born His sons; the fairest of her daughters Eve. Under a tuft of shade that on a green Stood whispering soft, by a fresh fountain-side, They sat them down;... ... About them frisking played All beasts of the earth, since wild, and of all chase In wood or wilderness, forest or den. Sporting the lion ramped, and in his paw Dandled the kid; bears, tigers, ounces, pards, Gamboled before them; the unwieldy elephant, To make them mirth, used all his might, and wreathed His lithe proboscis; close the serpent sly, Insinuating, wove with Gordian twine His braided train, and of his fatal guile Gave proof unheeded. Others on the grass Couched, and, now filled with pasture, gazing sat, Or bedward ruminating; for the sun, Declined, was hastening now with prone career To the Ocean Isles, and in the ascending scale Of Heaven the stars that usher evening rose.

John Milton.

From "Paradise Lost."

The Tiger

Tiger, tiger, burning bright In the forests of the night! What immortal hand or eye Could frame thy fearful symmetry?

In what distant deeps or skies Burnt the ardor of thine eyes? On what wings dare he aspire— What the hand dare seize the fire?

And what shoulder, and what art Could twist the sinews of thy heart? And when thy heart began to beat, What dread hand form'd thy dread feet?

What the hammer, what the chain, In what furnace was thy brain? What the anvil? What dread grasp Dare its deadly terrors clasp?

When the stars threw down their spears, And watered heaven with their tears, Did he smile his work to see? Did he who made the lamb make thee?

Tiger, tiger, burning bright In the forests of the night, What immortal hand or eye Dare frame thy fearful symmetry?

William Blake.

The Spacious Firmament on High

The spacious firmament on high, With all the blue ethereal sky, And spangled heavens, a shining frame. Their great Original proclaim. The unwearied sun from day to day Does his Creator's power display, And publishes to every land The work of an Almighty hand.

Soon as the evening shades prevail, The moon takes up the wondrous tale, And nightly to the listening earth Repeats the story of her birth; Whilst all the stars that round her burn, And all the planets in their turn, Confirm the tidings as they roll, And spread the truth from pole to pole.

What though in solemn silence, all Move round this dark, terrestrial ball? What though nor real voice nor sound Amidst their radiant orbs be found? In Reason's ear they all rejoice, And utter forth a glorious voice, Forever singing as they shine: "The hand that made us is divine!"

Joseph Addison.

INTERLEAVES

Green Things Growing

"Oh, the fluttering and the pattering of those green things growing! How they talk each to each, when none of us are knowing;"

"Every clod feels a stir of might, An instinct within it that reaches and towers, And groping blindly above it for light, Climbs to a soul in grass and flowers;"

"... Lean against a streamlet's rushy banks, And watch intently Nature's gentle doings; They will be found softer than ringdoves' cooings."

"Dear, tell them, that if eyes were made for seeing, Then beauty is its own excuse for being."

"They know the time to go! The fairy clocks strike their inaudible hour In field and woodland, and each punctual flower Bows at the signal an obedient head And hastes to bed."

"If so the sweetness of the wheat Into my soul might pass, And the clear courage of the grass."

"Flower in the crannied wall, I pluck you out of the crannies; Hold you here, root and all, in my hand, Little flower—but if I could understand What you are, root and all, and all in all, I should know what God and man is."

III
GREEN THINGS GROWING
Green Things Growing

Oh, the green things growing, the green things growing, The faint sweet smell of the green things growing! I should like to live, whether I smile or grieve, Just to watch the happy life of my green things growing.

Oh, the fluttering and the pattering of those green things growing! How they talk each to each, when none of us are knowing; In the wonderful white of the weird moonlight Or the dim dreamy dawn when the cocks are crowing.

I love, I love them so,—my green things growing! And I think that they love me, without false showing; For by many a tender touch, they comfort me so much, With the soft mute comfort of green things growing.

Dinah Maria Mulock.

The Sigh of Silence

I stood tiptoe upon a little hill; The air was cooling and so very still, That the sweet buds which with a modest pride Pull droopingly, in slanting curve aside, Their scanty-leaved, and finely-tapering stems, Had not yet lost their starry diadems Caught from the early sobbing of the morn. The clouds were pure and white as flocks new-shorn, And fresh from the clear brook; sweetly they slept On the blue fields of heaven, and then there crept A little noiseless noise among the leaves, Born of the very sigh that silence heaves; For not the faintest motion could be seen Of all the shades that slanted o'er the green.

John Keats.

Under the Greenwood Tree

Under the greenwood tree, Who loves to lie with me, And tune his merry note Unto the sweet bird's throat, Come hither, come hither, come hither! Here shall he see No enemy But winter and rough weather.

Who doth ambition shun, And loves to live i' the sun, Seeking the food he eats, And pleased with what he gets, Come hither, come hither, come hither! Here shall he see No enemy But winter and rough weather.

William Shakespeare.

From "As You Like It."

The Planting of the Apple Tree

Come, let us plant the apple tree. Cleave the tough greensward with the spade; Wide let its hollow bed be made; There gently lay the roots, and there Sift the dark mold with kindly care, And press it o'er them tenderly, As, round the sleeping infant's feet We softly fold the cradle sheet; So plant we the apple tree.

What plant we in this apple tree? Buds, which the breath of summer days Shall lengthen into leafy sprays; Boughs where the thrush, with crimson breast, Shall haunt and sing and hide her nest; We plant, upon the sunny lea, A shadow for the noontide hour, A shelter from the summer shower, When we plant the apple tree.

What plant we in this apple tree? Sweets for a hundred flowery springs To load the May wind's restless wings, When, from the orchard row, he pours Its fragrance through our open doors; A world of blossoms for the bee, Flowers for the sick girl's silent room, For the glad infant sprigs of bloom, We plant with the apple tree.

What plant we in this apple tree? Fruits that shall swell in sunny June, And redden in the August noon, And drop, when gentle airs come by, That fan the blue September sky, While children come, with cries of glee, And seek them where the fragrant grass Betrays their bed to those who pass, At the foot of the apple tree.

And when, above this apple tree, The winter stars are quivering bright, And winds go howling through the night, Girls, whose young eyes o'erflow with mirth, Shall peel its fruit by cottage hearth, And guests in prouder homes shall see, Heaped with the grape of Cintra's vine And golden orange of the line, The fruit of the apple tree.

The fruitage of this apple tree Winds, and our flag of stripe and star, Shall bear to coasts that lie afar, Where men shall wonder at the view, And ask in what fair groves they grew; And sojourners beyond the sea Shall think of childhood's careless day And long, long hours of summer play, In the shade of the apple tree.

Each year shall give this apple tree A broader flush of roseate bloom, A deeper maze of verdurous gloom, And loosen, when the frost clouds lower, The crisp brown leaves in thicker shower. The years shall come and pass, but we Shall hear no longer, where we lie, The summer's songs, the autumn's sigh, In the boughs of the apple tree.

And time shall waste this apple tree. Oh, when its aged branches throw Thin shadows on the ground below, Shall fraud and force and iron will Oppress the weak and helpless still? What shall the tasks of mercy be, Amid the toils, the strifes, the tears, Of those who live when length of years Is wasting this apple tree?

"Who planted this old apple tree?" The children of that distant day Thus to some aged man shall say; And, gazing on its mossy stem, The gray-haired man shall answer them: "A poet of the land was he, Born in the rude but good old times; 'Tis said he made some quaint old rhymes On planting the apple tree."

William Cullen Bryant.

By courtesy of D. Appleton & Co., publishers of Bryant's Complete Poetical Works.

An Apple Orchard in the Spring

25

Have you seen an apple orchard in the spring? In the spring? An English apple orchard in the spring? When the spreading trees are hoary With their wealth of promised glory, And the mavis sings its story, In the spring.

Have you plucked the apple blossoms in the spring? In the spring? And caught their subtle odors in the spring? Pink buds pouting at the light, Crumpled petals baby white, Just to touch them a delight— In the spring.

Have you walked beneath the blossoms in the spring? In the spring? Beneath the apple blossoms in the spring? When the pink cascades are falling, And the silver brooklets brawling, And the cuckoo bird soft calling, In the spring.

If you have not, then you know not, in the spring, In the spring, Half the color, beauty, wonder of the spring, No sweet sight can I remember Half so precious, half so tender, As the apple blossoms render In the spring.

William Martin.

Mine Host of "The Golden Apple"

A goodly host one day was mine, A Golden Apple his only sign, That hung from a long branch, ripe and fine.

My host was the bountiful apple-tree; He gave me shelter and nourished me With the best of fare, all fresh and free.

And light-winged guests came not a few, To his leafy inn, and sipped the dew, And sang their best songs ere they flew.

I slept at night on a downy bed Of moss, and my Host benignly spread His own cool shadow over my head.

When I asked what reckoning there might be, He shook his broad boughs cheerily:— A blessing be thine, green Apple-tree!

Thomas Westwood.

The Tree

I love thee when thy swelling buds appear, And one by one their tender leaves unfold, As if they knew that warmer suns were near, Nor longer sought to hide from winter's cold; And when with darker growth thy leaves are seen To veil from view the early robin's nest, I love to lie beneath thy waving screen, With limbs by summer's heat and toil oppressed; And when the autumn winds have stripped thee bare, And round thee lies the smooth, untrodden snow, When naught is thine that made thee once so fair, I love to watch thy shadowy form below, And through thy leafless arms to look above On stars that brighter beam when most we need their love.

Jones Very.

A Young Fir-Wood

These little firs to-day are things To clasp into a giant's cap, Or fans to suit his lady's lap. From many winters, many springs Shall cherish them in strength and sap, Till they be marked upon the map, A wood for the wind's wanderings. All seed is in the sower's hands: And what at first was trained to spread Its shelter for some single head,— Yea, even such fellowship of wands,— May hide the sunset, and the shade Of its great multitude be laid Upon the earth and elder sands.

Dante G. Rossetti.

The Snowing of the Pines

Softer than silence, stiller than still air Float down from high pine-boughs the slender leaves. The forest floor its annual boon receives That comes like snowfall, tireless, tranquil, fair. Gently they glide, gently they clothe the bare Old rocks with grace. Their fall a mantle weaves Of paler yellow than autumnal sheaves Or those strange blossoms the witch-hazels wear. Athwart long aisles the sunbeams pierce their way; High up, the crows are gathering for the night; The delicate needles fill the air; the jay Takes through their golden mist his radiant flight; They fall and fall, till at November's close The snow-flakes drop as lightly—snows on snows.

Thomas Wentworth Higginson.

The Procession of the Flowers

First came the primrose, On the bank high. Like a maiden looking forth From the window of a tower When the battle rolls below, So look'd she, And saw the storms go by.

Then came the wind-flower In the valley left behind, As a wounded maiden, pale With purple streaks of woe, When the battle has roll'd by Wanders to and fro, So totter'd she, Dishevell'd in the wind.

Then came the daisies, On the first of May, Like a banner'd show's advance While the crowd runs by the way, With ten thousand flowers about them they came trooping through the fields.

As a happy people come, So came they, As a happy people come When the war has roll'd away, With dance and tabor, pipe and drum, And all make holiday.

Then came the cowslip, Like a dancer in the fair, She spread her little mat of green, And on it danced she. With a fillet bound about her brow, A fillet round her happy brow, A golden fillet round her brow, And rubies in her hair.

Sydney Dobell.

Sweet Peas

Here are sweet peas, on tiptoe for a flight: With wings of gentle flush o'er delicate white, And taper fingers catching at all things, To bind them all about with tiny rings. Linger awhile upon some bending planks That lean against a streamlet's rushy banks, And watch intently Nature's gentle doings: They will be found softer than ringdove's cooings. How silent comes the water round that bend! Not the minutest whisper does it send To the o'erhanging sallows: blades of grass Slowly across the chequer'd shadows pass.

John Keats.

A Snowdrop

Only a tender little thing, So velvet soft and white it is; But march himself is not so strong, With all the great gales that are his.

In vain his whistling storms he calls, In vain the cohorts of his power Ride down the sky on mighty blasts— He cannot crush the little flower.

Its white spear parts the sod, the snows Than that white spear less snowy are, The rains roll off its crest like spray, It lifts again its spotless star.

Harriet Prescott Spofford.

Almond Blossom

Blossom of the almond trees, April's gift to April's bees, Birthday ornament of spring, Flora's fairest daughterling; Coming when no flowerets dare Trust the cruel outer air; When the royal kingcup bold Dares not don his coat of gold; And the sturdy black-thorn spray Keeps his silver for the May;— Coming when no flowerets would, Save thy lowly sisterhood, Early violets, blue and white, Dying for their love of light. Almond blossom, sent to teach us That the spring-days soon will reach us, Lest, with longing over-tried, We die, as the violets died— Blossom, clouding all the tree With thy crimson broidery, Long before a leaf of green O'er the bravest bough is seen; Ah! when winter winds are swinging All thy red bells into ringing, With a bee in every bell, Almond blossom, we greet thee well.

Edwin Arnold.

Wild Rose

Some innocent girlish Kisses by a charm Changed to a flight of small pink Butterflies, To waver under June's delicious skies Across gold-sprinkled meads—the merry swarm A smiling powerful word did next transform To little Roses mesh'd in green, allies Of earth and air, and everything we prize For mirthful, gentle, delicate, and warm.

William Allingham.

Tiger-Lilies

I like not lady-slippers, Nor yet the sweet-pea blossoms, Nor yet the flaky roses, Red, or white as snow; I like the chaliced lilies, The heavy Eastern lilies, The gorgeous tiger-lilies, That in our garden grow!

For they are tall and slender; Their mouths are dashed with carmine, And when the wind sweeps by them, On their emerald stalks They bend so proud and graceful,— They are Circassian women, The favorites of the Sultan, Adown our garden walks!

And when the rain is falling, I sit beside the window And watch them glow and glisten,— How they burn and glow! O for the burning lilies, The tender Eastern lilies, The gorgeous tiger-lilies, That in our garden grow!

Thomas Bailey Aldrich.

To the Fringed Gentian

Thou blossom bright with autumn dew, And colored with the heaven's own blue, That openest, when the quiet light Succeeds the keen and frosty night;

Thou comest not when violets lean O'er wandering brooks and springs unseen, Or columbines in purple dressed, Nod o'er the ground-bird's hidden nest.

Thou waitest late, and com'st alone, When woods are bare, and birds are flown, And frosts and shortening days portend The aged Year is near his end.

Then doth thy sweet and quiet eye Look through its fringes to the sky, Blue—blue—as if that sky let fall A flower from its cerulean wall. I would that thus, when I shall see The hour of death draw near to me, Hope, blossoming within my heart, May look to heaven as I depart.

William Cullen Bryant.

By courtesy of D. Appleton & Co., publishers of Bryant's Complete Poetical Works.

To a Mountain Daisy
On Turning One Down With the Plough in April.

Wee, modest, crimson-tipped flow'r, Thou's met me in an evil hour; For I maun crush amang the stoure Thy slender stem; To spare thee now is past my pow'r, Thou bonnie gem!

Alas! it's no thy neebor sweet, The bonnie lark, companion meet! Bending thee 'mang the dewy weet, Wi' spreckl'd breast, When upward-springing, blithe, to greet The purpling east.

Cauld blew the bitter-biting north Upon thy early, humble birth; Yet cheerfully thou glinted forth Amid the storm, Scarce rear'd above the parent earth Thy tender form. The flaunting flow'rs our gardens yield, High shelt'ring woods and wa's maun shield; But thou, beneath the random bield O' clod or stane, Adorns the histie stibble-field, Unseen, alane.

There, in thy scanty mantle clad, Thy snawie bosom sun-ward spread, Thou lifts thy unassuming head In humble guise; But now the share uptears thy bed, And low thou lies.

Robert Burns.

Bind-Weed

In the deep shadow of the porch A slender bind-weed springs, And climbs, like airy acrobat, The trellises, and swings And dances in the golden sun In fairy loops and rings.

Its cup-shaped blossoms, brimmed with dew, Like pearly chalices, Hold cooling fountains, to refresh The butterflies and bees; And humming-birds on vibrant wings Hover, to drink at ease.

And up and down the garden-beds, Mid box and thyme and yew, And spikes of purple lavender, And spikes of larkspur blue, The bind-weed tendrils win their way, And find a passage through.

With touches coaxing, delicate, And arts that never tire, They tie the rose-trees each to each, The lilac to the brier, Making for graceless things a grace, With steady, sweet desire.

Till near and far the garden growths, The sweet, the frail, the rude, Draw close, as if with one consent, And find each other good, Held by the bind-weed's pliant loops, In a dear brotherhood.

Like one fair sister, slender, arch, A flower in bloom and poise, Gentle and merry and beloved, Making no stir or noise, But swaying, linking, blessing all A family of boys.

Susan Coolidge.

The Rhodora

In May, when sea-winds pierced our solitudes, I found the fresh Rhodora in the woods, Spreading its leafless blooms in a damp nook, To please the desert and the sluggish brook: The purple petals, fallen in the pool Made the black waters with their beauty gay; Here might the red-bird come his plumes to cool, And court the flower that cheapens his array. Rhodora! if the sages ask thee why This charm is wasted on the earth and sky, Dear, tell them, that if eyes were made for seeing, Then beauty is its own excuse for being. Why thou wert there, O rival of the rose! I never thought to ask; I never knew, But in my simple ignorance suppose The selfsame Power that brought me there, brought you.

Ralph Waldo Emerson.

A Song of Clover

I wonder what the Clover thinks,— Intimate friend of Bob-o'-links, Lover of Daisies slim and white, Waltzer with Buttercups at night; Keeper of Inn for traveling Bees, Serving to them wine-dregs and lees, Left by the Royal Humming Birds, Who sip and pay with fine-spun words; Fellow with all the lowliest, Peer of the gayest and the best; Comrade of winds, beloved of sun, Kissed by the Dew-drops, one by one; Prophet of Good-Luck mystery By sign of four which few may see; Symbol of Nature's magic zone, One out of three, and three in one; Emblem of comfort in the speech Which poor men's babies early reach; Sweet by the roadsides, sweet by rills, Sweet in the meadows, sweet on hills, Sweet in its white, sweet in its red,— Oh, half its sweetness cannot be said;— Sweet in its every living breath, Sweetest, perhaps, at last, in death! Oh! who knows what the Clover thinks? No one! unless the Bob-o'-links!

"Saxe Holm."

To the Dandelion

(Extract)

Dear common flower, that grow'st beside the way, Fringing the dusty road with harmless gold, First pledge of blithesome May, Which children pluck, and, full of pride uphold, High-hearted buccaneers, o'erjoyed that they An Eldorado in the grass have found, Which not the rich earth's ample round May match in wealth, thou art more dear to me Than all the prouder summer-blooms may be.

James Russell Lowell.

To Daffodils

Fair Daffodils, we weep to see You haste away so soon; As yet the early-rising sun Has not attained his noon. Stay, stay, Until the hastening day Has run But to the even-song; And, having prayed together, we Will go with you along.

We have short time to stay, as you, We have as short a spring; As quick a growth to meet decay, As you, or anything. We die As your hours do, and dry Away, Like to the summer's rain; Or as the pearls of morning's dew, Ne'er to be found again.

Robert Herrick.

The Daffodils

I wandered lonely as a cloud That floats on high o'er vales and hills, When all at once I saw a crowd,— A host, of golden daffodils, Beside the lake, beneath the trees, Fluttering and dancing in the breeze.

Continuous as the stars that shine And twinkle on the milky way, They stretched in never-ending line Along the margin of a bay: Ten thousand saw I at a glance, Tossing their heads in sprightly dance.

The waves beside them danced, but they Outdid the sparkling waves in glee; A poet could not but be gay In such a jocund company. I gazed, and gazed, but little thought What wealth the show to me had brought:

For oft, when on my couch I lie In vacant or in pensive mood, They flash upon that inward eye Which is the bliss of solitude; And then my heart with pleasure fills, And dances with the daffodils.

William Wordsworth.

The White Anemone

'Tis the white anemone, fashioned so Like to the stars of the winter snow, First thinks, "If I come too soon, no doubt I shall seem but the snow that stayed too long, So 'tis I that will be Spring's unguessed scout," And wide she wanders the woods among. Then, from out the mossiest hiding-places, Smile meek moonlight-colored faces Of pale primroses puritan, In maiden sisterhood demure; Each virgin floweret faint and wan With the bliss of her own sweet breath so pure.

* * * *

Owen Meredith.

(Edward Robert Bulwer-Lytton.)

The Grass

The grass so little has to do,— A sphere of simple green, With only butterflies to brood, And bees to entertain,

And stir all day to pretty tunes The breezes fetch along, And hold the sunshine in its lap And bow to everything;

And thread the dews all night, like pearls, And make itself so fine,— A duchess were too common For such a noticing.

And even when it dies, to pass In odors so divine, As lowly spices gone to sleep, Or amulets of pine.

And then to dwell in sovereign barns, And dream the days away,— The grass so little has to do, I wish I were the hay!
Emily Dickinson.

The Corn-Song

Heap high the farmer's wintry hoard! Heap high the golden corn! No richer gift has Autumn poured From out her lavish horn!

Let other lands, exulting, glean The apple from the pine, The orange from its glossy green, The cluster from the vine;

We better love the hardy gift Our rugged vales bestow, To cheer us when the storm shall drift Our harvest-fields with snow.

Through vales of grass and meads of flowers, Our ploughs their furrows made, While on the hills the sun and showers Of changeful April played.

We dropped the seed o'er hill and plain, Beneath the sun of May, And frightened from our sprouting grain The robber crows away.

All through the long, bright days of June Its leaves grew green and fair, And waved in hot midsummer's noon Its soft and yellow hair.

And now with autumn's moonlit eves, Its harvest-time has come, We pluck away the frosted leaves, And bear the treasure home.

There richer than the fabled gift Apollo showered of old, Fair hands the broken grain shall sift, And knead its meal of gold.

Let vapid idlers loll in silk Around their costly board; Give us the bowl of samp and milk, By homespun beauty poured!

Where'er the wide old kitchen hearth Sends up its smoky curls, Who will not thank the kindly earth, And bless our farmer girls!

Then shame on all the proud and vain, Whose folly laughs to scorn The blessing of our hardy grain, Our wealth of golden corn!

Let earth withhold her goodly root, Let mildew blight the rye, Give to the worm the orchard's fruit, The wheat field to the fly:

But let the good old crop adorn The hills our fathers trod; Still let us for his golden corn, Send up our thanks to God!
John Greenleaf Whittier.

Columbia's Emblem

Blazon Columbia's emblem The bounteous, golden Corn! Eons ago, of the great sun's glow And the joy of the earth, 'twas born. From Superior's shore to Chili, From the ocean of dawn to the west, With its banners of green and silken sheen It sprang at the sun's behest; And by dew and shower, from its natal hour, With honey and wine 'twas fed, Till on slope and plain the gods were fain To share the feast outspread: For the rarest boon to the land they loved Was the Corn so rich and fair, Nor star nor breeze o'er the farthest seas Could find its like elsewhere.

In their holiest temples the Incas Offered the heaven-sent Maize— Grains wrought of gold, in a silver fold, For the sun's enraptured gaze; And its harvest came to the wandering tribes As the gods' own gift and seal, And Montezuma's festal bread Was made of its sacred meal. Narrow their cherished fields; but ours Are broad as the continent's breast. And, lavish as leaves, the rustling sheaves Bring plenty and joy and rest; For they strew the plains and crowd the wains When the reapers meet at morn, Till blithe cheers ring and west winds sing A song for the garnered Corn.

29

The rose may bloom for England, The lily for France unfold; Ireland may honor the shamrock, Scotland her thistle bold; But the shield of the great Republic, The glory of the West, Shall bear a stalk of the tasseled Corn— The sun's supreme bequest! The arbutus and the golden rod The heart of the North may cheer, And the mountain laurel for Maryland Its royal clusters rear, And jasmine and magnolia The crest of the South adorn; But the wide Republic's emblem Is the bounteous, golden Corn!

Edna Dean Proctor.

Scythe Song

Mowers, weary and brown, and blithe, What is the word methinks ye know, Endless over-word that the Scythe Sings to the blades of the grass below? Scythes that swing in the grass and clover, Something, still, they say as they pass; What is the word that, over and over, Sings the Scythe to the flowers and grass?

Hush, ah hush, the Scythes are saying, *Hush, and heed not, and fall asleep; Hush*, they say to the grasses swaying, *Hush*, they sing to the clover deep! *Hush*—'tis the lullaby Time is singing— *Hush, and heed not, for all things pass, Hush, ah hush!* and the Scythes are swinging Over the clover, over the grass!

Andrew Lang.

By courtesy of Longmans, Green & Co.

Time to Go

They know the time to go! The fairy clocks strike their inaudible hour In field and woodland, and each punctual flower Bows at the signal an obedient head And hastes to bed.

The pale Anemone Glides on her way with scarcely a good-night; The Violets tie their purple nightcaps tight; Hand clasped in hand, the dancing Columbines, In blithesome lines,

Drop their last courtesies, Flit from the scene, and couch them for their rest; The Meadow Lily folds her scarlet vest And hides it 'neath the Grasses' lengthening green; Fair and serene,

Her sister Lily floats On the blue pond, and raises golden eyes To court the golden splendor of the skies,— The sudden signal comes, and down she goes To find repose

In the cool depths below. A little later, and the Asters blue Depart in crowds, a brave and cheery crew; While Golden-rod, still wide awake and gay, Turns him away,

Furls his bright parasol, And, like a little hero, meets his fate. The Gentians, very proud to sit up late, Next follow. Every Fern is tucked and set 'Neath coverlet, Downy and soft and warm. No little seedling voice is heard to grieve Or make complaints the folding woods beneath; No lingerer dares to stay, for well they know The time to go.

Teach us your patience, brave, Dear flowers, till we shall dare to part like you, Willing God's will, sure that his clock strikes true, That his sweet day augurs a sweeter morrow, With smiles, not sorrow.

Susan Coolidge.

The Death of the Flowers

The melancholy days have come, the saddest of the year, Of wailing winds, and naked woods, and meadows brown and sere. Heaped in the hollows of the grove, the withered leaves lie dead; They rustle to the eddying gust, and to the rabbit's tread. The robin and the wren are flown, and from the shrubs the jay, And from the wood-top calls the crow, through all the gloomy day.

Where are the flowers, the fair young flowers, that lately sprang and stood In brighter light and softer airs, a beauteous sisterhood? Alas! they all are in their graves, the gentle race of flowers Are lying in their lowly beds, with the fair and good of ours. The rain is falling where they lie, but the cold, November rain, Calls not, from out the gloomy earth, the lovely ones again.

The wind-flower and the violet, they perished long ago, And the brier-rose and the orchids died amid the summer glow; But on the hill the golden-rod, and the aster in the wood, And the yellow sun-flower by the brook in autumn beauty stood, Till fell the frost from the clear, cold heaven, as falls the plague on men, And the brightness of their smile was gone, from upland, glade, and glen.

And now, when comes the calm, mild day, as still such days will come, To call the squirrel and the bee from out their winter home; When the sound of dropping nuts is heard, though all the trees are still, And twinkle in the smoky light the waters of the rill, The south wind searches for the flowers whose fragrance late he bore, And sighs to find them in the wood and by the stream no more.

William Cullen Bryant.

By courtesy of D. Appleton & Co., publishers of Bryant's Complete Poetical Works.

Autumn's Mirth

'Tis all a myth that Autumn grieves, For, watch the rain among the leaves; With silver fingers dimly seen It makes each leaf a tambourine, And swings and leaps with elfin mirth To kiss the brow of mother earth; Or, laughing 'mid the trembling grass, It nods a greeting as you pass. Oh! hear the rain amid the leaves, 'Tis all a myth that Autumn grieves!

'Tis all a myth that Autumn grieves, For, list the wind among the sheaves; Far sweeter than the breath of May, Or storied scents of old Cathay, It blends the perfumes rare and good Of spicy pine and hickory wood And with a voice in gayest chime, It prates of rifled mint and thyme. Oh! scent the wind among the sheaves, 'Tis all a myth that Autumn grieves!

'Tis all a myth that Autumn grieves, Behold the wondrous web she weaves! By viewless hands her thread is spun Of evening vapors shyly won. Across the grass from side to side A myriad unseen shuttles glide Throughout the night, till on the height Aurora leads the laggard light. Behold the wondrous web she weaves, 'Tis all a myth that Autumn grieves!

Samuel Minturn Peck.

INTERLEAVES
On the Wing

Our "little brothers of the air," have you named them all without a gun, as Emerson asks in "Forbearance"? Shy, glancing eyes peer from nests half-hidden in leaves; the forest is vocal with melody, the air is tremulous with the whirr of tiny wings.

Poet-singers have written undying lines about their brother minstrels of the wood, and the "blithe lark," especially, has a proud place in poetry, apostrophized as he is by Shakespeare, Shelley, Frederick Tennyson, Wordsworth, and The Ettrick Shepherd.

As the skylark's note dies away we hear the saucy chatter of Cranch's Bobolink, the twitter of Keats's Goldfinches, the mournful cry of Celia Thaxter's Sandpiper, and the revolving wheel of Emily Dickinson's Humming-bird, with its resonance of emerald, its rush of cochineal. The feathered warblers, Robin, Bluebird, Swallow, speed their southern flight, but there are other songs of summer, voices of sweet and tiny cousins, heard at the lazy noontide; chirpings, rustlings of the green little vaulters in the sunny grass. And if the wee grasshoppers and those warm little housekeepers the crickets, have served as themes for Keats and Leigh Hunt, so has the humble bee provoked his tribute from the poets:

"His feet are shod with gauze, His helmet is of gold; His breast a single onyx With chrysophrase inlaid."

Come within earshot of his drowsy hum, his breezy bass,—Father Tabb's publican bee,

"Collecting the tax On honey and wax,"

or Emerson's yellow-breeched philosopher,

"Seeing only what is fair, Sipping only what is sweet."

IV
ON THE WING
Sing On, Blithe Bird!

I've plucked the berry from the bush, the brown nut from the tree, But heart of happy little bird ne'er broken was by me. I saw them in their curious nests, close couching, slyly peer With their wild eyes, like glittering beads, to note if harm were near; I passed them by, and blessed them all; I felt that it was good To leave unmoved the creatures small whose home was in the wood.

And here, even now, above my head, a lusty rogue doth sing; He pecks his swelling breast and neck, and trims his little wing. He will not fly; he knows full well, while chirping on that spray, I would not harm him for a world, or interrupt his lay. Sing on, sing on, blithe bird! and fill my heart with summer gladness; It has been aching many a day with measures full of sadness!

William Motherwell.

To a Skylark

Hail to thee, blithe spirit! Bird thou never wert— That from heaven or near it Pourest thy full heart In profuse strains of unpremeditated art.

Higher still and higher From the earth thou springest Like a cloud of fire; The blue deep thou wingest, And singing still dost soar, and soaring ever singest.

In the golden light'ning Of the sunken sun, O'er which clouds are bright'ning, Thou dost float and run, Like an embodied joy whose race is just begun.

The pale purple even Melts around thy flight; Like a star of heaven In the broad daylight, Thou art unseen, but yet I hear thy shrill delight—

Keen as are the arrows Of that silver sphere Whose intense lamp narrows In the white dawn clear, Until we hardly see, we feel, that it is there.

All the earth and air With thy voice is loud, As, when night is bare, From one lonely cloud The moon rains out her beams, and heaven is overflow'd.

31

What thou art we know not; What is most like thee? From rainbow clouds there flow not Drops so bright to see As from thy presence showers a rain of melody:—

Like a poet hidden In the light of thought, Singing hymns unbidden, Till the world is wrought To sympathy with hopes and fears it heeded not:

Like a high-born maiden In a palace tower, Soothing her love-laden Soul in secret hour With music sweet as love which overflows her bower:

Like a glow-worm golden In a dell of dew, Scattering unbeholden Its aërial hue Among the flowers and grass which screen it from the view:

Like a rose embow'red By its own green leaves, By warm winds deflow'red, Till the scent it gives Makes faint with too much sweet these heavy-wingèd thieves.

Sound of vernal showers On the twinkling grass, Rain-awak'ned flowers,— All that ever was, Joyous and clear and fresh,— thy music doth surpass.

Teach us, sprite or bird, What sweet thoughts are thine: I have never heard Praise of love or wine That panted forth a flood of rapture so divine.

Chorus hymeneal Or triumphal chant, Matched with thine, would be all But an empty vaunt— A thing wherein we feel there is some hidden want.

What objects are the fountains Of thy happy strain? What fields, or waves, or mountains? What shapes of sky or plain? What love of thine own kind? what ignorance of pain?

With thy clear keen joyance Languor cannot be: Shadow of annoyance Never came near thee: Thou lovest, but ne'er knew love's sad satiety.

Waking or asleep, Thou of death must deem Things more true and deep Than we mortals dream, Or how could thy notes flow in such a crystal stream?

We look before and after, And pine for what is not: Our sincerest laughter With some pain is fraught; Our sweetest songs are those that tell of saddest thought.

Yet, if we could scorn Hate and pride and fear, If we were things born Not to shed a tear, I know not how thy joy we ever should come near.

Better than all measures Of delightful sound, Better than all treasures That in books are found, Thy skill to poet were, thou scorner of the ground!

Teach me half the gladness That thy brain must know; Such harmonious madness From my lips would flow The world should listen then as I am listening now.

Percy Bysshe Shelley.

Sir Lark and King Sun: A Parable

"Good morrow, my lord!" in the sky alone, Sang the lark as the sun ascended his throne. "Shine on me, my lord; I only am come, Of all your servants, to welcome you home. I have flown right up, a whole hour, I swear, To catch the first shine of your golden hair."

"Must I thank you then," said the king, "Sir Lark, For flying so high and hating the dark? You ask a full cup for half a thirst: Half was love of me, and half love to be first. There's many a bird makes no such haste, But waits till I come: that's as much to my taste."

And King Sun hid his head in a turban of cloud, And Sir Lark stopped singing, quite vexed and cowed; But he flew up higher, and thought, "Anon The wrath of the king will be over and gone; And his crown, shining out of its cloudy fold, Will change my brown feathers to a glory of gold."

So he flew—with the strength of a lark he flew; But, as he rose, the cloud rose too; And not one gleam of the golden hair Came through the depths of the misty air; Till, weary with flying, with sighing sore, The strong sun-seeker could do no more.

His wings had had no chrism of gold; And his feathers felt withered and worn and old; He faltered, and sank, and dropped like a stone. And there on his nest, where he left her, alone Sat his little wife on her little eggs, Keeping them warm with wings and legs.

Did I say alone? Ah, no such thing! Full in her face was shining the king. "Welcome, Sir Lark! You look tired," said he; "Up is not always the best way to me. While you have been singing so high and away, I've been shining to your little wife all day."

He had set his crown all about the nest, And out of the midst shone her little brown breast; And so glorious was she in russet gold, That for wonder and awe Sir Lark grew cold. He popped his head under her wing, and lay As still as a stone, till King Sun was away.

George MacDonald.

The Skylark

How the blithe Lark runs up the golden stair That leans thro' cloudy gates from Heaven to Earth, And all alone in the empyreal air Fills it with jubilant sweet songs of mirth; How far he seems, how far With the light upon his wings, Is it a bird or star That shines and sings?

*   *   *   *

And now he dives into a rainbow's rivers; In streams of gold and purple he is drown'd; Shrilly the arrows of his song he shivers, As tho' the stormy drops were turned to sound: And now he issues thro', He scales a cloudy tower; Faintly, like falling dew, His fast notes shower.

*   *   *   *

Frederick Tennyson.

By courtesy of John Lane.

The Skylark

Bird of the wilderness, Blithesome and cumberless, Sweet be thy matin o'er moorland and lea! Emblem of happiness, Blest is thy dwelling-place,— Oh, to abide in the desert with thee! Wild is thy lay and loud Far in the downy cloud, Love gives it energy, love gave it birth! Where, on thy dewy wing, Where art thou journeying? Thy lay is in heaven, thy love is on earth.

O'er fell and fountain sheen, O'er moor and mountain green, O'er the red streamer that heralds the day, Over the cloudlet dim, Over the rainbow's rim, Musical cherub, soar, singing, away! Then, when the gloaming comes, Low in the heather blooms Sweet will thy welcome and bed of love be! Emblem of happiness, Blest is thy dwelling-place— Oh, to abide in the desert with thee!

James Hogg.

(The Ettrick Shepherd.)

The Bobolinks

When Nature had made all her birds, With no more cares to think on, She gave a rippling laugh, and out There flew a Bobolinkon.

She laughed again; out flew a mate; A breeze of Eden bore them Across the fields of Paradise, The sunrise reddening o'er them.

Incarnate sport and holiday, They flew and sang forever; Their souls through June were all in tune, Their wings were weary never.

Their tribe, still drunk with air and light, And perfume of the meadow, Go reeling up and down the sky, In sunshine and in shadow.

One springs from out the dew-wet grass; Another follows after; The morn is thrilling with their songs And peals of fairy laughter.

From out the marshes and the brook, They set the tall reeds swinging, And meet and frolic in the air, Half prattling and half singing.

When morning winds sweep meadow-lands In green and russet billows. And toss the lonely elm-tree's boughs. And silver all the willows,

I see you buffeting the breeze, Or with its motion swaying, Your notes half drowned against the wind, Or down the current playing.

When far away o'er grassy flats, Where the thick wood commences, The white-sleeved mowers look like specks, Beyond the zigzag fences,

And noon is hot, and barn-roofs gleam White in the pale blue distance, I hear the saucy minstrels still In chattering persistence.

When eve her domes of opal fire Piles round the blue horizon, Or thunder rolls from hill to hill A Kyrie Eleison,

Still merriest of the merry birds, Your sparkle is unfading,— Pied harlequins of June,—no end Of song and masquerading.

*   *   *   *

Hope springs with you: I dread no more Despondency and dulness; For Good Supreme can never fail That gives such perfect fulness.

The life that floods the happy fields With song and light and color Will shape our lives to richer states, And heap our measures fuller.

Christopher Pearse Cranch.

To a Waterfowl

Whither 'midst falling dew, While glow the heavens with the last steps of day, Far, through their rosy depths, dost thou pursue Thy solitary way?

Vainly the fowler's eye Might mark thy distant flight to do thee wrong, As, darkly painted on the crimson sky, Thy figure floats along.

Seek'st thou the plashy brink Of weedy lake, or marge of river wide, Or where the rocky billows rise and sink On the chafed ocean-side?

There is a Power whose care Teaches thy way along that pathless coast,— The desert and illimitable air,— Lone wandering, but not lost.

All day thy wings have fanned, At that far height, the cold, thin atmosphere, Yet stoop not, weary, to the welcome land, Though the dark night is near.

And soon that toil shall end; Soon shalt thou find a summer home, and rest, And scream among thy fellows; reeds shall bend, Soon, o'er thy sheltered nest.

Thou'rt gone, the abyss of heaven Hath swallowed up thy form; yet, on my heart Deeply hath sunk the lesson thou hast given, And shall not soon depart.

He who, from zone to zone, Guides through the boundless sky thy certain flight, In the long way that I must tread alone, Will lead my steps aright.

William Cullen Bryant.

By courtesy of D. Appleton & Co., publishers of Bryant's Complete Poetical Works.

Goldfinches

Sometimes goldfinches one by one will drop From low-hung branches; little space they stop, But sip, and twitter, and their feathers sleek, Then off at once, as in a wanton freak; Or perhaps, to show their black and golden wings, Pausing upon their yellow flutterings. Were I in such a place, I sure should pray That naught less sweet might call my thoughts away Than the soft rustle of a maiden's gown Fanning away the dandelion's down.

John Keats.

The Sandpiper

Across the narrow beach we flit, One little sandpiper and I; And fast I gather, bit by bit, The scattered driftwood, bleached and dry. The wild waves reach their hands for it, The wild wind raves, the tide runs high, As up and down the beach we flit,— One little sandpiper and I.

Above our heads the sullen clouds Scud black and swift across the sky; Like silent ghosts in misty shrouds Stand out the white lighthouses high. Almost as far as eye can reach I see the close-reefed vessels fly, As fast we flit along the beach,— One little sandpiper and I.

I watch him as he skims along, Uttering his sweet and mournful cry; He starts not at my fitful song, Or flash of fluttering drapery. He has no thought of any wrong; He scans me with a fearless eye; Stanch friends are we, well tried and strong, The little sandpiper and I.

Comrade, where wilt thou be to-night When the loosed storm breaks furiously? My driftwood fire will burn so bright! To what warm shelter canst thou fly? I do not fear for thee, though wroth The tempest rushes through the sky; For are we not God's children both, Thou, little sandpiper, and I?

Celia Thaxter.

The Eagle
(Fragment)

He clasps the crag with hookèd hands; Close to the sun in lonely lands, Ring'd with the azure world, he stands.

The wrinkled sea beneath him crawls; He watches from his mountain walls; And like a thunderbolt he falls.

Alfred, Lord Tennyson.

Child's Talk in April

I wish you were a pleasant wren, And I your small accepted mate; How we'd look down on toilsome men! We'd rise and go to bed at eight Or it may be not quite so late.

Then you should see the nest I'd build, The wondrous nest for you and me; The outside rough perhaps, but filled With wool and down; ah, you should see The cosy nest that it would be.

We'd have our change of hope and fear, Some quarrels, reconcilements sweet: I'd perch by you to chirp and cheer, Or hop about on active feet, And fetch you dainty bits to eat.

We'd be so happy by the day. So safe and happy through the night, We both should feel, and I should say, It's all one season of delight, And we'll make merry whilst we may.

Perhaps some day there'd be an egg When spring had blossomed from the snow: I'd stand triumphant on one leg; Like chanticleer I'd almost crow To let our little neighbours know.

Next you should sit and I would sing Through lengthening days of sunny spring; Till, if you wearied of the task, I'd sit; and you should spread your wing From bough to bough; I'd sit and bask.

Fancy the breaking of the shell, The chirp, the chickens wet and bare, The untried proud paternal swell; And you with housewife-matron air Enacting choicer bills of fare.

Fancy the embryo coats of down, The gradual feathers soft and sleek; Till clothed and strong from tail to crown, With virgin warblings in their beak, They too go forth to soar and seek.

So would it last an April through And early summer fresh with dew, Then should we part and live as twain: Love-time would bring me back to you And build our happy nest again.

Christina G. Rossetti.

The Flight of the Birds

Whither away, Robin, Whither away? Is it through envy of the maple-leaf, Whose blushes mock the crimson of thy breast, Thou wilt not stay? The summer days were long, yet all too brief The happy season thou hast been our guest: Whither away?

Whither away, Bluebird, Whither away? The blast is chill, yet in the upper sky Thou still canst find the color of thy wing, The hue of May. Warbler, why speed thy southern flight? ah, why, Thou too, whose song first told us of the Spring? Whither away?

Whither away, Swallow, Whither away? Canst thou no longer tarry in the North, Here, where our roof so well hath screened thy nest? Not one short day? Wilt thou—as if thou human wert—go forth And wanton far from them who love thee best? Whither away?

Edmund Clarence Stedman.

The Shepherd's Home

My banks they are furnished with bees, Whose murmur invites one to sleep; My grottoes are shaded with trees, And my hills are white over with sheep. I seldom have met with a loss, Such health do my fountains bestow; My fountains all bordered with moss, Where the harebells and violets blow.

Not a pine in the grove is there seen, But with tendrils of woodbine is bound; Not a beech's more beautiful green, But a sweetbrier entwines it around. Not my fields in the prime of the year, More charms than my cattle unfold; Not a brook that is limpid and clear, But it glitters with fishes of gold.

I have found out a gift for my fair, I have found where the wood pigeons breed, But let me such plunder forbear, She will say 'twas a barbarous deed; For he ne'er could be true, she averred, Who would rob a poor bird of its young; And I loved her the more when I heard Such tenderness fall from her tongue.

William Shenstone.

To a Cricket

Voice of Summer, keen and shrill, Chirping round my winter fire, Of thy song I never tire, Weary others as they will; For thy song with Summer's filled— Filled with sunshine, filled with June; Firelight echo of that noon Heard in fields when all is stilled In the golden light of May, Bringing scents of new-mown hay, Bees, and birds, and flowers away: Prithee, haunt my fireside still, Voice of Summer, keen and shrill!

William C. Bennett.

On the Grasshopper and Cricket

The poetry of earth is never dead: When all the birds are faint with the hot sun, And hide in cooling trees, a voice will run From hedge to hedge about the new-mown mead; That is the Grasshopper's—he takes the lead In summer luxury,—he has never done With his delights; for when tired out with fun, He rests at ease beneath some pleasant weed. The poetry of earth is ceasing never: On a lone winter evening, when the frost Has wrought a silence, from the stove there shrills The Cricket's song, in warmth increasing ever, And seems to one, in drowsiness half lost, The Grasshopper's among some grassy hills.

John Keats.

The Tax-Gatherer

"And pray, who are you?" Said the violet blue To the Bee, with surprise At his wonderful size, In her eye-glass of dew.

"I, madam," quoth he, "Am a publican Bee, Collecting the tax Of honey and wax. Have you nothing for me?"

John B. Tabb.

To the Grasshopper and the Cricket

Green little vaulter in the sunny grass, Catching your heart up at the feel of June,— Sole voice that's heard amidst the lazy noon, When even the bees lag at the summoning brass; And you, warm little housekeeper, who class With those who think the candles come too soon, Loving the fire, and with your tricksome tune Nick the glad silent moments as they pass! O sweet and tiny cousins, that belong, One to the fields, the other to the hearth, Both have your sunshine; both, though small, are strong At your clear hearts; and both seem given to earth To sing in thoughtful ears their natural song,— In doors and out, summer and winter, Mirth.

Leigh Hunt.

The Bee

Like trains of cars on tracks of plush I hear the level bee: A jar across the flowers goes, Their velvet masonry

Withstands until the sweet assault Their chivalry consumes, While he, victorious, tilts away To vanquish other blooms. His feet are shod with gauze, His helmet is of gold; His breast, a single onyx With chrysoprase, inlaid.

His labor is a chant, His idleness a tune; Oh, for a bee's experience Of clovers and of noon!

Emily Dickinson.

The Humble-Bee

Burly, dozing humble-bee, Where thou art is clime for me. Let them sail for Porto Rique, Far-off heats through seas to seek; I will follow thee alone, Thou animated torrid zone! Zigzag steerer, desert cheerer, Let me chase thy waving lines; Keep me nearer, me thy hearer, Singing over shrubs and vines.

Insect lover of the sun, Joy of thy dominion! Sailor of the atmosphere; Swimmer through the waves of air; Voyager of light and noon; Epicurean of June,— Wait, I prithee, till I come Within earshot of thy hum,— All without is martyrdom.

When the south wind, in May days, With a net of shining haze Silvers the horizon wall, And with softness touching all, Tints the human countenance With a color of romance, And, infusing subtle heats, Turns the sod to violets, Thou, in sunny solitudes, Rover of the underwoods, The green silence dost displace With thy mellow, breezy bass.

Hot midsummer's petted crone, Sweet to me thy drowsy tone Tells of countless sunny hours, Long days, and solid banks of flowers; Of gulfs of sweetness without bound In Indian wildernesses found; Of Syrian peace, immortal leisure, Firmest cheer, and bird-like pleasure.

Aught unsavory or unclean Hath my insect never seen; But violets and bilberry bells, Maple-sap and daffodels, Grass with green flag half-mast high, Succory to match the sky, Columbine with horn of honey, Scented fern, and agrimony, Clover, catchfly, adder's-tongue And brier-roses, dwelt among; All beside was unknown waste, All was picture as he passed.

Wiser far than human seer, Yellow-breeched philosopher! Seeing only what is fair, Sipping only what is sweet, Thou dost mock at fate and care, Leave the chaff and take the wheat; When the fierce northwestern blast Cools sea and land so far and fast, Thou already slumberest deep; Woe and want thou canst outsleep: Want and woe, which torture us, Thy sleep makes ridiculous.

Ralph Waldo Emerson.

All Things Wait Upon Thee

Innocent eyes not ours And made to look on flowers, Eyes of small birds, and insects small; Morn after summer morn The sweet rose on her thorn Opens her bosom to them all. The last and least of things, That soar on quivering wings, Or crawl among the grass blades out of sight, Have just as clear a right To their appointed portion of delight As queens or kings.

Christina G. Rossetti.

Providence

Lo, the lilies of the field, How their leaves instruction yield! Hark to Nature's lesson given By the blessed birds of heaven! Every bush and tufted tree Warbles sweet philosophy: Mortal, fly from doubt and sorrow, God provideth for the morrow.

Say, with richer crimson glows The kingly mantle than the rose? Say, have kings more wholesome fare Than we citizens of air? Barns nor hoarded grain have we, Yet we carol merrily. Mortal, fly from doubt and sorrow, God provideth for the morrow.

One there lives, whose guardian eye Guides our humble destiny; One there lives, who, Lord of all, Keeps our feathers lest they fall. Pass we blithely then the time, Fearless of the snare and lime, Free from doubt and faithless sorrow: God provideth for the morrow.

Reginald Heber.

INTERLEAVES

The Inglenook

"With his flute of reeds a stranger Wanders piping through the village, Beckons to the fairest maiden, And she follows where he leads her, Leaving all things for the stranger."

The ancient arrowmaker is left standing lonely at the door of his wigwam, but Laughing Water and Hiawatha have gone to make a new household among the myriad homes of earth.

It matters not whether the inglenook be in wigwam or cabin, cottage or palace, if *Love Dwells Within* be graven upon the threshold, for "where a true wife comes, there home is always around her." She is the Domina or House Lady, and under the benediction of her gaze arise sweet order, peace, and restful charm. The "gudeman," too; "his very foot has music in't when he comes up the stair," and like the fire on the hearth he diffuses warmth and comfort and good cheer. By and by a cradle swings to and fro in the sheltered corner of the fireside; baby feet have come to stray on life's untrodden brink; baby eyes whose speech make dumb the wise smile up into the mother's as she sings her lullaby:

"The Queen has sceptre, crown, and ball, You are my sceptre, crown, and all. And it's O! sweet, sweet, and a lullaby."

The dog and the cat snooze peacefully on the hearth, the kettle hums, the kitchen clock ticks drowsily. The circle of love widens to take in all who are helping to make home beautiful—the farm boy, the milkmaid, and even the whinnying mare and friendly cow.

The poetry of the inglenook is simple, unpretentious, humble, but it has a tender charm of its own because it sings of a heaven far on this side of the stars:

"By men called home."

V

THE INGLENOOK

A New Household

O Fortunate, O happy day, When a new household finds its place Among the myriad homes of earth, Like a new star just sprung to birth, And rolled on its harmonious way Into the boundless realms of space!

*   *   *   *

Henry Wadsworth Longfellow.
From "The Hanging of the Crane."

Two Heavens

For there are two heavens, sweet, Both made of love,—one, inconceivable Ev'n by the other, so divine it is; The other, far on this side of the stars, By men called home.

Leigh Hunt.

A Song of Love

Say, what is the spell, when her fledglings are cheeping, That lures the bird home to her nest? Or wakes the tired mother, whose infant is weeping, To cuddle and croon it to rest? What the magic that charms the glad babe in her arms, Till it cooes with the voice of the dove? 'Tis a secret, and so let us whisper it low— And the name of the secret is Love! For I think it is Love, For I feel it is Love, For I'm sure it is nothing but Love!

Say, whence is the voice that when anger is burning, Bids the whirl of the tempest to cease? That stirs the vexed soul with an aching—a yearning For the brotherly hand-grip of peace? Whence the music that fills all our being—that thrills Around us, beneath, and above? 'Tis a secret: none knows how it comes, or it goes— But the name of the secret is Love! For I think it is Love, For I feel it is Love, For I'm sure it is nothing but Love!

Say, whose is the skill that paints valley and hill, Like a picture so fair to the sight? That flecks the green meadow with sunshine and shadow, Till the little lambs leap with delight? 'Tis a secret untold to hearts cruel and cold, Though 'tis sung, by the angels above, In notes that ring clear for the ears that can hear— And the name of the secret is Love! For I think it is Love, For I feel it is Love, For I'm sure it is nothing but Love!

Lewis Carroll.

Mother's Song

My heart is like a fountain true That flows and flows with love to you. As chirps the lark unto the tree So chirps my pretty babe to me. And it's O! sweet, sweet! and a lullaby.

There's not a rose where'er I seek, As comely as my baby's cheek. There's not a comb of honey-bee, So full of sweets as babe to me. And it's O! sweet, sweet! and a lullaby.

There's not a star that shines on high, Is brighter than my baby's eye. There's not a boat upon the sea, Can dance as baby does to me. And it's O! sweet, sweet! and a lullaby.

No silk was ever spun so fine As is the hair of baby mine— My baby smells more sweet to me Than smells in spring the elder tree. And it's O! sweet, sweet! and a lullaby.

A little fish swims in the well, So in my heart does baby dwell. A little flower blows on the tree, My baby is the flower to me. And it's O! sweet, sweet! and a lullaby.

The Queen has sceptre, crown and ball, You are my sceptre, crown and all. For all her robes of royal silk, More fair your skin, as white as milk. And it's O! sweet, sweet! and a lullaby.

Ten thousand parks where deer run, Ten thousand roses in the sun, Ten thousand pearls beneath the sea, My baby more precious is to me. And it's O! sweet, sweet! and a lullaby.

West of England Lullaby.

The Bonniest Bairn in a' the Warl'

The bonniest bairn in a' the warl' Has skin like the drifted snaw, An' rosy wee cheeks sae saft an' sleek— There never was ither sic twa; Its een are just bonnie wee wander'd stars, Its leggies are plump like a farl, An' ilk ane maun see't, an' a' maun declare't The cleverest bairn, The daintiest bairn, The rosiest, cosiest, cantiest bairn, The dearest, queerest, Rarest, fairest, Bonniest bairn in a' the warl'.

37

The bonniest bairn in a' the warl' Ye ken whaur the ferlie lives? It's doon in yon howe, it's owre yon knowe— In the laps o' a thousand wives; It's up an' ayont in yon castle brent, The heir o' the belted earl; It's sookin' its thoomb in yon gipsy tent— The cleverest bairn, The daintiest bairn, The rosiest, cosiest, cantiest bairn, The dearest, queerest, Rarest, fairest, Bonniest bairn in a' the warl'.

*   *   *   *

Robert Ford.

Cuddle Doon

The bairnies cuddle doon at nicht, Wi' muckle faucht an' din; Oh, try an' sleep, ye waukrife rogues, Your father's comin' in. They never heed a word I speak; I try to gi'e a froon, But aye I hap them up, an' cry, "O, bairnies, cuddle doon."

Wee Jamie wi' the curly heid— He aye sleeps neist the wa', Bangs up an' cries, "I want a piece"; The rascal starts them a'. I rin an' fetch them pieces, drinks, They stop awee the soun'; Then draw the blankets up and cry, "Noo, weanies, cuddle doon."

But ere five minutes gang, wee Rab Cries oot frae 'neath the claes, "Mither, mak' Tam gie ower at ance— He's kittlin' wi' his taes." The mischief's in that Tam for tricks, He'd bother half the toon: But aye I hap them up an' cry, "O, bairnies, cuddle doon."

At length they hear their father's fit, An', as he steeks the door, They turn their faces to the wa', While Tam pretends to snore. "Hae a' the weans been gude?" he asks, As he pits aff his shoon; "The bairnies, John, are in their beds, An' lang since cuddled doon."

An' just afore we bed oorsel's, We look at oor wee lambs; Tam has his airm roun' wee Rab's neck, An' Rab his airm roun' Tam's. I lift wee Jamie up the bed, An', as I straik each croon, I whisper, till my heart fills up, "O, bairnies, cuddle doon."

The bairnies cuddle doon at nicht, Wi' mirth that's dear to me; But sune the big warl's cark an' care Will quaten doon their glee. Yet come what will to ilka ane, May He who sits aboon Aye whisper, though their pows be bauld, "O, bairnies, cuddle doon."

Alexander Anderson.

I Am Lonely

The world is great: the birds all fly from me, The stars are golden fruit upon a tree All out of reach: my little sister went, And I am lonely.

The world is great: I tried to mount the hill Above the pines, where the light lies so still, But it rose higher: little Lisa went And I am lonely.

The world is great: the wind comes rushing by, I wonder where it comes from; sea birds cry And hurt my heart: my little sister went, And I am lonely.

The world is great: the people laugh and talk, And make loud holiday: how fast they walk! I'm lame, they push me: little Lisa went, And I am lonely.

George Eliot.

From "The Spanish Gypsy."

Brother and Sister

But were another childhood-world my share, I would be born a little sister there.

I

I cannot choose but think upon the time When our two lives grew like two buds that kiss At lightest thrill from the bee's swinging chime, Because the one so near the other is.

He was the elder and a little man Of forty inches, bound to show no dread, And I the girl that puppy-like now ran, Now lagged behind my brother's larger tread.

I held him wise, and when he talked to me Of snakes and birds, and which God loved the best, I thought his knowledge marked the boundary Where men grew blind, though angels knew the rest.

If he said "Hush!" I tried to hold my breath; Wherever he said "Come!" I stepped in faith.

II

Long years have left their writing on my brow, But yet the freshness and the dew-fed beam Of those young mornings are about me now, When we two wandered toward the far-off stream With rod and line. Our basket held a store Baked for us only, and I thought with joy That I should have my share, though he had more, Because he was the elder and a boy.

The firmaments of daisies since to me Have had those mornings in their opening eyes, The bunchéd cowslip's pale transparency Carries that sunshine of sweet memories,

And wild-rose branches take their finest scent From those blest hours of infantine content.

III

Our mother bade us keep the trodden ways, Stroked down my tippet, set my brother's frill, Then with the benediction of

38

her gaze Clung to us lessening, and pursued us still

Across the homestead to the rookery elms, Whose tall old trunks had each a grassy mound, So rich for us, we counted them as realms With varied products: here were earth-nuts found,

And here the Lady-fingers in deep shade; Here sloping toward the Moat the rushes grew, The large to split for pith, the small to braid; While over all the dark rooks cawing flew, And made a happy strange solemnity, A deep-toned chant from life unknown to me.

*   *   *   *

IX

We had the selfsame world enlarged for each By loving difference of girl and boy: The fruit that hung on high beyond my reach He plucked for me, and oft he must employ

A measuring glance to guide my tiny shoe Where lay firm stepping-stones, or call to mind "This thing I like my sister may not do, For she is little, and I must be kind."

Thus boyish Will the nobler mastery learned Where inward vision over impulse reigns, Widening its life with separate life discerned, A Like unlike, a Self that self restrains.

His years with others must the sweeter be For those brief days he spent in loving me.

*   *   *   *

George Eliot.

Home

O Falmouth is a fine town with ships in the bay, And I wish from my heart it's there I was to-day; I wish from my heart I was far away from here, Sitting in my parlour and talking to my dear. For it's home, dearie, home—it's home I want to be. Our topsails are hoisted, and we'll away to sea. O the oak and the ash and the bonnie birken tree They're all growing green in the old countree.

In Baltimore a-walking a lady I did meet With her babe on her arm as she came down the street; And I thought how I sailed, and the cradle standing ready For the pretty little babe that has never seen its daddie. And it's home, dearie, home,—

O, if it be a lass, she shall wear a golden ring; And if it be a lad, he shall fight for his king; With his dirk and his hat and his little jacket blue He shall walk the quarter-deck as his daddie used to do. And it's home, dearie, home,—

O, there's a wind a-blowing, a-blowing from the west, And that of all the winds is the one I like the best, For it blows at our backs, and it shakes our pennon free, And it soon will blow us home to the old countree. For it's home, dearie, home— it's home I want to be. Our topsails are hoisted, and we'll away to sea. O the oak and the ash and the bonnie birken tree They're all growing green in the old countree.

William Ernest Henley.

Love Will Find Out the Way

Over the mountains And over the waves, Under the fountains And under the graves; Under floods that are deepest, Which Neptune obey, Over rocks that are steepest, Love will find out the way.

Where there is no place For the glow-worm to lie, Where there is no space For receipt of a fly; Where the midge dares not venture Lest herself fast she lay, If Love come, he will enter And will find out the way.

*   *   *   *

Old English.

The Sailor's Wife

And are ye sure the news is true? And are ye sure he's weel? Is this a time to think o' wark? Ye jades, lay by your wheel; Is this the time to spin a thread. When Colin's at the door? Reach down my cloak, I'll to the quay, And see him come ashore. For there's nae luck about the house, There's nae luck at a'; There's little pleasure in the house When our gudeman's awa.

And gie to me my bigonet, My bishop's satin gown; For I maun tell the baillie's wife That Colin's in the town. My Turkey slippers maun gae on, My stockins pearly blue; It's a' to pleasure our gudeman, For he's baith leal and true.

Rise, lass, and mak a clean fireside, Put on the muckle pot; Gie little Kate her button gown And Jock his Sunday coat; And mak their shoon as black as slaes, Their hose as white as snaw; It's a' to please my ain gudeman, For he's been long awa.

There's twa fat hens upo' the coop Been fed this month and mair; Mak haste and thraw their necks about, That Colin weel may fare; And spread the table neat and clean, Gar ilka thing look braw, For wha can tell how Colin fared When he was far awa?

Sae true his heart, sae smooth his speech, His breath like caller air; His very foot has music in't As he comes up the stair. And will I see his face again? And will I hear him speak? I'm downright dizzy wi' the thought, In troth I'm like to greet!

If Colin's weel, and weel content, I hae nae mair to crave; And gin I live to keep him sae, I'm blest aboon the lave: And will I see his face again? And will I hear him speak? I'm downright dizzy wi' the thought, In troth I'm like to greet. For there's nae

luck about the house, There's nae luck at a'; There's little pleasure in the house When our gudeman's awa.
William J. Mickle.

Evening at the Farm

Over the hill the farm-boy goes. His shadow lengthens along the land, A giant staff in a giant hand; In the poplar-tree, above the spring, The katydid begins to sing; The early dews are falling;— Into the stone-heap darts the mink; The swallows skim the river's brink; And home to the woodland fly the crows, When over the hill the farm-boy goes, Cheerily calling, "Co', boss! co', boss! co'! co'! co'!" Farther, farther, over the hill, Faintly calling, calling still, "Co', boss! co', boss! co'! co'!"

Into the yard the farmer goes, With grateful heart, at the close of day: Harness and chain are hung away; In the wagon-shed stand yoke and plough, The straw's in the stack, the hay in the mow, The cooling dews are falling;— The friendly sheep his welcome bleat, The pigs come grunting to his feet, And the whinnying mare her master knows, When into the yard the farmer goes, His cattle calling,— "Co', boss! co', boss! co'! co'!" While still the cow-boy, far away, Goes seeking those that have gone astray,— "Co', boss! co', boss! co'! co'!"

Now to her task the milkmaid goes. The cattle come crowding through the gate, Lowing, pushing, little and great; About the trough, by the farm-yard pump, The frolicsome yearlings frisk and jump, While the pleasant dews are falling;— The new milch heifer is quick and shy, But the old cow waits with tranquil eye, And the white stream into the bright pail flows, When to her task the milkmaid goes, Soothingly calling, "So, boss! so, boss! so! so! so!" The cheerful milkmaid takes her stool, And sits and milks in the twilight cool. Saying "So! so, boss! so! so!"

To supper at last the farmer goes. The apples are pared, the paper read, The stories are told, then all to bed. Without, the crickets' ceaseless song Makes shrill the silence all night long; The heavy dews are falling. The housewife's hand has turned the lock; Drowsily ticks the kitchen clock; The household sinks to deep repose, But still in sleep the farm-boy goes Singing, calling,— "Co', boss! co', boss! co'! co'! co'!" And oft the milkmaid, in her dreams, Drums in the pail with the flashing streams, Murmuring "So, boss! so!"
John Townsend Trowbridge.

Home Song

Stay, stay at home, my heart, and rest; Home-keeping hearts are happiest, For those that wander they know not where Are full of trouble and full of care, To stay at home is best.

Weary and homesick and distressed, They wander east, they wander west, And are baffled, and beaten and blown about By the winds of the wilderness of doubt; To stay at home is best.

Then stay at home, my heart, and rest; The bird is safest in its nest: O'er all that flutter their wings and fly A hawk is hovering in the sky; To stay at home is best.
Henry Wadsworth Longfellow.

Etude Rêaliste

I
A baby's feet, like seashells pink, Might tempt, should heaven see meet, An angel's lips to kiss, we think,— A baby's feet.
Like rose-hued sea-flowers toward the heat They stretch and spread and wink Their ten soft buds that part and meet.
No flower-bells that expand and shrink Gleam half so heavenly sweet, As shine on life's untrodden brink,— A baby's feet.
II
A baby's hands, like rosebuds furled, Where yet no leaf expands, Ope if you touch, though close upcurled,— A baby's hands.
Then, even as warriors grip their brands When battle's bolt is hurled, They close, clenched hard like tightening bands.
No rose-buds yet by dawn impearled Match, even in loveliest lands, The sweetest flowers in all the world,— A baby's hands.
III
A baby's eyes, ere speech begin, Ere lips learn words or sighs, Bless all things bright enough to win A baby's eyes.
Love while the sweet thing laughs and lies, And sleep flows out and in, Sees perfect in them Paradise!
Their glance might cast out pain and sin, Their speech make dumb the wise, By mute glad godhead felt within A baby's eyes. Algernon Charles Swinburne.

We Are Seven

———A simple child, That lightly draws its breath, And feels its life in every limb, What should it know of death?

I met a little cottage girl: She was eight years old, she said; Her hair was thick with many a curl That clustered round her head.

She had a rustic, woodland air, And she was wildly clad: Her eyes were fair, and very fair;— Her beauty made me glad.

"Sisters and brothers, little Maid, How many may you be?" "How many? Seven in all," she said, And wondering looked at me.

"And where are they? I pray you tell." She answered, "Seven are we; And two of us at Conway dwell, And two are gone to sea.

"Two of us in the churchyard lie, My sister and my brother; And, in the churchyard cottage, I Dwell near them with my mother."

"You say that two at Conway dwell, And two are gone to sea, Yet ye are seven! I pray you tell, Sweet Maid, how this may be."

Then did the little maid reply, "Seven boys and girls are we; Two of us in the churchyard lie, Beneath the churchyard tree."

"You run about, my little Maid, Your limbs they are alive; If two are in the churchyard laid Then ye are only five."

"Their graves are green, they may be seen," The little Maid replied, "Twelve steps or more from my mother's door, And they are side by side.

"My stockings there I often knit, My kerchief there I hem; And there upon the ground I sit And sing a song to them.

"And often after sunset, Sir, When it is light and fair, I take my little porringer And eat my supper there.

"The first that died was sister Jane; In bed she moaning lay, Till God released her of her pain; And then she went away.

"So in the churchyard she was laid; And, when the grass was dry, Together round her grave we played, My brother John and I.

"And when the ground was white with snow And I could run and slide, My brother John was forced to go, And he lies by her side."

"How many are you, then," said I, "If they two are in heaven?" Quick was the little Maid's reply, "O Master! we are seven."

"But they are dead; those two are dead! Their spirits are in heaven!" 'Twas throwing words away: for still The little Maid would have her will, And said, "Nay, we are seven!"

William Wordsworth.

INTERLEAVES
Fairy Songs and Songs of Fancy

Most of these songs come to you from the masters of English poetry. Nations, like individuals, have their "play-spells," and Shakespeare, Drayton, and "rare Ben Jonson" belong to that wonderful age of Elizabeth when more than ten score of poets were making England a veritable nest of singing-birds.

Dowden says of the exquisite songs scattered through Shakespeare's plays, that if they do not make their own way, like the notes in the wildwood, no words will open the dull ear to take them in. Of Drayton we give you here "The Arming of Pigwiggen," from "Nymphidia," and later on "The Battle of Agincourt," called, respectively, the best fantastic poem and the best war poem in the language.

Then comes Milton the sublime; Milton set apart among poets; so that the adjective Miltonic has come to be a synonym for gravity, loftiness, and majesty. After Milton, Dryden, often called the greatest poet of a little age; but if he lacked the true sublimity he reverenced in the great Puritan, he was still the first, and perhaps the greatest, master of satirical poetry. Then, more than half a century afterward, comes Coleridge with his dreamy grace and his touch of the supernatural; his marvellous poetic gift, of sudden blossoming and sad and premature decay. Contemporary with Coleridge was Shelley, the master singer of his time, pouring out, like his own skylark, "his full heart in profuse strains of unpremeditated art."

When these two voices were hushed the Victorian era was dawning and the laurel worn by Wordsworth was placed on the brow of a poet who, by his perfect grace of manner, melody of rhythm, finished skill, clear insight, and nobility of thought, gave his name to the Tennysonian age.

VI
FAIRY SONGS AND SONGS OF FANCY
FAIRY LAND
I

Puck and the Fairy

Puck. How now, spirit! whither wander you?

Fairy. Over hill, over dale, Thorough bush, thorough brier, Over park, over pale, Thorough flood, thorough fire, I do wander everywhere, Swifter than the moonè's sphere; And I serve the fairy queen, To dew her orbs upon the green; The cowslips tall her pensioners be; In their gold coats, spots you see; Those be rubies, fairy favors, In those freckles live their savors; I must go seek some dewdrops here, And hang a pearl in every cowslip's ear. Farewell, thou lob of spirits; I'll be gone: Our queen and all her elves come here anon.

From "Midsummer-Night's Dream."

II

Lullaby for Titania

You spotted snakes with double tongue, Thorny hedgehogs, be not seen; Newts and blind-worms, do no wrong; Come not near our fairy queen.

Philomel, with melody, Sing in our sweet lullaby; Lulla, lulla, lullaby; lulla, lulla, lullaby! Never harm, Nor spell nor charm, Come our lovely lady nigh; So, good-night, with lullaby.

Weaving spiders, come not here; Hence, you long-legg'd spinners, hence! Beetles black, approach not near; Worm nor snail, do no offence.

Philomel, with melody, Sing in our sweet lullaby; Lulla, lulla, lullaby; lulla, lulla, lullaby! Never harm, Nor spell nor charm, Come our lovely lady nigh; So, good-night, with lullaby.

From "Midsummer-Night's Dream."

III

Oberon and Titania to the Fairy Train

Oberon. Through the house give glimmering light, By the dead and drowsy fire; Every elf and fairy sprite, Hop as light as bird from brier; And this ditty after me Sing, and dance it trippingly. *Titania.* First, rehearse your song by rote, To each word a warbling note: Hand in hand with fairy grace Will we sing and bless this place.

From "Midsummer-Night's Dream."

William Shakespeare.

IV

Ariel's Songs

I

Come unto these yellow sands, And then take hands: Court'sied when you have and kiss'd, (The wild waves whist) Foot it featly here and there; And sweet Sprites, the burthen bear. Hark, hark! Bow, wow, The watch-dog's bark: Bow, wow, Hark, hark! I hear The strain of strutting chanticleer Cry, Cock-a-diddle-dow!

II

Where the bee sucks, there suck I: In a cowslip's bell I lie; There I couch when owls do cry. On the bat's back I do fly, After summer merrily. Merrily, merrily, shall I live now, Under the blossom that hangs on the bough!

III

Full fathom five thy father lies; Of his bones are coral made; Those are pearls that were his eyes: Nothing of him that doth fade But doth suffer a sea-change Into something rich and strange. Sea-nymphs hourly ring his knell: Ding-dong. Hark! now I hear them— Ding-dong, bell!

William Shakespeare.

From "The Tempest."

Orpheus With His Lute

Orpheus with his lute made trees, And the mountain tops that freeze, Bow themselves when he did sing: To his music, plants and flowers Ever sprung; as sun and showers There had made a lasting spring.

Every thing that heard him play, Even the billows of the sea, Hung their heads, and then lay by. In sweet music is such art, Killing care and grief of heart Fall asleep or hearing, die.

William Shakespeare.

From "King Henry VIII."

The Arming of Pigwiggen

(He) quickly arms him for the field, A little cockle-shell his shield, Which he could very bravely wield, Yet could it not be piersed: His spear a bent both stiff and strong, And well near of two inches long; The pile was of a horsefly's tongue, Whose sharpness naught reversed.

And put him on a coat of mail, Which was of a fish's scale, That when his foe should him assail, No point should be prevailing. His rapier was a hornet's sting, It was a very dangerous thing; For if he chanc'd to hurt the king, It would be long in healing.

His helmet was a beetle's head, Most horrible and full of dread, That able was to strike one dead, Yet it did well become him: And for a plume a horse's hair, Which being tosséd by the air, Had force to strike his foe with fear, And turn his weapon from him.

Himself he on an earwig set, Yet scarce he on his back could get, So oft and high he did curvet Ere he himself could settle: He made him turn, and stop, and bound, To gallop, and to trot the round, He scarce could stand on any ground, He was so full of mettle.

Michael Drayton.

From "Nymphidia."

Hesperus' Song

Queen and huntress, chaste and fair, Now the sun is laid to sleep, Seated in thy silver chair, State in wonted manner keep. Hesperus entreats thy light, Goddess, excellently bright.

Earth, let not thy envious shade Dare itself to interpose; Cynthia's shining orb was made Heaven to clear, when day did close; Bless us then with wishèd sight, Goddess, excellently bright.

Lay thy bow of pearl apart, And thy crystal-shining quiver; Give unto the flying hart Space to breathe, how short soever: Thou that mak'st a day of night, Goddess, excellently bright.

Ben Jonson.

From "Cynthia's Revels."

L'Allegro
(Extracts)
* * * *

Haste thee, nymph, and bring with thee Jest and youthful Jollity, Quips, and Cranks, and wanton Wiles, Nods, and Becks, and Wreathèd Smiles. Such as hang on Hebe's cheek, And love to live in dimple sleek; Sport that wrinkled Care derides, And Laughter holding both his sides. Come, and trip it as you go On the light fantastic toe, And in thy right hand lead with thee The Mountain Nymph, sweet Liberty; And if I give thee honor due, Mirth, admit me of thy crew, To live with her, and live with thee, In unreprovèd pleasures free; To hear the Lark begin his flight, And singing startle the dull night, From his watch-tower in the skies, Till the dappled dawn doth rise; Then to come in spite of sorrow, And at my window bid good-morrow, Through the Sweet-Briar, or the Vine, Or the twisted Eglantine: While the Cock with lively din Scatters the rear of darkness thin, And to the stack, or the Barn-door, Stoutly struts his Dames before: Oft listening how the Hounds and horn Cheerly rouse the slumb'ring morn, From the side of some hoar hill, Through the high wood echoing shrill: Some time walking not unseen By Hedgerow Elms, on Hillocks green, Right against the Eastern gate, Where the great Sun begins his state, Robed in flames and Amber light, The clouds in thousand liveries dight. While the Plowman near at hand Whistles o'er the furrowed land, And the Milkmaid singeth blithe, And the Mower whets his scythe, And every Shepherd tells his tale Under the Hawthorn in the dale. Straight mine eye hath caught new pleasures Whilst the landskip round it measures, Russet Lawns, and Fallows gray, Where the nibbling flock do stray, Mountains on whose barren breast The laboring clouds do often rest, Meadows trim with Daisies pied, Shallow Brooks, and Rivers wide. Towers and Battlements it sees Bosomed high in tufted Trees, Where perhaps some beauty lies, The Cynosure of neighboring eyes. Hard by, a Cottage chimney smokes, From betwixt two aged Oaks, Where Corydon and Thyrsis met, Are at their savory dinner set Of Herbs, and other Country Messes, Which the neat-handed Phillis dresses; And then in haste her Bower she leaves With Thestylis to bind the Sheaves; Or, if the earlier season lead, To the tanned Haycock in the Mead. Sometimes with secure delight The upland Hamlets will invite, When the merry Bells ring round, And the jocund rebecks sound To many a youth, and many a maid, Dancing in the Checkered shade; And young and old come forth to play On a Sunshine Holy-day Till the livelong daylight fail; Then to the Spicy Nut-brown Ale, With stories told of many a feat, How Fairy Mab the junkets eat, She was pinched, and pulled, she said, And he by Friars' Lanthorn led, Tells how the drudging Goblin sweat, To earn his Cream-bowl duly set, When in one night, ere glimpse of morn, His shadowy Flail hath threshed the Corn, That ten day-laborers could not end; Then lies him down the Lubbar Fiend, And stretched out all the Chimney's length, Basks at the fire his hairy strength, And Crop-full out of doors he flings, Ere the first Cock his Matin rings. Thus done the Tales, to bed they creep By whispering Winds soon lulled asleep. Towered Cities please us then, And the busy hum of men, Where throngs of Knights and Barons bold In weeds of Peace high triumphs hold, With store of Ladies, whose bright eyes Rain influence, and judge the prize Of Wit, or Arms, while both contend To win her Grace, whom all commend. There let Hymen oft appear In Saffron robe, with Taper clear, And pomp, and feast, and revelry, With mask, and antique Pageantry; Such sights as youthful Poets dream On summer eves by haunted stream. Then to the well-trod stage anon, If Jonson's learnèd sock be on, Or sweetest Shakespeare, fancy's child. Warble his native Wood-notes wild. And ever against eating Cares, Lap me in soft Lydian airs, Married to immortal verse, Such as the meeting soul may pierce In notes, with many a winding bout Of linkèd sweetness long drawn out, With wanton heed, and giddy cunning, The melting voice through mazes running, Untwisting all the chains that tie The hidden soul of harmony; That Orpheus' self may heave his head From golden slumber on a bed Of heaped Elysian flowers, and hear Such strains as would have won the ear Of Pluto, to have quite set free His half-regained Eurydice. These delights, if thou canst give, Mirth, with thee I mean to live.

John Milton.

Sabrina Fair

The Spirit sings: Sabrina fair, Listen where thou art sitting Under the glassy, cool, translucent wave, In twisted braids of lilies knitting The loose train of thy amber-dropping hair; Listen for dear honor's sake, Goddess of the silver lake, Listen, and save! Listen, and appear to us, In name of great Oceanus;

*   *   *   *

By all the Nymphs that Nightly dance Upon thy streams with wily glance, Rise, rise, and heave thy rosy head From thy coral-paven bed, And bridle in thy headlong wave, Till thou our summons answered have. Listen, and save.

By the rushy-fringèd bank, Where grows the Willow and the Osier dank, My sliding Chariot stays, Thick set with agate, and the azure sheen Of turkis blue, and emerald green, That in the channel strays; Whilst from off the waters fleet Thus I set my printless feet O'er the Cowslip's Velvet head, That bends not as I tread; Gentle swain, at thy request I am here.

John Milton.

From "Comus."

Alexander's Feast

'Twas at the royal feast, for Persia won By Philip's warlike son: Aloft in awful state The godlike hero sate On his imperial throne: His valiant peers were placed around; Their brows with roses and with myrtles bound: (So should desert in arms be crowned.) The lovely Thais, by his side, Sate like a blooming Eastern bride In flower of youth and beauty's pride. Happy, happy, happy pair! None but the brave, None but the brave, None but the brave deserves the fair.

Chorus.

Happy, happy, happy pair! None but the brave, None but the brave, None but the brave deserves the fair.

Timotheus, placed on high Amid the tuneful quire, With flying fingers touched the lyre: The trembling notes ascend the sky, And heavenly joys inspire. The song began from Jove, Who left his blissful seats above, (Such is the power of mighty love.) A dragon's fiery form belied the god: Sublime on radiant spires he rode. The listening crowd admire the lofty sound, A present deity, they shout around; A present deity, the vaulted roofs rebound: With ravish'd ears The monarch hears, Assumes the god, Affects to nod, And seems to shake the spheres.

Chorus.

With ravish'd ears The monarch hears, Assumes the god, Affects to nod, And seems to shake the spheres.

John Dryden.

From "Ode on St. Cecilia's Day."

Kubla Khan

In Xanadu did Kubla Khan A stately pleasure-dome decree: Where Alph, the sacred river, ran Through caverns measureless to man, Down to a sunless sea. So twice five miles of fertile ground With walls and towers were girdled round: And there were gardens bright with sinuous rills Where blossomed many an incense-bearing tree; And here were forests ancient as the hills, Enfolding sunny spots of greenery.

But O! that deep romantic chasm which slanted Down the green hill athwart a cedarn cover! A savage place! as holy and enchanted As e'er beneath a waning moon was haunted By woman wailing for her demon-lover! And from this chasm, with ceaseless turmoil seething, As if this earth in fast thick pants were breathing, A mighty fountain momently was forced: Amid whose swift, half-intermitted burst Huge fragments vaulted like rebounding hail, Or chaffy grain beneath the thresher's flail: And 'mid these dancing rocks at once and ever It flung up momently the sacred river. Five miles meandering with a mazy motion Through wood and dale, the sacred river ran, Then reached the caverns measureless to man, And sank in tumult to a lifeless ocean: And 'mid this tumult Kubla heard from far Ancestral voices prophesying war!

The shadow of the dome of pleasure Floated midway on the waves; Where was heard the mingled measure From the fountain and the caves. It was a miracle of rare device, A sunny pleasure-dome with caves of ice! A damsel with a dulcimer In a vision once I saw: It was an Abyssinian maid, And on her dulcimer she played, Singing of Mount Abora. Could I revive within me Her sympathy and song, To such a deep delight 'twould win me, That with music loud and long, I would build that dome in air, That sunny dome! Those caves of ice! And all who heard should see them there, And all should cry, Beware! Beware! His flashing eyes, his floating hair! Weave a circle round him thrice, And close your eyes with holy dread, For he on honey-dew hath fed, And drunk the milk of Paradise.

Samuel Taylor Coleridge.

The Magic Car Moved On

The Fairy and the Soul proceeded; The silver clouds disparted; And, as the car of magic they ascended, Again the speechless music swelled, Again the coursers of the air Unfurled their azure pennons, and the Queen, Shaking the beamy reins, Bade them pursue their way.

The magic car moved on. The night was fair, and countless stars Studded heaven's dark-blue vault,— The eastern wave grew pale With the first smile of morn. The magic car moved on. From the celestial hoofs The atmosphere in flaming sparkles flew; And, where the burning wheels Eddied above the mountain's loftiest peak, Was traced a line of lightning. Now far above a rock, the utmost verge Of the wide earth, it flew— The rival of the Andes, whose dark brow Loured o'er the silver sea.

Far far below the chariot's path, Calm as a slumbering babe, Tremendous Ocean lay. The mirror of its stillness showed The pale and waning stars, The chariot's fiery track, And the grey light of morn Tingeing those fleecy clouds That cradled in their folds the infant dawn. The chariot seemed to fly Through the abyss of an immense concave, Radiant with million constellations, tinged With shades of infinite colour, And semicircled with a belt Flashing incessant meteors.

The magic car moved on. As they approached their goal, The coursers seemed to gather speed. The sea no longer was distinguished; earth Appeared a vast and shadowy sphere; The sun's unclouded orb Rolled through the black concave; Its rays of rapid light Parted around the chariot's swifter course, And fell like ocean's feathery spray Dashed from the boiling surge Before a vessel's prow. The magic car moved on. Earth's distant orb appeared The smallest light that twinkles in the heavens Whilst round the chariot's way Innumerable systems rolled, And countless spheres diffused An ever-varying glory. It was a sight of wonder: some Were hornèd like the crescent moon; Some shed a mild and silver beam Like Hesperus o'er the western sea; Some dashed athwart with trains of flame, Like worlds to death and ruin driven; Some shone like stars, and, as the chariot passed, Bedimmed all other light.

Percy Bysshe Shelley.

From "Queen Mab."

Arethusa

Arethusa arose From her couch of snows In the Acroceraunian mountains,— From cloud and from crag, With many a jag, Shepherding her bright fountains. She leapt down the rocks With her rainbow locks Streaming among the streams; Her steps paved with green The downward ravine Which slopes to the western gleams: And gliding and springing, She went, ever singing, In murmurs as soft as sleep; The Earth seemed to love her, And Heaven smiled above her, As she lingered towards the deep.

Then Alpheus bold, On his glacier cold, With his trident the mountains strook And opened a chasm In the rocks;—with the spasm All Erymanthus shook. And the black south wind It concealed behind The urns of the silent snow, And earthquake and thunder Did rend in sunder The bars of the springs below. The beard and the hair Of the River-god were Seen through the torrent's sweep, As he followed the light Of the fleet nymph's flight To the brink of the Dorian deep.

"Oh! save me! Oh! guide me! And bid the deep hide me! For he grasps me now by the hair!" The loud Ocean heard, To its blue depth stirred, And divided at her prayer; And under the water The Earth's white daughter Fled like a sunny beam, Behind her descended, Her billows unblended With the brackish Dorian stream. Like a gloomy stain On the emerald main, Alpheus rushed behind,— As an eagle pursuing A dove to its ruin Down the streams of the cloudy wind. Under the bowers Where the Ocean Powers Sit on their pearlèd thrones; Through the coral woods Of the weltering floods; Over heaps of unvalued stones; Through the dim beams Which amid the streams Weave a network of colored light; And under the caves Where the shadowy waves Are as green as the forest's night; Outspeeding the shark, And the swordfish dark,— Under the ocean foam, And up through the rifts Of the mountain clifts,— They passed to their Dorian home.

And now from their fountains In Enna's mountains, Down one vale where the morning basks, Like friends once parted Grown single-hearted, They ply their watery tasks. At sunrise they leap From their cradles steep In the cave of the shelving hill; At noontide they flow Through the woods below And the meadows of asphodel; And at night they sleep In the rocking deep Beneath the Ortygian shore;— Like the spirits that lie In the azure sky, When they love but live no more.

Percy Bysshe Shelley.

The Culprit Fay
(Extracts)
III
Fairy Dawn
* * * *

'Tis the hour of fairy ban and spell: The wood-tick has kept the minutes well; He has counted them all with click and stroke, Deep in the heart of the mountain oak, And he has awakened the sentry elve Who sleeps with him in the haunted tree, To bid him ring the hour of twelve, And call the fays to their revelry; Twelve small strokes on his tinkling bell— ('Twas made of the white snail's pearly shell)— "Midnight comes, and all is well! Hither, hither, wing your way! 'Tis the dawn of the fairy-day."

IV
The Assembling of the Fays

They come from beds of lichen green, They creep from the mullein's velvet screen; Some on the backs of beetles fly From the silver tops of moon-touched trees, Where they swung in their cobweb hammocks high, And rocked about in the evening breeze; Some from the humbird's downy nest— They had driven him out by elfin power, And, pillowed on plumes of his rainbow breast, Had slumbered there till the charmèd hour; Some had lain in the scoop of the rock, With glittering ising-stars inlaid; And some had opened the four-o'clock, And stole within its purple shade. And now they throng the moonlight glade, Above—below—on every side, Their little minim forms arrayed, In the tricksy pomp of fairy pride.

45

VI

The Throne of the Lily-King

The throne was reared upon the grass, Of spice-wood and of sassafras; On pillars of mottled tortoise-shell Hung the burnished canopy— And over it gorgeous curtains fell Of the tulip's crimson drapery. The monarch sat on his judgment-seat, On his brow the crown imperial shone, The prisoner Fay was at his feet, And his peers were ranged around the throne, He waved his sceptre in the air, He looked around and calmly spoke; His brow was grave and his eye severe, But his voice in a softened accent broke:

VII

The Fay's Crime

Fairy! Fairy! list and mark: Thou hast broke thine elfin chain; Thy flame-wood lamp is quenched and dark, And thy wings are dyed with a deadly stain— Thou hast sullied thine elfin purity In the glance of a mortal maiden's eye, Thou hast scorned our dread decree, And thou shouldst pay the forfeit high, But well I know her sinless mind Is pure as the angel forms above, Gentle and meek, and chaste and kind, Such as a spirit well might love; Fairy! had she spot or taint, Bitter had been thy punishment.

VIII

The Fay's Sentence

"Thou shalt seek the beach of sand Where the water bounds the elfin land; Thou shalt watch the oozy brine Till the sturgeon leaps in the bright moonshine, Then dart the glistening arch below, And catch a drop from his silver bow. The water-sprites will wield their arms And dash around, with roar and rave, And vain are the woodland spirits' charms, They are the imps that rule the wave. Yet trust thee in thy single might: If thy heart be pure and thy spirit right, Thou shalt win the warlock fight.

IX

"If the spray-bead gem be won, The stain of thy wing is washed away: But another errand must be done Ere thy crime be lost for aye; Thy flame-wood lamp is quenched and dark, Thou must reillume its spark. Mount thy steed and spur him high To the heaven's blue canopy; And when thou seest a shooting star, Follow it fast, and follow it far— The last faint spark of its burning train Shall light the elfin lamp again. Thou hast heard our sentence, Fay; Hence! to the water-side, away!"

X

The Fay's Departure

The goblin marked his monarch well; He spake not, but he bowed him low, Then plucked a crimson colen-bell, And turned him round in act to go. The way is long, he cannot fly, His soiléd wing has lost its power, And he winds adown the mountain high, For many a sore and weary hour. Through dreary beds of tangled fern, Through groves of nightshade dark and dern, Over the grass and through the brake, Where toils the ant and sleeps the snake; Now over the violet's azure flush He skips along in lightsome mood; And now he thrids the bramble-bush, Till its points are dyed in fairy blood. He has leaped the bog, he has pierced the brier, He has swum the brook, and waded the mire, Till his spirits sank, and his limbs grew weak, And the red waxed fainter in his cheek. He had fallen to the ground outright, For rugged and dim was his onward track, But there came a spotted toad in sight, And he laughed as he jumped upon her back: He bridled her mouth with a silkweed twist, He lashed her sides with an osier thong; And now, through evening's dewy mist, With leap and spring they bound along, Till the mountain's magic verge is past, And the beach of sand is reached at last.

Joseph Rodman Drake.

A Myth

A floating, a floating Across the sleeping sea, All night I heard a singing bird Upon the topmast tree.

"Oh, came you from the isles of Greece Or from the banks of Seine? Or off some tree in forests free That fringe the western main?"

"I came not off the old world, Nor yet from off the new; But I am one of the birds of God Which sing the whole night through."

"Oh, sing and wake the dawning! Oh, whistle for the wind! The night is long, the current strong, My boat it lags behind."

"The current sweeps the old world, The current sweeps the new; The wind will blow, the dawn will glow, Ere thou hast sailed them through."

Charles Kingsley.

The Fairy Folk

Up the airy mountain, Down the rushy glen We daren't go a-hunting, For fear of little men; Wee folk, good folk, Trooping all together; Green jacket, red cap, And white owl's feather.

Down along the rocky shore Some make their home, They live on crispy pancakes Of yellow tide-foam; Some in the reeds Of the black mountain-lake, With frogs for their watch-dogs, All night awake.

High on the hill-top The old King sits; He is now so old and gray He's nigh lost his wits. With a bridge of white mist

46

Columbkill he crosses, On his stately journeys From Slieveleague to Rosses; Or going up with music, On cold starry nights, To sup with the Queen Of the gay Northern Lights.

They stole little Bridget For seven years long; When she came down again Her friends were all gone. They took her lightly back, Between the night and morrow; They thought that she was fast asleep, But she was dead with sorrow. They have kept her ever since Deep within the lakes, On a bed of flag leaves, Watching till she wakes.

By the craggy hillside, Through the mosses bare, They have planted thorn-trees For pleasure here and there. Is any man so daring As dig one up in spite? He shall find the thornies set In his bed at night.

Up the airy mountain, Down the rushy glen, We daren't go a-hunting For fear of little men; Wee folk, good folk, Trooping all together; Green jacket, red cap, And white owl's feather.

William Allingham.

The Merman

I

Who would be A merman bold, Sitting alone, Singing alone Under the sea, With a crown of gold, On a throne?

II

I would be a merman bold, I would sit and sing the whole of the day; I would fill the sea-halls with a voice of power; But at night I would roam abroad and play With the mermaids in and out of the rocks, Dressing their hair with the white sea-flower; And holding them back by their flowing locks I would kiss them often under the sea, And kiss them again till they kiss'd me Laughingly, laughingly; And then we would wander away, away, To the pale-green sea-groves straight and high, Chasing each other merrily.

III

There would be neither moon nor star; But the wave would make music above us afar— Low thunder and light in the magic night— Neither moon nor star. We would call aloud in the dreamy dells, Call to each other and whoop and cry All night, merrily, merrily. They would pelt me with starry spangles and shells, Laughing and clapping their hands between, All night, merrily, merrily, But I would throw to them back in mine Turkis and agate and almondine; Then leaping out upon them unseen I would kiss them often under the sea, And kiss them again till they kiss'd me Laughingly, laughingly. O, what a happy life were mine Under the hollow-hung ocean green! Soft are the moss-beds under the sea; We would live merrily, merrily.

Alfred, Lord Tennyson.

The Mermaid

I

Who would be A mermaid fair, Singing alone, Combing her hair Under the sea, In a golden curl With a comb of pearl, On a throne?

II

I would be a mermaid fair; I would sing to myself the whole of the day; With a comb of pearl I would comb my hair; And still as I combed I would sing and say, "Who is it loves me? who loves not me?" I would comb my hair till my ringlets would fall Low adown, low adown, From under my starry sea-bud crown Low adown and around, And I should look like a fountain of gold Springing alone With a shrill inner sound, Over the throne In the midst of the hall; Till that great sea-snake under the sea From his coiled sleeps in the central deeps Would slowly trail himself sevenfold Round the hall where I sate, and look in at the gate With his large calm eyes for the love of me. And all the mermen under the sea Would feel their immortality Die in their hearts for the love of me.

III

But at night I would wander away, away, I would fling on each side my low-flowing locks, And lightly vault from the throne and play With the mermen in and out of the rocks; We would run to and fro, and hide and seek, On the broad sea-wolds in the crimson shells, Whose silvery spikes are nearest the sea. But if any came near I would call and shriek, And adown the steep like a wave I would leap From the diamond ledges that jut from the dells; For I would not be kiss'd by all who would list, Of the bold merry mermen under the sea; They would sue me, and woo me, and flatter me, In the purple twilights under the sea; But the king of them all would carry me, Woo me, win me, and marry me, In the branching jaspers under the sea; Then all the dry pied things that be In the hueless mosses under the sea Would curl round my silver feet silently, All looking up for the love of me. And if I should carol aloud from aloft All things that are forked and horned and soft Would lean out from the hollow sphere of the sea, All looking down for the love of me.

Alfred, Lord Tennyson.

Bugle Song

The splendor falls on castle walls, And snowy summits old in story; The long light shakes across the lakes, And the wild cataract leaps in glory. Blow, bugle, blow, set the wild echoes flying: Blow, bugle; answer, echoes, dying, dying, dying.

Oh hark! oh hear! how thin and clear, And thinner, clearer, farther going! Oh sweet and far from cliff and scar The horns of Elfland faintly blowing! Blow, let us hear the purple glens replying: Blow, bugle; answer, echoes, dying, dying, dying.

O Love, they die in yon rich sky, They faint on hill, or field, or river: Our echoes roll from soul to soul, And grow forever and forever: Blow, bugle, blow, set the wild echoes flying, And answer, echoes, answer, dying, dying, dying.

Alfred, Lord Tennyson.

From "The Princess."

The Raven

Once upon a midnight dreary, while I pondered, weak and weary, Over many a quaint and curious volume of forgotten lore, While I nodded, nearly napping, suddenly there came a tapping, As of some one gently rapping, rapping at my chamber door. "'Tis some visitor," I muttered, "tapping at my chamber door— Only this, and nothing more."

Ah, distinctly I remember it was in the bleak December, And each separate dying ember wrought its ghost upon the floor. Eagerly I wished the morrow;—vainly I had sought to borrow From my books surcease of sorrow—sorrow for the lost Lenore— For the rare and radiant maiden whom the angels name Lenore— Nameless here for evermore.

And the silken sad uncertain rustling of each purple curtain Thrilled me—filled me with fantastic terrors never felt before; So that now, to still the beating of my heart, I stood repeating "'Tis some visitor entreating entrance at my chamber door— Some late visitor entreating entrance at my chamber door;— This it is, and nothing more."

Presently my soul grew stronger; hesitating then no longer, "Sir," said I, "or Madam, truly your forgiveness I implore; But the fact is I was napping, and so gently you came rapping, And so faintly you came tapping, tapping at my chamber door, That I scarce was sure I heard you"—here I opened wide the door;—— Darkness there, and nothing more.

Deep into that darkness peering, long I stood there wondering, fearing, Doubting, dreaming dreams no mortal ever dared to dream before; But the silence was unbroken, and the darkness gave no token, And the only word there spoken was the whispered word, "Lenore!" This I whispered, and an echo murmured back the word, "Lenore!" Merely this, and nothing more.

Back into the chamber turning, all my soul within me burning, Soon again I heard a tapping somewhat louder than before. "Surely," said I, "surely that is something at my window lattice; Let me see, then, what thereat is, and this mystery explore— Let my heart be still a moment and this mystery explore;— 'Tis the wind, and nothing more!"

Open here I flung the shutter, when, with many a flirt and flutter, In there stepped a stately raven of the saintly days of yore. Not the least obeisance made he; not an instant stopped or stayed he; But, with mien of lord or lady, perched above my chamber door— Perched upon a bust of Pallas just above my chamber door— Perched, and sat, and nothing more.

Then this ebony bird beguiling my sad fancy into smiling, By the grave and stern decorum of the countenance it wore, "Though thy crest be shorn and shaven, thou," I said, "art sure no craven, Ghastly grim and ancient raven wandering from the Nightly shore— Tell me what thy lordly name is on the Night's Plutonian shore!" Quoth the raven, "Nevermore."

Much I marvelled this ungainly fowl to hear discourse so plainly, Though its answer little meaning—little relevancy bore; For we cannot help agreeing that no living human being Ever yet was blessed with seeing bird above his chamber door— Bird or beast upon the sculptured bust above his chamber door, With such name as "Nevermore."

But the raven, sitting lonely on the placid bust, spoke only That one word, as if his soul in that one word he did outpour. Nothing further then he uttered—not a feather then he fluttered— Till I scarcely more than muttered "Other friends have flown before— On the morrow he will leave me, as my hopes have flown before." Then the bird said "Nevermore."

Startled at the stillness broken by reply so aptly spoken, "Doubtless," said I, "what it utters is its only stock and store, Caught from some unhappy master whom unmerciful disaster Followed fast and followed faster till his songs one burden bore— Till the dirges of his hope that melancholy burden bore Of 'Never—nevermore.'"

But the raven still beguiling all my sad soul into smiling, Straight I wheeled a cushioned seat in front of bird and bust and door; Then, upon the velvet sinking, I betook myself to linking Fancy unto fancy, thinking what this ominous bird of yore— What this grim, ungainly, ghastly, gaunt and ominous bird of yore Meant in croaking "Nevermore."

This I sat engaged in guessing, but no syllable expressing To the fowl whose fiery eyes now burned into my bosom's core; This and more I sat divining, with my head at ease reclining On the cushion's velvet lining that the lamp-light gloated o'er, But whose velvet violet lining with the lamp-light gloating o'er, She shall press, ah, nevermore!

Then, methought, the air grew denser, perfumed from an unseen censer Swung by angels whose faint foot-falls tinkled on the tufted floor. "Wretch," I cried, "thy God hath lent thee—by these angels he hath sent thee Respite—respite and nepenthe from thy memories of Lenore! Quaff, oh quaff this kind nepenthe, and forget this lost Lenore!" Quoth the raven, "Nevermore."

"Prophet," said I, "thing of evil!—prophet still, if bird or devil!— Whether Tempter sent, or whether tempest tossed thee here ashore, Desolate yet all undaunted, on this desert land enchanted— On this home by Horror haunted—tell me truly, I implore— Is there—is there balm in Gilead?—tell me—tell me, I implore! Quoth the raven, "Nevermore."

"Prophet!" said I, "thing of evil—prophet still, if bird or devil! By that Heaven that bends above us—by that God we both adore— Tell this soul with sorrow laden if, within the distant Aidenn, It shall clasp a sainted maiden whom the angels name Lenore— Clasp a rare and radiant maiden whom the angels name Lenore?" Quoth the raven, "Nevermore."

"Be that word our sign of parting, bird or fiend!" I shrieked, upstarting— "Get thee back into the tempest and the Night's Plutonian shore! Leave no black plume as a token of that lie thy soul hath spoken! Leave my loneliness unbroken! quit the bust above my door! Take thy beak from out my heart, and take thy form from off my door!" Quoth the raven, "Nevermore."

And the raven, never flitting, still is sitting, still is sitting On the pallid bust of Pallas, just above my chamber door; And his eyes have all the seeming of a demon's that is dreaming, And the lamp-light o'er him streaming throws his shadow on the floor; And my soul from out that shadow that lies floating on the floor Shall be lifted—nevermore!

Edgar Allan Poe.

The Bells

I

Hear the sledges with the bells— Silver bells! What a world of merriment their melody foretells! How they tinkle, tinkle, tinkle, In the icy air of night! While the stars, that oversprinkle All the heavens, seem to twinkle With a crystalline delight; Keeping time, time, time, In a sort of Runic rhyme, To the tintinnabulation that so musically wells From the bells, bells, bells, bells, Bells, bells, bells— From the jingling and the tinkling of the bells.

II

Hear the mellow wedding bells, Golden bells! What a world of happiness their harmony foretells! Through the balmy air of night How they ring out their delight! From the molten-golden notes, And all in tune, What a liquid ditty floats To the turtle-dove that listens, while she gloats On the moon! Oh, from out the sounding cells, What a gush of euphony voluminously wells! How it swells! How it dwells On the Future! how it tells Of the rapture that impels To the swinging and the ringing Of the bells, bells, bells, Of the bells, bells, bells, bells, Bells, bells, bells— To the rhyming and the chiming of the bells!

III

Hear the loud alarum bells— Brazen bells! What a tale of terror, now, their turbulency tells! In the startled ear of night How they scream out their affright! Too much horrified to speak, They can only shriek, shriek, Out of tune, In the clamorous appealing to the mercy of the fire, In a mad expostulation with the deaf and frantic fire, Leaping higher, higher, higher, With a desperate desire, And a resolute endeavor Now—now to sit or never, By the side of the pale-faced moon. Oh, the bells, bells, bells! What a tale their terror tells Of despair! How they clang, and clash, and roar! What a horror they outpour On the bosom of the palpitating air! Yet the ear it fully knows, By the twanging, And the clanging, How the danger ebbs and flows; Yet the ear distinctly tells, In the jangling And the wrangling, How the danger sinks and swells, By the sinking or the swelling in the anger of the bells— Of the bells— Of the bells, bells, bells, bells, Bells, bells, bells,— In the clamor and the clangor of the bells.

IV

Hear the tolling of the bells— Iron bells! What a world of solemn thought their monody compels! In the silence of the night, How we shiver with affright At the melancholy menace of their tone! For every sound that floats From the rust within their throats Is a groan.

And the people—ah, the people— They that dwell up in the steeple, All alone, And who tolling, tolling, tolling, In that muffled monotone, Feel a glory in so rolling On the human heart a stone— They are neither man nor woman— They are neither brute or human— They are Ghouls: And their king it is who tolls; And he rolls, rolls, rolls, Rolls A pæan from the bells! And his merry bosom swells With the pæan of the bells! And he dances and he yells; Keeping time, time, time In a sort of Runic rhyme, To the pæan of the bells— Of the bells: Keeping time, time, time In a sort of Runic rhyme, To the throbbing of the bells, Of the bells, bells, bells,— To the sobbing of the bells; Keeping time, time, time, As he knells, knells, knells, In a happy Runic rhyme, To the rolling of the bells,— Of the bells, bells, bells,— To the tolling of the bells, Of the bells, bells, bells, bells, Bells, bells, bells,— To the moaning and the groaning of the bells.

Edgar Allan Poe.

INTERLEAVES
Sports and Pastimes

In ancient tapestries, centuries old, you sometimes see, wrought in delicate needlework that is faded with the lapse of years, pictures of the sports of the period. There will be quaint scenes showing otter and bear hunting, swans' nesting, hawking, chasing the deer, and the like; in-door scenes, too, depicting pretty pages strumming musical instruments, and lovely ladies at their tambour or 'broidery frames.

The poetry of each passing age preserves pictures of its plays and diversions still more perfectly than worn and tattered tapestry, and the verses we have chosen cover a bewildering variety of pastimes and recreations. The poets have sounded the praises of almost every kind of sport: angling, swimming, skating, bubble-blowing, going a-Maying, walking, riding, whittling, nutting, the country pleasures of "the barefoot boy," the joys of reading, the delights of music, and the exhilarations of cruising and travelling. One poem of the immediate present, Beeching's "Bicycling Song," shows us that the sport of the moment need not of necessity be too commonplace to be wrought into verse. At first thought the amusements of these latter days are so swift and breathless, so complicated with steam, electricity, and other great forces of the new era, that they seem less poetic than the picturesque frolics of milkmaids and shepherds, the games of the old Greeks or the gay sports of the days of chivalry. But after all, as Lowell said, "there is as much poetry in the iron horses that eat fire as in those of Diomed that fed on men. If you cut an apple across, you may trace in it the lines of the blossom that the bee hummed around in May; and so the soul of poetry survives in things prosaic."

VII
SPORTS AND PASTIMES
Blowing Bubbles
See, the pretty Planet! Floating sphere! Faintest breeze will fan it Far or near;
World as light as feather; Moonshine rays, Rainbow tints together, As it plays;
Drooping, sinking, failing, Nigh to earth, Mounting, whirling, sailing, Full of mirth;
Life there, welling, flowing, Waving round; Pictures coming, going, Without sound.
Quick now, be this airy Globe repell'd! Never can the fairy Star be held.
Touch'd—it in a twinkle Disappears! Leaving but a sprinkle, As of tears.
William Allingham.

Bicycling Song
With lifted feet, hands still, I am poised, and down the hill Dart, with heedful mind; The air goes by in a wind.

Swifter and yet more swift, Till the heart with a mighty lift Makes the lungs laugh, the throat cry:— "O bird, see; see, bird, I fly.

"Is this, is this your joy? O bird, then I, though a boy, For a golden moment share Your feathery life in air!"

Say, heart, is there aught like this In a world that is full of bliss? 'Tis more than skating, bound Steel-shod to the level ground.

Speed slackens now, I float Awhile in my airy boat; Till, when the wheels scarce crawl, My feet to the treadles fall.

Alas, that the longest hill Must end in a vale; but still, Who climbs with toil, wheresoe'er, Shall find wings waiting there.
Henry Charles Beeching.

Going A Maying
Get up, get up for shame! The blooming morn Upon her wings presents the god unshorn: See how Aurora throws her fair Fresh-quilted colours through the air: Get up, sweet-slug-a-bed, and see The dew-bespangled herb and tree! Each flower has wept and bowed toward the east, Above an hour since, yet you not drest, Nay, not so much as out of bed? When all the birds have matins said, And sung their thankful hymns, 'tis sin, Nay, profanation, to keep in, Whenas a thousand virgins on this day, Spring, sooner than the lark, to fetch in May.

Rise, and put on your foliage, and be seen To come forth, like the Spring-time fresh and green, And sweet as Flora. Take no care For jewels for your gown or hair: Fear not; the leaves will strew Gems in abundance upon you: Besides, the childhood of the day has kept, Against you come, some orient pearls unwept. Come, and receive them while the light Hangs on the dew-locks of the night. And Titan on the eastern hill Retires himself, or else stands still Till you come forth! Wash, dress, be brief in praying: Few beads are best, when once we go a Maying.

Come, my Corinna, come; and coming, mark How each field turns a street, each street a park, Made green, and trimmed with trees! see how Devotion gives each house a bough Or branch! each porch, each door, ere this, An ark, a tabernacle is, Made up of white-thorn neatly interwove, As if here were those cooler shades of love. Can such delights be in the street, And open fields, and we not see't? Come, we'll abroad: and let's obey The proclamation made for May. And sin no more, as we have done, by staying, But, my Corinna, come, let's go a Maying.

There's not a budding boy or girl, this day, But is got up, and gone to bring in May. A deal of youth, ere this is come Back and with white-thorn laden home. Some have despatched their cakes and cream, Before that we have left to dream: And some have wept, and woo'd, and plighted troth, And chose their priest, ere we can cast off sloth: Many a green-gown has been given, Many a kiss, both odd and even: Many a glance, too, has been sent From out the eye, love's firmament: Many a jest told of the keys betraying This night, and locks picked: yet we're not a Maying.

Come, let us go, while we are in our prime, And take the harmless folly of the time! We shall grow old apace, and die

Before we know our liberty. Our life is short, and our days run As fast away as does the sun. And as a vapour, or a drop of rain, Once lost, can ne'er be found again, So when or you or I are made A fable, song, or fleeting shade, All love, all liking, all delight, Lies drowned with us in endless night. Then, while time serves, and we are but decaying, Come, my Corinna, come, let's go a Maying.

Robert Herrick.

Jog On, Jog On

Jog on, jog on the foot path-way, And merrily hent the stile-a, Your merry heart goes all the day, Your sad tires in a mile-a.

Your paltry money-bags of gold— What need have we to stare for, When little or nothing soon is told, And we have the less to care for.

Then cast away care, let sorrow cease, A fig for melancholy; Let's laugh and sing, or, if you please, We'll frolic with sweet Dolly.

From The Winter's Tale.

First stanza by William Shakespeare. Last two stanzas by unknown author in "Antidote Against Melancholy,".

A Vagabond Song

There is something in the Autumn that is native to my blood— Touch of manner, hint of mood; And my heart is like a rhyme, With the yellow and the purple and the crimson keeping time.

The scarlet of the maples can shake me like a cry Of bugles going by. And my lonely spirit thrills To see the frosty asters like smoke upon the hills.

There is something in October sets the gipsy blood astir; We must rise and follow her, When from every hill of flame She calls and calls each vagabond by name.

Bliss Carman.

Swimming

And mightier grew the joy to meet full-faced Each wave, and mount with upward plunge, and taste The rapture of its rolling strength, and cross Its flickering crown of snows that flash and toss Like plumes in battle's blithest charge, and thence To match the next with yet more strenuous sense; Till on his eyes the light beat hard and bade His face turn west and shoreward through the glad Swift revel of the waters golden-clad, And back with light reluctant heart he bore Across the broad-backed rollers in to shore.

Algernon C. Swinburne.

From "Tristram of Lyonesse."

Swimming

How many a time have I Cloven, with arm still lustier, breast more daring, The wave all roughened; with a swimmer's stroke Flinging the billows back from my drenched hair, And laughing from my lip the audacious brine, Which kissed it like a wine-cup, rising o'er The waves as they arose, and prouder still The loftier they uplifted me; and oft, In wantonness of spirit, plunging down Into their green and glassy gulfs, and making My way to shells and seaweed, all unseen By those above, till they waxed fearful; then Returning with my grasp full of such tokens As showed that I had searched the deep; exulting, With a far-dashing stroke, and drawing deep The long suspended breath, again I spurned The foam which broke around me, and pursued My track like a sea-bird.—I was a boy then.

George Gordon, Lord Byron.

From "The Two Foscari."

The Angler's Reveille

What time the rose of dawn is laid across the lips of night, And all the drowsy little stars have fallen asleep in light; 'Tis then a wandering wind awakes, and runs from tree to tree, And borrows words from all the birds to sound the reveille.

This is the carol the Robin throws Over the edge of the valley; Listen how boldly it flows, Sally on sally:

Tirra-lirra, Down the river, Laughing water All a-quiver. Day is near, Clear, clear. Fish are breaking, Time for waking. Tup, tup, tup! Do you hear? All clear— Wake up!

The phantom flood of dreams has ebbed and vanished with the dark, And like a dove the heart forsakes the prison of the ark; Now forth she fares through friendly woods and diamond-fields of dew, While every voice cries out "Rejoice!" as if the world were new.

This is the ballad the Bluebird sings, Unto his mate replying, Shaking the tune from his wings While he is flying:

Surely, surely, surely, Life is dear Even here. Blue above, You to love, Purely, purely, purely.

There's wild azalea on the hill, and roses down the dell, And just one spray of lilac still abloom beside the well; The columbine adorns the rocks, the laurel buds grow pink, Along the stream white arums gleam, and violets bend to drink.

This is the song of the Yellowthroat, Fluttering gaily beside you; Hear how each voluble note Offers to guide you:

Which way, sir? I say, sir, Let me teach you, I beseech you! Are you wishing Jolly fishing? This way, sir! I'll teach you.

Then come, my friend, forget your foes, and leave your fears behind, And wander forth to try your luck, with cheerful, quiet mind; For be your fortune great or small, you'll take what God may give, And all the day your heart shall say, "'Tis luck enough to live."

This is the song the Brown Thrush flings, Out of his thicket of roses; Hark how it warbles and rings, Mark how it closes:

Luck, luck, What luck? Good enough for me! I'm alive, you see. Sun shining, No repining; Never borrow Idle sorrow; Drop it! Cover it up! Hold your cup! Joy will fill it, Don't spill it, Steady, be ready, Good luck!

Henry van Dyke.

From "The Toiling of Felix." By permission of Charles Scribner's Sons.

The Angler's Invitation

Come when the leaf comes, angle with me, Come when the bee hums over the lea, Come with the wild flowers— Come with the wild showers— Come when the singing bird calleth for thee!

Then to the stream side, gladly we'll hie, Where the grey trout glide silently by, Or in some still place Over the hill face Hurrying onward, drop the light fly.

Then, when the dew falls, homeward we'll speed To our own loved walls down on the mead, There, by the bright hearth, Holding our night mirth, We'll drink to sweet friendship in need and in deed.

Thomas Tod Stoddart.

Skating

And in the frosty season, when the sun Was set, and, visible, for many a mile, The cottage-windows through the twilight blazed, I heeded not the summons. Happy time It was indeed for all of us: for me It was a time of rapture! Clear and loud The village clock tolled six. I wheeled about, Proud and exulting, like an untired horse That cares not for its home. All shod with steel, We hissed along the polished ice, in games Confederate, imitative of the chase And woodland pleasures,—the resounding horn, The pack loud bellowing, and the hunted hare. So through the darkness and the cold we flew, And not a voice was idle. With the din Meanwhile the precipices rang aloud. The leafless trees and every icy crag Tinkled like iron; while the distant hills Into the tumult sent an alien sound Of melancholy, not unnoticed; while the stars Eastward were sparkling clear, and in the west The orange sky of evening died away.

Not seldom from the uproar I retired Into a silent bay; or sportively Glanced sideways, leaving the tumultuous throng, To cut across the reflex of a star,— Image, that, flying still before me, gleamed Upon the glassy plain. And oftentimes, When we had given our bodies to the wind, And all the shadowy banks on either side Came sweeping through the darkness, spinning still The rapid line of motion, then at once Have I, reclining back upon my heels, Stopped short; yet still the solitary cliffs Wheeled by me, even as if the earth had rolled With visible motion her diurnal round. Behind me did they stretch in solemn train, Feebler and feebler; and I stood and watched Till all was tranquil as a summer sea.

William Wordsworth.

From "The Prelude."

Reading

... We get no good By being ungenerous, even to a book, And calculating profits ... so much help By so much reading. It is rather when We gloriously forget ourselves and plunge Soul-forward, headlong, into a book's profound, Impassioned for its beauty and salt of truth— 'Tis then we get the right good from a book.

Elizabeth B. Browning.

From "Aurora Leigh."

On First Looking Into Chapman's Homer

Much have I travelled in the realms of gold, And many goodly states and kingdoms seen; Round many western islands have I been Which bards in fealty to Apollo hold. Oft of one wide expanse had I been told That deep-browed Homer ruled as his demesne: Yet did I never breathe its pure serene Till I heard Chapman speak out loud and bold; Then felt I like some watcher of the skies When a new planet swims into his ken; Or like stout Cortez, when with eagle eyes He stared at the Pacific—and all his men Looked at each other with a wild surmise— Silent, upon a peak in Darien.

John Keats.

Music's Silver Sound

When griping grief the heart doth wound, And doleful dump the mind oppress, Then music, with her silver sound, With speedy help doth lend redress.

William Shakespeare.

From "Romeo and Juliet."

The Power of Music

For do but note a wild and wanton herd, Or race of youthful and unhandled colts, Fetching mad bounds, bellowing and neighing loud, Which is the hot condition of their blood; If they but hear perchance a trumpet sound, Or any air of music touch their ears, You shall perceive them make a mutual stand, Their savage eyes turn'd to a modest gaze, By the sweet power of music: therefore the poet Did feign that Orpheus drew trees, stones and floods; Since naught so stockish, hard, and full of rage, But music for the time doth change his nature. The man that hath no music in himself, Nor is not moved with concord of sweet sounds, Is fit for treasons, stratagems, and spoils; The motions of his spirit are dull as night, And his affections dark as Erebus: Let no such man be trusted.

William Shakespeare.

From "The Merchant of Venice."

Descend, Ye Nine

Descend, ye Nine! descend and sing; The breathing instruments inspire, Wake into voice each silent string, And sweep the sounding lyre! In a sadly pleasing strain, Let the warbling lute complain: Let the loud trumpet sound, Till the roofs all around The shrill echoes rebound; While in more lengthen'd notes and slow, The deep, majestic, solemn organs blow. Hark! the numbers soft and clear Gently steal upon the ear; Now louder, and yet louder rise, And fill with spreading sounds the skies; Exulting in triumph now swell the bold notes, In broken air, trembling, the wild music floats; Till, by degrees, remote and small, The strains decay, And melt away, In a dying, dying fall. By music, minds an equal temper know, Nor swell too high, nor sink too low. If in the breast tumultuous joys arise, Music her soft, assuasive voice applies; Or, when the soul is press'd with cares, Exalts her in enlivening airs. Warriors she fires with animated sounds; Pours balm into the bleeding lover's wounds: Melancholy lifts her head, Morpheus rouses from his bed, Sloth unfolds her arms and wakes, Listening Envy drops her snakes; Intestine war no more our passions wage, And giddy factions bear away their rage.

Alexander Pope.

From "Ode on St. Cecilia's Day."

Old Song

'Tis a dull sight To see the year dying, When winter winds Set the yellow wood sighing: Sighing, O sighing!

When such a time cometh I do retire Into an old room Beside a bright fire: O, pile a bright fire!

And there I sit Reading old things, Of knights and lorn damsels, While the wind sings— O, drearily sings!

I never look out Nor attend to the blast; For all to be seen Is the leaves falling fast: Falling, falling!

But close at the hearth, Like a cricket, sit I Reading of summer And chivalry— Gallant chivalry!

*   *   *   *

Then the clouds part, Swallows soaring between; The spring is alive, And the meadows are green!

I jump up like mad, Break the old pipe in twain, And away to the meadows, The meadows again!

Edward Fitzgerald.

The Barefoot Boy

Blessings on thee, little man, Barefoot boy, with cheek of tan! With thy upturned pantaloons, And thy merry whistled tunes; With thy red lip, redder still Kissed by strawberries on the hill; With the sunshine on thy face, Through thy torn brim's jaunty grace; From my heart I give thee joy,— I was once a barefoot boy! Prince thou art,—the grown-up man Only is republican. Let the million-dollared ride! Barefoot, trudging at his side, Thou hast more than he can buy In the reach of ear and eye,— Outward sunshine, inward joy: Blessings on thee, barefoot boy!

O for boyhood's painless play, Sleep that wakes in laughing day, Health that mocks the doctor's rules, Knowledge never learned of schools, Of the wild bee's morning chase, Of the wild-flower's time and place, Flight of fowl and habitude Of the tenants of the wood; How the tortoise bears his shell, How the woodchuck digs his cell, And the ground-mole sinks his well; How the robin feeds her young, How the oriole's nest is hung; Where the whitest lilies blow, Where the freshest berries grow, Where the groundnut trails its vine, Where the wood-grape's clusters shine: Of the black wasp's cunning way, Mason of his walls of clay, And the architectural plans Of gray hornet artisans!— For, eschewing books and tasks, Nature answers all he asks; Hand in hand with her he walks, Face to face with her he talks, Part and parcel of her joy,— Blessings on the barefoot boy!

O for boyhood's time of June, Crowding years in one brief moon, When all things I heard or saw, Me, their master, waited for. I was rich in flowers and trees, Humming-birds and honey-bees; For my sport the squirrel played, Plied the snouted mole his spade; For my taste the blackberry cone Purpled over hedge and stone; Laughed the brook for my delight Through the day and through the night, Whispering at the garden wall, Talked with me from fall to fall; Mine the sand-rimmed pickerel pond, Mine the walnut slopes beyond, Mine, on bending orchard trees, Apples of Hesperides! Still as my horizon grew, Larger grew my riches too; All the world I saw or knew Seemed a complex Chinese toy, Fashioned for a barefoot boy!

O for festal dainties spread, Like my bowl of milk and bread,— Pewter spoon and bowl of wood, On the door-stone, gray and rude! O'er me like a regal tent, Cloudy ribbed, the sunset bent, Purple-curtained, fringed with gold, Looped in many a wind-swung fold; While for music came the play Of the pied frogs' orchestra; And to light the noisy choir, Lit the fly his lamp of fire. I was monarch: pomp and joy Waited on the barefoot boy!

Cheerily, then, my little man, Live and laugh as boyhood can! Though the flinty slopes be hard, Stubble-speared the new-mown sward, Every morn shall lead thee through Fresh baptisms of the dew; Every evening from thy feet Shall the cool wind kiss the heat: All too soon these feet must hide In the prison cells of pride, Lose the freedom of the sod, Like a colt's for work be shod, Made to tread the mills of toil, Up and down in ceaseless moil: Happy if their track be found Never on forbidden ground; Happy if they sink not in Quick and treacherous sands of sin. Ah! that thou couldst know thy joy, Ere it passes, barefoot boy!

John Greenleaf Whittier.

Leolin and Edith

These had been together from the first, Leolin's first nurse was, five years after, hers; So much the boy foreran: but when his date Doubled her own, for want of playmates he

*　　*　　*　　*

Had tost his ball and flown his kite, and roll'd His hoop to pleasure Edith, with her dipt Against the rush of the air in the prone swing, Made blossom-ball or daisy-chain, arranged Her garden, sow'd her name and kept it green In living letters, told her fairy-tales, Show'd her the fairy footings on the grass, The little dells of cowslip, fairy palms, The petty marestail forest, fairy pines, Or from the tiny pitted target blew What looked a flight of fairy arrows aim'd All at one mark, all hitting: make-believes For Edith and himself.

Alfred, Lord Tennyson.

From "Aylmer's Field."

Going A-Nutting

No clouds are in the morning sky, The vapors hug the stream,— Who says that life and love can die In all this northern gleam? At every turn the maples burn, The quail is whistling free, The partridge whirs, and the frosted burs Are dropping for you and me. Ho! hilly ho! heigh O! Hilly ho! In the clear October morning.

Along our path the woods are bold, And glow with ripe desire; The yellow chestnut showers its gold, The sumachs spread their fire; The breezes feel as crisp as steel, The buckwheat tops are red: Then down the lane, love, scurry again, And over the stubble tread! Ho! hilly ho! heigh O! Hilly ho! In the clear October morning.

Edmund Clarence Stedman.

Whittling

The Yankee boy, before he's sent to school, Well knows the mysteries of that magic tool, The pocket-knife. To that his wistful eye Turns, while he hears his mother's lullaby; His hoarded cents he gladly gives to get it, Then leaves no stone unturned till he can whet it; And in the education of the lad No little part that implement hath had. His pocket-knife to the young whittler brings A growing knowledge of material things.

Projectiles, music, and the sculptor's art, His chestnut whistle and his shingle cart, His elder pop-gun, with its hickory rod, Its sharp explosion and rebounding wad, His corn-stalk fiddle, and the deeper tone That murmurs from his pumpkin-stalk trombone, Conspire to teach the boy. To these succeed His bow, his arrow of a feathered reed, His windmill, raised the passing breeze to win, His water-wheel, that turns upon a pin, Or, if his father lives upon the shore, You'll see his ship, "beam ends upon the floor," Full rigged, with raking masts, and timbers staunch, And waiting, near the wash-tub, for a launch. Thus, by his genius and his jack-knife driven Ere long he'll solve you any problem given; Make any gimcrack, musical or mute, A plough, a couch, an organ, or a flute; Make you a locomotive or a clock, Cut a canal, or build a floating-dock, Or lead forth beauty from a marble block;— Make anything, in short, for sea or shore, From a child's rattle to a seventy-four;— Make it, said I?—Ay, when he undertakes it, He'll make the thing and the machine that makes it.

And when the thing is made,—whether it be To move on earth, in air, or on the sea; Whether on water, o'er the waves to glide, Or, upon land to roll, revolve, or slide; Whether to whirl or jar, to strike or ring, Whether it be a piston or a spring, Wheel, pulley, tube sonorous, wood or brass, The thing designed shall surely come to pass; For, when his hand's upon it, you may know That there's go in it, and he'll make it go.

John Pierpont.

Hunting Song

Waken, lords and ladies gay, On the mountain dawns the day; All the jolly chase is here With hawk and horse and hunting-spear! Hounds are in their couples yelling, Hawks are whistling, horns are knelling. Merrily, merrily mingle they, "Waken, lords and ladies gay."

Waken, lords and ladies gay, The mist has left the mountain gray, Springlets in the dawn are steaming, Diamonds on the brake are gleaming, And foresters have busy been To track the buck in thicket green; Now we come to chant our lay "Waken, lords and ladies gay."

Waken, lords and ladies gay, To the greenwood haste away; We can show you where he lies, Fleet of foot and tall of size; We can show the marks he made When 'gainst the oak his antlers fray'd; You shall see him brought to bay; "Waken, lords and ladies gay."

Louder, louder chant the lay Waken, lords and ladies gay! Tell them youth and mirth and glee Run a course as well as we; Time, stern huntsman! who can balk, Stanch as hound and fleet as hawk; Think of this, and rise with day, Gentle lords and ladies gay!

Sir Walter Scott.

The Hunter's Song

Rise! Sleep no more! 'Tis a noble morn! The dews hang thick on the fringéd thorn, And the frost shrinks back like a beaten hound, Under the steaming, steaming ground. Behold where the billowy clouds flow by, And leave us alone in the clear gray sky! Our horses are ready and steady,—So, ho! I'm gone like a dart from the Tartar's bow. *Hark, hark!—who calleth the maiden Morn From her sleep in the woods and the stubble corn? The horn—the horn! The merry sweet ring of the hunter's horn!*

Now through the copse where the fox is found And over the stream at a mighty bound, And over the high lands and over the low, O'er furrows, o'er meadows the hunters go! Away! as the hawk flies full at his prey So flieth the hunter,—away, away! From the burst at the corn till set of sun, When the red fox dies, and the day is done! *Hark, hark!—What sound on the wind is borne? 'Tis the conquering voice of the hunter's horn. The horn,—the horn! The merry bold voice of the hunter's horn!*

Sound, sound the horn! To the hunter good What's the gully deep, or the roaring flood? Right over he bounds, as the wild stag bounds, At the heels of his swift, sure, silent hounds. O what delight can a mortal lack When he once is firm on his horse's back, With his stirrups short and his snaffle strong, And the blast of the horn for his morning song! *Hark, hark! Now home! and dream till morn Of the bold sweet sound of the hunter's horn! The horn, the horn! Oh, the sound of all sounds is the hunter's horn!*

Barry Cornwall.

(Bryan Waller Procter.)

The Blood Horse

Gamarra is a dainty steed, Strong, black, and of a noble breed, Full of fire, and full of bone, With all his line of fathers known; Fine his nose, his nostrils thin, But blown abroad by the pride within! His mane is like a river flowing, And his eyes like embers glowing In the darkness of the night, And his pace as swift as light.

Look—how 'round his straining throat Grace and shifting beauty float; Sinewy strength is in his reins, And the red blood gallops through his veins; Richer, redder, never ran Through the boasting heart of man. He can trace his lineage higher Than the Bourbon dare aspire,— Douglas, Guzman, or the Guelph, Or O'Brien's blood itself!

He, who hath no peer, was born, Here, upon a red March morn; But his famous fathers dead Were Arabs all, and Arab bred, And the last of that great line Trod like one of a race divine! And yet,—he was but friend to one, Who fed him at the set of sun, By some lone fountain fringed with green: With him, a roving Bedouin, He lived (none else would he obey Through all the hot Arabian day),— And died untamed upon the sands Where Balkh amidst the desert stands!

Barry Cornwall.

(Bryan Waller Procter.)

The Northern Seas

Up! up! let us a voyage take; Why sit we here at ease? Find us a vessel tight and snug, Bound for the Northern Seas.

I long to see the Northern Lights, With their rushing splendors, fly, Like living things, with flaming wings, Wide o'er the wondrous sky.

I long to see those icebergs vast, With heads all crowned with snow; Whose green roots sleep in the awful deep, Two hundred fathoms low.

I long to hear the thundering crash Of their terrific fall; And the echoes from a thousand cliffs, Like lonely voices call.

There shall we see the fierce white bear, The sleepy seals aground, And the spouting whales that to and fro Sail with a dreary sound.

There may we tread on depths of ice, That the hairy mammoth hide; Perfect as when, in times of old, The mighty creature died.

And while the unsetting sun shines on Through the still heaven's deep blue, We'll traverse the azure waves, the herds Of the dread sea-horse to view.

We'll pass the shores of solemn pine, Where wolves and black bears prowl, And away to the rocky isles of mist To rouse the northern fowl.

Up there shall start ten thousand wings, With a rushing, whistling din; Up shall the auk and fulmar start,— All but the fat penguin.

And there, in the wastes of the silent sky, With the silent earth below, We shall see far off to his lonely rock The lonely eagle go.

Then softly, softly will we tread By island streams, to see Where the pelican of the silent North Sits there all silently.
William Howitt.

The Needle

The gay belles of fashion may boast of excelling In waltz or cotillion, at whist or quadrille; And seek admiration by vauntingly telling Of drawing, and painting, and musical skill; But give me the fair one, in country or city, Whose home and its duties are dear to her heart, Who cheerfully warbles some rustical ditty, While plying the needle with exquisite art: The bright little needle—the swift-flying needle, The needle directed by beauty and art. If Love have a potent, a magical token, A talisman, ever resistless and true— A charm that is never evaded or broken, A witchery certain the heart to subdue— 'T is this—and his armory never has furnished So keen and unerring, or polished a dart; Let Beauty direct it, so pointed and burnished, And, oh! it is certain of touching the heart: The bright little needle—the swift-flying needle, The needle directed by beauty and art.

Be wise, then, ye maidens, nor seek admiration By dressing for conquest, and flirting with all; You never, whate'er be your fortune or station, Appear half so lovely at rout or at ball, As gayly convened at a work-covered table, Each cheerfully active and playing her part, Beguiling the task with a song or a fable, And plying the needle with exquisite art: The bright little needle—the swift-flying needle, The needle directed by beauty and art.
Samuel Woodworth.

INTERLEAVES
A Garden of Girls

Enter a procession of charming girls; wee ones like Nikolina and Jessie, others, like Peggy, just entering their teens. Some are so saintly we can almost see the halos above their lovely heads—like Mrs. Browning's human angel in the first poem, or like Shakespeare's Silvia, who excels each mortal thing; others are just happy children, like Little Bell.

The poets, as you will see, have delighted to paint the beauties of this rosebud garden. There is sweet Phyllis, the little dairymaid, whose hand seemed milk, in milk it was so white; Annie Laurie, with her brow like the snowdrift and her voice like wind in summer sighing; merry Margaret, like midsummer flower; but you will note that in all of them sunny hair and dewy eyes are not where the beauty lies. "Love deep and kind" leaves good gifts behind, with Bell and with Mally, too, who is rare and fair and every way complete, and who is also modest and discreet. On the other hand, Burns does not describe Nannie by so much as a single word, but it is easy to conjure up her picture, so eloquently he paints the dreariness of the world "when Nannie's awa'."

Will you not add to this garden of girls others whom you would like to see blooming beside them? Remember, it is a rosebud garden, and the new-comers must be not only beautiful, but sweet and fragrant with pretty, womanly virtues.

"She walks—the lady of my delight A shepherdess of sheep. Her flocks are thoughts. She keeps them white; She guards them from the steep. She feeds them on the fragrant height, And folds them in for sleep."

VIII
A GARDEN OF GIRLS
A Portrait

"One Name is Elizabeth."—Jonson.

I will paint her as I see her: Ten times have the lilies blown, Since she looked upon the sun.

And her face is lily-clear— Lily-shaped, and drooped in duty To the law of its own beauty.

Oval cheeks encolored faintly, Which a trail of golden hair Keeps from fading off to air:

And a forehead fair and saintly, Which two blue eyes undershine, Like meek prayers before a shrine.

Face and figure of a child,— Though too calm, you think, and tender, For the childhood you would lend her.

Yet child-simple, undefiled, Frank, obedient,—waiting still On the turnings of your will.

Moving light, as all young things— As young birds, or early wheat When the wind blows over it.

Only free from flutterings Of loud mirth that scorneth measure— Taking love for her chief pleasure:

Choosing pleasures (for the rest) Which come softly—just as she, When she nestles at your knee.

Quiet talk she liketh best, In a bower of gentle looks,— Watering flowers, or reading books.

And her voice, it murmurs lowly, As a silver stream may run, Which yet feels, you feel, the sun.

And her smile, it seems half holy, As if drawn from thoughts more fair Than our common jestings are.

And if any poet knew her, He would sing of her with falls Used in lovely madrigals.

And if any painter drew her, He would paint her unaware With a halo round her hair.

And if reader read the poem, He would whisper—"You have done a Consecrated little Una!"

And a dreamer (did you show him That same picture) would exclaim, "'Tis my angel, with a name!"

And a stranger,—when he sees her In the street even—smileth stilly, Just as you would at a lily.

And all voices that address her, Soften, sleeken every word, As if speaking to a bird.

And all fancies yearn to cover The hard earth whereon she passes. With the thymy scented grasses.

And all hearts do pray, "God love her!" Ay, and always, in good sooth, We may all be sure he doth.

Elizabeth Barrett Browning.

Little Bell

Piped the blackbird on the beechwood spray: "Pretty maid, slow wandering this way, What's your name?" quoth he— "What's your name? Oh, stop and straight unfold, Pretty maid with showery curls of gold,"— "Little Bell," said she.

Little Bell sat down beneath the rocks— Tossed aside her gleaming golden locks— "Bonny bird," quoth she, "Sing me your best song before I go." "Here's the very finest song I know, Little Bell," said he.

And the blackbird piped; you never heard Half so gay a song from any bird;— Full of quips and wiles, Now so round and rich, now soft and slow, All for love of that sweet face below, Dimpled o'er with smiles.

And the while the bonny bird did pour His full heart out freely o'er and o'er, 'Neath the morning skies, In the little childish heart below, All the sweetness seemed to grow and grow, And shine forth in happy overflow From the blue, bright eyes.

Down the dell she tripped; and through the glade Peeped the squirrel from the hazel shade, And from out the tree Swung and leaped and frolicked, void of fear, While bold blackbird piped, that all might hear, "Little Bell!" piped he.

Little Bell sat down amid the fern: "Squirrel, squirrel, to your task return; Bring me nuts!" quoth she. Up, away, the frisky squirrel hies, Golden wood lights glancing in his eyes; And adown the tree, Great ripe nuts, kissed brown by July sun, In the little lap drop, one by one: Hark, how blackbird pipes to see the fun! "Happy Bell!" pipes he.

Little Bell looked up and down the glade: "Squirrel, squirrel, if you're not afraid, Come and share with me!" Down came squirrel, eager for his fare, Down came bonny blackbird, I declare. Little Bell gave each his honest share, Ah the merry three!

And the while these frolic playmates twain Piped and frisked from bough to bough again, 'Neath the morning skies, In the little childish heart below, All the sweetness seemed to grow and grow, And shine out in happy overflow, From her blue, bright eyes.

By her snow-white cot at close of day, Knelt sweet Bell, with folded palms to pray: Very calm and clear Rose the praying voice to where, unseen, In blue heaven, an angel shape serene Paused awhile to hear.

"What good child is this," the angel said, "That, with happy heart, beside her bed Prays so lovingly?" Low and soft, oh! very low and soft, Crooned the blackbird in the orchard croft, "Bell, *dear* Bell!" crooned he.

"Whom God's creatures love," the angel fair Murmured, "God doth bless with angels' care; Child, thy bed shall be Folded safe from harm. Love, deep and kind, Shall watch around, and leave good gifts behind, Little Bell, for thee."

Thomas Westwood.

A Child of Twelve

A child most infantine Yet wandering far beyond that innocent age In all but its sweet looks and mien divine.

*   *   *   *

She moved upon this earth a shape of brightness, A power, that from its objects scarcely drew One impulse of her being—in her lightness Most like some radiant cloud of morning dew, Which wanders through the waste air's pathless blue, To nourish some far desert; she did seem Beside me, gathering beauty as she grew, Like the bright shade of some immortal dream Which walks, when tempest sleeps, the wave of life's dark stream. As mine own shadow was this child to me.

*   *   *   *

This playmate sweet, This child of twelve years old.

Percy Bysshe Shelley

From "The Revolt of Islam."

Chloe

It was the charming month of May, When all the flowers were fresh and gay, One morning by the break of day, The youthful charming Chloe From peaceful slumbers she arose, Girt on her mantle and her hose, And o'er the flowery mead she goes, The youthful charming Chloe. Lovely was she by the dawn, Youthful Chloe, charming Chloe, Tripping o'er the pearly lawn, The youthful charming Chloe.

The feather'd people you might see, Perch'd all around on every tree, In notes of sweetest melody They hail the charming Chloe; Till painting gay the eastern skies, The glorious sun began to rise, Out-rivall'd by the radiant eyes Of youthful, charming Chloe. Lovely was she by the dawn, Youthful Chloe, charming Chloe, Tripping o'er the pearly lawn, The youthful, charming Chloe.

Robert Burns.

O Mally's Meek, Mally's Sweet

As I was walking up the street, A barefit maid I chanced to meet; But O the road was very hard For that fair maiden's tender feet. O Mally's meek, Mally's sweet, Mally's modest and discreet, Mally's rare, Mally's fair, Mally's every way complete.

It were more meet that those fine feet Were weel laced up in silken shoon, And 'twere more fit that she should sit Within yon chariot gilt aboon.

Her yellow hair, beyond compare, Comes trinkling down her swan-white neck, And her two eyes, like stars in skies, Would keep a sinking ship frae wreck. O Mally's meek, Mally's sweet, Mally's modest and discreet, Mally's rare, Mally's fair, Mally's every way complete.

Robert Burns.

Who Is Silvia?

Who is Silvia? What is she, That all our swains commend her? Holy, fair, and wise is she; The heaven such grace did lend her, That she might admirèd be.

Is she kind as she is fair? For beauty lives with kindness: Love doth to her eyes repair, To help him of his blindness; And, being helped, inhabits there.

Then to Silvia let us sing, That Silvia is excelling; She excels each mortal thing Upon the dull earth dwelling; To her let us garlands bring.

William Shakespeare.

From "The Two Gentlemen of Verona."

To Mistress Margaret Hussey

Merry Margaret As midsummer flower— Gentle as falcon, Or hawk of the tower; With solace and gladness, Much mirth and no madness, All good and no badness; So joyously, So maidenly, So womanly Her demeaning,— In everything Far, far passing That I can indite Or suffice to write, Of merry Margaret, As midsummer flower, Gentle as falcon Or hawk of the tower; As patient and as still, And as full of good-will, As fair Isiphil, Coliander, Sweet Pomander, Good Cassander; Steadfast of thought, Well made, well wrought; Far may be sought Ere you can find So courteous, so kind, As merry Margaret, This midsummer flower— Gentle as falcon Or hawk of the tower.

John Skelton.

Ruth

She stood breast-high amid the corn, Clasp'd by the golden light of morn, Like the sweetheart of the sun, Who many a glowing kiss had won.

On her cheek an autumn flush. Deeply ripened;—such a blush In the midst of brown was born, Like red poppies grown with corn.

Round her eyes her tresses fell, Which were blackest none could tell, But long lashes veil'd a light That had else been all too bright.

And her hat, with shady brim, Made her tressy forehead dim;— Thus she stood amid the stooks, Praising God with sweetest looks.

"Sure," I said, "Heav'n did not mean Where I reap thou shouldst but glean; Lay thy sheaf adown and come, Share my harvest and my home."

Thomas Hood.

My Peggy

My Peggy is a young thing, Just entered in her teens, Fair as the day, and sweet as May, Fair as the day, and always gay, My Peggy is a young thing, And I'm not very auld, Yet well I like to meet her at The wauking of the fauld.

* * * *

My Peggy sings sae saftly, When on my pipe I play; By a' the rest it is confest, By a' the rest, that she sings best. My Peggy sings sae saftly, And in her sangs are tauld, With innocence, the wale of sense, At wauking of the fauld.

Allan Ramsay.

From "The Gentle Shepherd."

Annie Laurie

Maxwelton braes are bonnie Where early fa's the dew, And it's there that Annie Laurie Gie'd me her promise true,— Gie'd me her promise true, Which ne'er forgot will be; And for bonnie Annie Laurie I'd lay me doune and dee.

Her brow is like the snawdrift, Her throat is like the swan, Her face it is the fairest That e'er the sun shone on,— That e'er the sun shone on; And dark blue is her e'e; And for bonnie Annie Laurie I'd lay me doune and dee.

Like dew on the gowan lying Is the fa' o' her fairy feet; Like the winds in summer sighing, Her voice is low and sweet,— Her voice is low and sweet; And she's a' the world to me; And for bonnie Annie Laurie I'd lay me doune and dee.

William Douglas of Fingland.

Lucy

Three years she grew in sun and shower; Then Nature said, "A lovelier flower On earth was never sown: This child I to myself will take; She shall be mine, and I will make A lady of my own.

"Myself will to my darling be Both law and impulse: and with me The girl, in rock and plain, In earth and heaven, in glade and bower, Shall feel an overseeing power To kindle or restrain.

"She shall be sportive as the fawn That, wild with glee, across the lawn, Or up the mountain springs; And hers shall be the breathing balm, And hers the silence and the calm Of mute, insensate things.

"The floating clouds their state shall lend To her; for her the willow bend; Nor shall she fail to see E'en in the motions of the storm Grace that shall mold the maiden's form By silent sympathy.

"The stars of midnight shall be dear To her; and she shall lean her ear In many a secret place Where rivulets dance their wayward round, And beauty born of murmuring sound Shall pass into her face.

"And vital feelings of delight Shall rear her form to stately height, Her virgin bosom swell; Such thoughts to Lucy I will give While she and I together live Here in this happy dell."

Thus Nature spake—the work was done— How soon my Lucy's race was run! She died, and left to me This heath, this calm and quiet scene; The memory of what has been, And nevermore will be.

William Wordsworth.

Jessie

Jessie is both young and fair, Dewy eyes and sunny hair; Sunny hair and dewy eyes Are not where her beauty lies.

Jessie is both kind and true, Heart of gold and will of yew; Will of yew and heart of gold— Still her charms are scarcely told.

If she yet remain unsung, Pretty, constant, docile, young. What remains not here compiled? Jessie is a little child!

Bret Harte.

Olivia

She gamboll'd on the greens A baby-germ, to when The maiden blossoms of her teens Could number five from ten.

I swear, by leaf, and wind, and rain— And hear me with thine ears— That tho' I circle in the grain Five hundred rings of years,

Yet, since I first could cast a shade, Did never creature pass So slightly, musically made, So light upon the grass.

*   *   *   *

Then ran she, gamesome as the colt, And livelier than a lark She sent her voice thro' all the holt Before her, and the park.

A light wind chased her on the wing, And in the chase grew wild, As close as might be would he cling About the darling child.

But light as any wind that blows, So fleetly did she stir, The flower she touch'd on, dipt and rose, And turned to look at her.

Alfred, Lord Tennyson.

From "The Talking Oak."

Nikolina

O tell me, little children, have you seen her— The tiny maid from Norway, Nikolina? O, her eyes are blue as cornflow'rs mid the corn, And her cheeks are rosy red as skies of morn!

Nikolina! swift she turns if any call her, As she stands among the poppies, hardly taller, Breaking off their scarlet cups for you, With spikes of slender larkspur, burning blue.

In her little garden many a flower is growing— Red, gold, and purple in the soft wind blowing But the child that stands amid the blossoms gay Is sweeter, quainter, brighter e'en than they.

Celia Thaxter.

The Solitary Reaper

Behold her, single in the field, Yon solitary Highland Lass! Reaping and singing by herself; Stop here, or gently pass! Alone she cuts and binds the grain, And sings a melancholy strain; O listen! for the vale profound Is overflowing with the sound.

No nightingale did ever chaunt More welcome notes to weary bands Of travelers in some shady haunt, Among Arabian sands; A voice so thrilling ne'er was heard, In springtime from the cuckoo bird, Breaking the silence of the seas Among the farthest Hebrides.

Will no one tell me what she sings?— Perhaps the plaintive numbers flow For old, unhappy, far-off things, And battles long ago: Or is it some more humble lay, Familiar matter of to-day? Some natural sorrow, loss or pain, That has been, and may be again?

Whate'er the theme, the maiden sang As if her song could have no ending; I saw her singing at her work, And o'er the sickle bending;— I listened, motionless and still; And, as I mounted up the hill, The music in my heart I bore, Long after it was heard no more.

William Wordsworth.

Helena and Hermia

We, Hermia,... Have with our needles created both one flower, Both on one sampler, sitting on one cushion, Both warbling of one song, both in one key; As if our hands, our sides, voices, and minds Had been incorporate. So we grew together, Like to a double cherry, seeming parted, But yet a union in partition, Two lovely berries moulded on one stem; So, with two seeming bodies, but one heart, Two of the first, like coats in heraldry Due but to one, and crownéd with one crest.

William Shakespeare.

From "A Midsummer Night's Dream."

Phyllis

In petticoat of green, Her hair about her eyne, Phyllis beneath an oak Sat milking her fair flock; 'Mongst that sweet-strained moisture, rare delight, Her hand seemed milk, in milk it was so white.

William Drummond.

So Sweet Is She

Have you seen but a bright lily grow, Before rude hands have touched it? Have you marked but the fall of the snow, Before the soil hath smutched it? Have you felt the wool of the beaver? Or swan's down ever? Or have smelt o' the bud of the brier? Or the nard i' the fire? Or have tasted the bag of the bee? Oh, so white! oh, so soft! oh, so sweet, is she!

Ben Jonson.

From "The Triumph of Charis."

I Love My Jean

Of a' the airts the wind can blaw, I dearly like the west, For there the bonnie lassie lives, The lassie I lo'e best; There wild woods grow, and rivers row, And monie a hill between; But day and night my fancy's flight Is ever wi' my Jean.

I see her in the dewy flowers, I see her sweet and fair; I hear her in the tunefu' birds, I hear her charm the air: There's not a bonnie flower that springs By fountain, shaw, or green; There's not a bonnie bird that sings, But minds me o' my Jean.

Robert Burns.

My Nannie's Awa'

Now in her green mantle blythe nature arrays, An' listens the lambkins that bleat o'er the braes, While birds warble welcome in ilka green shaw; But to me it's delightless—my Nannie's awa'.

The snaw-drap an' primrose our woodlands adorn, An' violets bathe in the weet o' the morn; They pain my sad bosom, sae sweetly they blaw, They mind me o' Nannie—an' Nannie's awa'.

Thou lav'rock that springs frae the dews of the lawn, The shepherd to warn o' the gray-breaking dawn, An' thou mellow mavis that hails the night-fa', Give over for pity—my Nannie's awa'.

Come, autumn, sae pensive, in yellow an' gray, An' soothe me wi' tidings o' nature's decay; The dark, dreary winter, an' wild-driving snaw, Alane can delight me—now Nannie's awa'.

Robert Burns.

INTERLEAVES

The World of Waters

"The sea has the sun for a harper." She has also among her myriad worshippers Swinburne, the poet-harpist, who sweeps all the strings of his noble instrument in her praise.

There can be no worthier introduction to a group of sea-poems than lines "all gold seven times refined," selected almost at random from a great poet whom you will be glad to read later on.

"Green earth has her sons and her daughters, And these have their guerdons; but we Are the wind's and the sun's and the water's, Elect of the sea."

"She is pure as the wind and the sun, And her sweetness endureth forever."

"For the wind, with his wings half open, at pause in the sky, neither fettered nor free, Leans waveward and flutters the ripple to laughter!"

"But for hours upon hours As a thrall she remains Spell-bound as with flowers And content in their chains, And her loud steeds fret not, and lift not a lock of their deep white manes."

"And all the rippling green grew royal gold Between him and the far sun's rising rim."

"Where the horn of the headland is sharper And her green floor glitters with fire, The sea has the sun for a harper, The sun has the sea for a lyre."

"The waves are a pavement of amber, By the feet of the sea-winds trod, To receive in a god's presence-chamber Our

father, the God."

IX
THE WORLD OF WATERS
To the Ocean

Roll on, thou deep and dark blue Ocean—roll! Ten thousand fleets sweep over thee in vain; Man marks the earth with ruin—his control Stops with the shore;—upon the watery plain The wrecks are all thy deed, nor doth remain A shadow of man's ravage, save his own, When for a moment, like a drop of rain, He sinks into thy depths with bubbling groan, Without a grave, unknell'd, uncoffin'd and unknown.

His steps are not upon thy paths—thy fields Are not a spoil for him—thou dost arise And shake him from thee; the vile strength he wields For earth's destruction thou dost all despise, Spurning him from thy bosom to the skies, And send'st him, shivering in thy playful spray, And howling, to his Gods, where haply lies His petty hope in some near port or bay, And dashest him again to earth—there let him lay.

The armaments which thunderstrike the walls Of rock-built cities, bidding nations quake, And monarchs tremble in their capitals, The oak leviathans, whose huge ribs make Their clay creator the vain title take Of lord of thee, and arbiter of war; These are thy toys, and, as the snowy flake, They melt into thy yeast of waves, which mar Alike the Armada's pride, or spoils of Trafalgar.

Thy shores are empires, changed in all save thee— Assyria, Greece, Rome, Carthage, what are they? Thy waters wasted them while they were free, And many a tyrant since: their shores obey The stranger, slave or savage; their decay Has dried up realms to deserts—not so thou. Unchangeable save to thy wild waves' play— Time writes no wrinkle on thine azure brow— Such as creation's dawn beheld, thou rollest now.

Thou glorious mirror, where the Almighty's form Glasses itself in tempests: in all time, Calm or convulsed—in breeze, or gale, or storm, Icing the pole, or in the torrid clime Dark-heaving;—boundless, endless, and sublime— The image of Eternity—the throne Of the Invisible; even from out thy slime The monsters of the deep are made; each zone Obeys thee; thou goest forth, dread, fathomless, alone.

George Gordon, Lord Byron.
From "Childe Harold's Pilgrimage."

A Life on the Ocean Wave

A life on the ocean wave, A home on the rolling deep, Where the scattered waters rave, And the winds their revels keep! Like an eagle caged I pine On this dull unchanging shore: Oh! give me the flashing brine, The spray and the tempest's roar!

Once more on the deck I stand Of my own swift-gliding craft: Set sail! farewell to the land! The gale follows fair abaft. We shoot through the sparkling foam Like an ocean-bird set free;— Like the ocean-bird, our home We'll find far out on the sea.

The land is no longer in view, The clouds have begun to frown; But with a stout vessel and crew, We'll say let the storm come down! And the song of our hearts shall be, While the winds and the waters rave, A home on the rolling sea! A life on the ocean wave.

Epes Sargent.
Harper's "Cyclopædia of British and American Poetry."

The Sea

The sea! the sea! the open sea! The blue, the fresh, the ever free! Without a mark, without a bound, It runneth the earth's wide regions round; It plays with the clouds; it mocks the skies; Or like a cradled creature lies.

I'm on the sea! I'm on the sea! I am where I would ever be; With the blue above, and the blue below, And silence wheresoe'er I go; If a storm should come and awake the deep, What matter? I shall ride and sleep.

I love, oh, how I love to ride On the fierce, foaming, bursting tide, When every mad wave drowns the moon, Or whistles aloft his tempest tune, And tells how goeth the world below, And why the sou'west blasts do blow.

I never was on the dull, tame shore, But I loved the great sea more and more, And backward flew to her billowy breast, Like a bird that seeketh its mother's nest; And a mother she was, and is, to me; For I was born on the open sea!

The waves were white, and red the morn, In the noisy hour when I was born; And the whale it whistled, the porpoise rolled, And the dolphins bared their backs of gold; And never was heard such an outcry wild As welcomed to life the ocean-child!

I've lived since then, in calm and strife, Full fifty summers, a sailor's life, With wealth to spend, and power to range, But never have sought nor sighed for change; And Death, whenever he comes to me, Shall come on the wild, unbounded sea!

Barry Cornwall.
(Bryan Waller Procter.)

A Sea-Song

A wet sheet and a flowing sea, A wind that follows fast, And fills the white and rustling sail And bends the gallant mast; And bends the gallant mast, my boys, While, like the eagle free, Away the good ship flies, and leaves Old England on the lee.

O for a soft and gentle wind! I heard a fair one cry; But give to me the snoring breeze And white waves heaving high; And white waves heaving high, my lads, The good ship tight and free— The world of waters is our home, And merry men are we.

There's tempest in yon hornèd moon, And lightning in yon cloud; But hark the music, mariners! The wind is piping loud; The wind is piping loud, my boys, The lightning flashes free— While the hollow oak our palace is, Our heritage the sea.

Allan Cunningham.

A Visit From the Sea

Far from the loud sea-beaches, Where he goes fishing and crying, Here in the inland garden, Why is the sea-gull flying?

Here are no fish to dive for: Here is the corn and lea; Here are the green trees rustling. Hie away home to sea!

Fresh is the river water, And quiet among the rushes; This is no home for the sea-gull, But for the rooks and thrushes.

Pity the bird that has wandered! Pity the sailor ashore! Hurry him home to the ocean, Let him come here no more!

High on the sea-cliff ledges The white gulls are trooping and crying; Here among rooks and roses, Why is the sea-gull flying?

Robert Louis Stevenson.

From "A Child's Garden of Verses." By permission of Charles Scribner's Sons.

Drifting

My soul to-day Is far away, Sailing the Vesuvian Bay; My wingèd boat, A bird afloat, Swings round the purple peaks remote:—

Round purple peaks It sails, and seeks Blue inlets and their crystal creeks, Where high rocks throw, Through deeps below, A duplicated golden glow.

Far, vague, and dim, The mountains swim; While on Vesuvius' misty brim, With outstretched hands, The gray smoke stands O'erlooking the volcanic lands.

Here Ischia smiles O'er liquid miles; And yonder, bluest of the isles, Calm Capri waits, Her sapphire gates Beguiling to her bright estates.

I heed not, if My rippling skiff Float swift or slow from cliff to cliff; With dreamful eyes My spirit lies Under the walls of Paradise.

Under the walls Where swells and falls The Bay's deep breast at intervals At peace I lie, Blown softly by, A cloud upon this liquid sky.

The day, so mild, Is Heaven's own child, With Earth and Ocean reconciled; The airs I feel Around me steal Are murmuring to the murmuring keel.

Over the rail My hand I trail Within the shadow of the sail, A joy intense, The cooling sense Glides down my drowsy indolence.

With dreamful eyes My spirit lies Where Summer sings and never dies,— O'erveiled with vines She glows and shines Among her future oil and wines.

Her children, hid The cliffs amid, Are gambolling with the gambolling kid, Or down the walls, With tipsy calls, Laugh on the rocks like waterfalls.

The fisher's child, With tresses wild, Unto the smooth, bright sand beguiled, With glowing lips Sings as she skips, Or gazes at the far-off ships.

Yon deep bark goes Where traffic blows, From lands of sun to lands of snows; This happier one,— Its course is run From lands of snow to lands of sun.

O happy ship, To rise and dip, With the blue crystal at your lip! O happy crew, My heart with you Sails, and sails, and sings anew!

No more, no more The worldly shore Upbraids me with its loud uproar: With dreamful eyes My spirit lies Under the walls of Paradise!

Thomas Buchanan Read.

By courtesy of J. B. Lippincott & Co.

Tacking Ship Off Shore

The weather-leech of the topsail shivers, The bowlines strain, and the lee-shrouds slacken, The braces are taut, the lithe boom quivers, And the waves with the coming squall-cloud blacken.

Open one point on the weather-bow, Is the light-house tall on Fire Island Head. There's a shade of doubt on the captain's brow, And the pilot watches the heaving lead.

I stand at the wheel, and with eager eye To sea and to sky and to shore I gaze, Till the muttered order of "Full and by!" Is suddenly changed for "Full for stays!"

The ship bends lower before the breeze, As her broadside fair to the blast she lays; And she swifter springs to the rising seas, As the pilot calls, "Stand by for stays!"

It is silence all, as each in his place, With the gathered coil in his hardened hands, By tack and bowline, by sheet and brace, Waiting the watchword impatient stands.

And the light on Fire Island Head draws near, As, trumpet-winged, the pilot's shout From his post on the bowsprit's heel I hear, With the welcome call of "Ready! About!"

No time to spare! It is touch and go; And the captain growls, "Down helm! hard down!" As my weight on the whirling spokes I throw, While heaven grows black with the storm-cloud's frown.

High o'er the knight-heads flies the spray, As we meet the shock of the plunging sea; And my shoulder stiff to the wheel I lay, As I answer, "Ay, ay, sir! Ha-a-rd a-lee!"

With the swerving leap of a startled steed The ship flies fast in the eye of the wind, The dangerous shoals on the lee recede, And the headland white we have left behind.

The topsails flutter, the jibs collapse, And belly and tug at the groaning cleats; And spanker slats, and the mainsail flaps; And thunders the order, "Tacks and sheets!"

'Mid the rattle of blocks and the tramp of the crew, Hisses the rain of the rushing squall: The sails are aback from clew to clew. And now is the moment for "Mainsail, haul!"

And the heavy yards, like a baby's toy, By fifty strong arms are swiftly swung: She holds her way, and I look with joy For the first white spray o'er the bulwarks flung.

"Let go, and haul!" 'Tis the last command, And the head-sails fill to the blast once more: Astern and to leeward lies the land, With its breakers white on the shingly shore.

What matters the reef, or the rain, or the squall? I steady the helm for the open sea; The first mate clamors, "Belay, there, all!" And the captain's breath once more comes free.

And so off shore let the good ship fly; Little care I how the gusts may blow, In my fo'castle bunk, in a jacket dry. Eight bells have struck, and my watch is below.

Walter Mitchell.

By courtesy of The Churchman.

Windlass Song

Heave at the windlass!—Heave O, cheerly, men! Heave all at once, with a will! The tide quickly making, Our cordage a-creaking, The water has put on a frill, Heave O!

Fare you well, sweethearts!—Heave O, cheerly, men! Fare you well, frolic and sport! The good ship all ready, Each dog-vane is steady, The wind blowing dead out of port, Heave O!

Once in blue water—Heave O, cheerly, men! Blow it from north or from south; She'll stand to it tightly, And curtsey politely, And carry a bone in her mouth, Heave O!

Short cruise or long cruise—Heave O, cheerly, men! Jolly Jack Tar thinks it one. No latitude dreads he Of White, Black, or Red Sea, Great icebergs, or tropical sun, Heave O!

One other turn, and Heave O, cheerly, men! Heave, and good-bye to the shore! Our money, how went it? We shared it and spent it; Next year we'll come back with some more, Heave O!

William Allingham.

The Coral Grove

Deep in the wave is a coral grove, Where the purple mullet and gold-fish rove; Where the sea-flower spreads its leaves of blue That never are wet with falling dew, But in bright and changeful beauty shine, Far down in the green and glassy brine.

The floor is of sand, like the mountain drift; And the pearl-shell spangle the flinty snow; From coral rocks the sea-plants lift Their boughs where the tides and billows flow. The water is calm and still below, For the winds and waves are absent there; And the sands are bright as the stars that glow In the motionless fields of upper air.

There, with its waving blade of green, The sea-flag streams through the silent water; And the crimson leaf of the dulse is seen To blush like a banner bathed in slaughter. There, with a light and easy motion, The fan-coral sweeps through the clear deep sea; And the yellow and scarlet tufts of ocean Are bending like corn on the upland lea; And life, in rare and beautiful forms, Is sporting amid those bowers of stone, And is safe when the wrathful Spirit of storms Has made the top of the wave his own.

And when the ship from his fury flies, Where the myriad voices of Ocean roar; When the wind-god frowns in the murky skies, And demons are waiting the wreck on shore,— Then, far below, in the peaceful sea, The purple mullet and gold-fish rove, While the waters murmur tranquilly Through the bending twigs of the coral grove.

James Gates Percival.

The Shell

See what a lovely shell, Small and pure as a pearl, Lying close to my foot, Frail, but a work divine, Made so fairily well With delicate spire and whorl, How exquisitely minute, A miracle of design! What is it? a learned man Could give it a clumsy name. Let him name it who can, The beauty would be the same.

The tiny cell is forlorn, Void of the little living will That made it stir on the shore. Did he stand at the diamond door Of his house in a rainbow frill? Did he push, when he was uncurled, A golden foot or a fairy horn Through his dim water-world? Slight, to be crush'd with a tap Of my finger-nail on the sand! Small, but a work divine! Frail, but of force to withstand, Year upon year, the shock Of cataract seas that snap The three-decker's oaken spine Athwart the ledges of rock, Here on the Breton strand!

Alfred, Lord Tennyson.

Bermudas

Where the remote Bermudas ride, In the ocean's bosom unespied, From a small boat, that rowed along, The listening winds received this song:

"What should we do but sing His praise, That led us through the watery maze, Unto an isle so long unknown, And yet far kinder than our own? Where He the huge sea-monsters wracks, That lift the deep upon their backs; He lands us on a grassy stage, Safe from the storms, and prelate's rage. He gave us this eternal spring, Which here enamels every thing, And sends the fowls to us in care, On daily visits through the air; He hangs in shades the orange bright, Like golden lamps in a green night, And does in the pomegranates close Jewels more rich than Ormus shows; He makes the figs our mouths to meet, And throws the melons at our feet; But apples plants of such a price, No tree could ever bear them twice; With cedars chosen by His hand, From Lebanon, He stores the land, And makes the hollow seas, that roar, Proclaim the ambergris on shore; He cast (of which we rather boast) The Gospel's pearl upon our coast, And in these rocks for us did frame A temple where to sound His name. Oh! let our voice His praise exalt, Till it arrive at Heaven's vault, Which, thence (perhaps) rebounding, may Echo beyond the Mexique Bay."

Thus sung they, in the English boat, An holy and a cheerful note; And all the way, to guide their chime, With falling oars they kept the time.

Andrew Marvell.

Where Lies the Land?

Where lies the land to which the ship would go? Far, far ahead is all her seamen know. And where the land she travels from? Away, Far, far behind, is all that they can say.

On sunny noons upon the deck's smooth face; Linked arm in arm, how pleasant here to pace; Or, o'er the stern reclining, watch below The foaming wake far widening as we go.

On stormy nights when wild north-westers rave, How proud a thing to fight with wind and wave! The dripping sailor on the reeling mast Exults to bear, and scorns to wish it past.

Where lies the land to which the ship would go? Far, far ahead, is all her seamen know. And where the land she travels from? Away, Far, far behind, is all that they can say.

Arthur Hugh Clough.

INTERLEAVES
For Home and Country

"Such is the patriot's boast, where'er we roam? His first, best country ever is at home."

This is the proud claim of Goldsmith's "Traveller," and the same passionate loyalty to the soil inspires all these poems of Fatherland. The Scotsman's heart is in the Highlands, the birthplace of valor, the country of worth; the English warrior boasts of his country:

"And o'er one-sixth of all the earth, and over all the main, Like some good Fairy, Freedom marks and blesses her domain;"

the Irish Minstrel-boy tears the chords of his faithful harp asunder lest they sound in the service of the foe, while the quick, alarming Yankee drum in Bret Harte's "Reveille" calls upon each freeman to defend the land of the pilgrim's pride, land where his fathers died.

Religion, war, and glory were the three souls of a perfect Christian knight, says Lamartine, and if Death's couriers, Fame and Honor, summon us to the field,

"Our business is like men to fight And hero-like to die."

In Kipling's "Recessional" and Lowell's "Fatherland" we hear a note as valiant, but more spiritual. The one makes us remember that

"The tumult and the shouting dies— The captains and the kings depart— Still stands Thine ancient sacrifice, An humble and a contrite heart."

The other leads us to still higher levels of thought, reminding us that wherever a single soul doth pine, or one man may help another, that spot of earth is thine and mine—that is the world-wide fatherland.

X

FOR HOME AND COUNTRY

The First, Best Country

But where to find the happiest spot below, Who can direct, when all pretend to know? The shuddering tenant of the frigid zone Boldly proclaims that happiest spot his own; Extols the treasures of his stormy seas, And his long nights of revelry and ease; The naked negro, panting at the line, Boasts of his golden sands and palmy wine, Basks in the glare, or stems the tepid wave, And thanks his gods for all the goods they gave. Such is the patriot's boast, where'er we roam, His first, best country ever is at home. And yet perhaps, if countries we compare, And estimate the blessings which they share, Though patriots flatter, still shall wisdom find An equal portion dealt to all mankind; As different good, by art or nature given, To different nations makes their blessings even.

Oliver Goldsmith.

From "The Traveller."

My Native Land

Breathes there the man with soul so dead, Who never to himself hath said, "This is my own—my native land!" Whose heart hath ne'er within him burned, As home his footsteps he hath turned, From wandering on a foreign strand? If such there breathe, go, mark him well! For him no minstrel's raptures swell. High though his titles, proud his name, Boundless his wealth as wish can claim,— Despite those titles, power, and pelf, The wretch, concentred all in self, Living shall forfeit fair renown, And, doubly dying, shall go down To the vile dust from whence he sprung, Unwept, unhonored, and unsung.

Sir Walter Scott.

From "The Lay of the Last Minstrel."

Loyalty

Hame, hame, hame! oh hame I fain wad be, O hame, hame, hame, to my ain countrie! When the flower is i' the bud and the leaf is on the tree, The lark shall sing me hame in my ain countrie; *Hame, hame, hame! oh hame I fain wad be, O hame, hame, hame, to my ain countrie!*

The green leaf o' loyaltie's begun for to fa', The bonnie white rose it is withering an' a'; But I'll water 't wi' the blude of usurping tyrannie, An' green it will grow in my ain countrie. *Hame, hame, hame! oh hame I fain wad be, O hame, hame, hame, to my ain countrie!*

The great now are gane, wha attempted to save; The new grass is springing on the tap o' their grave: But the sun thro' the mirk blinks blythe in my e'e, "I'll shine on ye yet in yere ain countrie." *Hame, hame, hame! oh hame I fain wad be, Hame, hame, hame, to my ain countrie!*

Allan Cunningham.

My Heart's in the Highlands

My heart's in the Highlands, my heart is not here; My heart's in the Highlands a-chasing the deer; Chasing the wild deer, and following the roe, My heart's in the Highlands wherever I go. Farewell to the Highlands, farewell to the North, The birthplace of valor, the country of worth; Wherever I wander, wherever I rove, The hills of the Highlands forever I love.

Farewell to the mountains high covered with snow; Farewell to the straths and green valleys below; Farewell to the forests and wild-hanging woods; Farewell to the torrents and loud-pouring floods. My heart's in the Highlands, my heart is not here, My heart's in the Highlands a-chasing the deer; Chasing the wild deer, and following the roe, My heart's in the Highlands wherever I go.

Robert Burns.

The Minstrel-Boy

The Minstrel-boy to the war is gone, In the ranks of death you'll find him; His father's sword he has girded on, And his wild harp slung behind him.— "Land of song!" said the warrior-bard, "Though all the world betrays thee, One sword, at least, thy rights shall guard, One faithful harp shall praise thee!"

The Minstrel fell!—but the foeman's chain Could not bring his proud soul under; The harp he loved ne'er spoke again, For he tore its chords asunder; And said, "No chains shall sully thee, Thou soul of love and bravery! Thy songs were made for the pure and free, They shall never sound in slavery!"

Thomas Moore.

The Harp That Once Through Tara's Halls

The harp that once through Tara's halls The soul of music shed, Now hangs as mute on Tara's walls As if that soul were fled. So sleeps the pride of former days, So glory's thrill is o'er, And hearts, that once beat high for praise, Now feel that pulse no more.

No more to chiefs and ladies bright The harp of Tara swells: The chord alone, that breaks at night; Its tale of ruin tells.

Thus Freedom now so seldom wakes, The only throb she gives Is when some heart indignant breaks, To show that still she lives.

Thomas Moore.

Fife and Drum

The trumpet's loud clangor Excites us to arms, With shrill notes of anger And mortal alarms.

The double, double, double beat Of the thundering drum, Cries, "Hark! the foes come; Charge, charge! 'tis too late to retreat."

John Dryden.

From "The Ode on St. Cecilia's Day."

The Cavalier's Song

A steed! a steed of matchlesse speed, A sword of metal keene! All else to noble heartes is drosse, All else on earth is meane. The neighyinge of the war-horse prowde, The rowlinge of the drum, The clangor of the trumpet lowde, Be soundes from heaven that come; And oh! the thundering presse of knightes, Whenas their war cryes swell, May tole from heaven an angel bright. And rouse a fiend from hell. Then mounte! then mounte, brave gallants all, And don your helmes amaine: Deathe's couriers, fame and honor, call Us to the field againe. No shrewish teares shall fill our eye When the sword-hilt's in our hand— Heart-whole we'll part, and no whit sighe For the fayrest of the land; Let piping swaine, and craven wight, Thus weepe and puling crye; Our business is like men to fight, And hero-like to die!

William Motherwell.

The Old Scottish Cavalier

Come listen to another song, Should make your heart beat high, Bring crimson to your forehead, And the luster to your eye;— It is a song of olden time, Of days long since gone by, And of a baron stout and bold As e'er wore sword on thigh! Like a brave old Scottish cavalier, All of the olden time!

He kept his castle in the north. Hard by the thundering Spey; And a thousand vassals dwelt around, All of his kindred they. And not a man of all that clan Had ever ceased to pray For the Royal race they laved so well, Though exiled far away From the steadfast Scottish cavaliers All of the olden time!

His father drew the righteous sword For Scotland and her claims, Among the loyal gentlemen And chiefs of ancient names, Who swore to fight or fall beneath The standard of King James, And died at Killiecrankie Pass With the glory of the Græmes; Like a true old Scottish cavalier All of the olden time!

He never owned the foreign rule, No master he obeyed, But kept his clan in peace at home, From foray and from raid; And when they asked him for his oath, He touched his glittering blade, And pointed to his bonnet blue, That bore the white cockade: Like a leal old Scottish cavalier, All of the olden time!

At length the news ran through the land— The Prince had come again! That night the fiery cross was sped O'er mountain and through glen; And our old baron rose in might, Like a lion from his den, And rode away across the hills To Charlie and his men, With the valiant Scottish cavaliers. All of the olden time!

He was the first that bent the knee When the Standard waved abroad, He was the first that charged the foe On Preston's bloody sod; And ever, in the van of fight, The foremost still he trod, Until on bleak Culloden's heath, He gave his soul to God, Like a good old Scottish cavalier, All of the olden time!

Oh never shall we know again A heart so stout and true— The olden times have passed away, And weary are the new: The fair white rose has faded From the garden where it grew, And no fond tears save those of heaven, The glorious bed bedew Of the last old Scottish cavalier All of the olden time!

William Edmondstoune Aytoun.

The Song of the Camp

"Give us a song!" the soldiers cried, The outer trenches guarding, When the heated guns of the camps allied Grew weary of bombarding.

The dark Redan, in silent scoff, Lay, grim and threatening, under; And the tawny mound of the Malakoff No longer belched its thunder.

There was a pause. A guardsman said: "We storm the forts to-morrow; Sing while we may, another day Will bring enough of sorrow."

They lay along the battery's side, Below the smoking cannon,— Brave hearts, from Severn and from Clyde, And from the banks of Shannon.

They sang of love, and not of fame; Forgot was Britain's glory; Each heart recalled a different name, But all sang "Annie Laurie."

Voice after voice caught up the song, Until its tender passion Rose like an anthem rich and strong,— Their battle eve confession.

Dear girl! her name he dared not speak; But as the song grew louder, Something upon the soldier's cheek Washed off the stains of powder.

Beyond the darkening ocean burned The bloody sunset's embers, While the Crimean valleys learned How English love remembers.

And once again a fire of hell Rained on the Russian quarters, With scream of shot and burst of shell, And bellowing of the mortars!

And Irish Nora's eyes are dim For a singer dumb and gory; And English Mary mourns for him Who sang of "Annie Laurie."

Sleep, soldiers! still in honored rest Your truth and valor wearing; The bravest are the tenderest,— The loving are the daring.

Bayard Taylor.

Border Ballad

March, march, Ettrick and Teviotdale; Why the de'il dinna ye march forward in order? March, march, Eskdale and Liddesdale! All the Blue Bonnets are over the Border! Many a banner spread Flutters above your head, Many a crest that is famous in story. Mount and make ready, then, Sons of the mountain glen, Fight for the Queen and our old Scottish glory.

Come from the hills where your hirsels are grazing; Come from the glen of the buck and the roe; Come to the crag where the beacon is blazing; Come with the buckler, the lance and the bow. Trumpets are sounding; War-steeds are bounding; Stand to your arms and march in good order. England shall many a day Tell of the bloody fray When the Blue Bonnets came over the Border.

Sir Walter Scott.

From "The Monastery."

Gathering Song of Donuil Dhu

Pibroch of Donuil Dhu, Pibroch of Donuil, Wake thy wild voice anew, Summon Clan Conuil. Come away, come away, Hark to the summons! Come in your war-array, Gentles and commons.

Come from deep glen, and From mountain so rocky; The war-pipe and pennon Are at Inverlochy. Come every hill-plaid, and True heart that wears one, Come every steel blade, and Strong hand that bears one.

Leave untended the herd, The flock without shelter; Leave the corpse uninterr'd, The bride at the altar; Leave the deer, leave the steer, Leave nets and barges: Come with your fighting gear, Broadswords and targes.

Come as the winds come, when Forests are rended, Come as the waves come, when Navies are stranded: Faster come, faster come, Faster and faster, Chief, vassal, page and groom, Tenant and master.

Fast they come, fast they come; See how they gather! Wide waves the eagle plume Blended with heather. Cast your plaids, draw your blades, Forward each man set! Pibroch of Donuil Dhu Knell for the onset!

Sir Walter Scott.

The Reveille

Hark! I hear the tramp of thousands, And of armèd men the hum; Lo! a nation's hosts have gathered Round the quick alarming drum,— Saying, "Come, Freemen, come! Ere your heritage be wasted," said the quick Alarming drum.

"Let me of my heart take counsel: War is not of life the sum; Who shall stay and reap the harvest When the autumn days shall come?" But the drum Echoed, "Come! Death shall reap the braver harvest," said the Solemn-sounding drum.

"But when won the coming battle, What of profit springs therefrom? What if conquest, subjugation, Even greater ills become?" But the drum Answered, "Come! You must do the sum to prove it," said the Yankee-answering drum.

"What if, 'mid the cannons' thunder, Whistling shot and bursting bomb, When my brothers fall around me, Should my heart grow cold and numb?" But the drum Answered, "Come! Better there in death united, than in life a recreant, — Come!"

Thus they answered,—hoping, fearing, Some in faith, and doubting some, Till a trumpet-voice proclaiming, Said, "My chosen people, come!" Then the drum, Lo! was dumb, For the great heart of the nation, throbbing, answered, "Lord, we come!"

Bret Harte.

Ye Mariners of England

Ye Mariners of England, That guard our native seas, Whose flag has braved, a thousand years, The battle and the breeze, Your glorious standard launch again, To match another foe! And sweep through the deep While the stormy winds do blow— While the battle rages loud and long, And the stormy winds do blow.

The spirit of your fathers Shall start from every wave! For the deck it was their field of fame, And Ocean was their grave. Where Blake and mighty Nelson fell Your manly hearts shall glow, As ye sweep through the deep While the stormy winds do blow— While the battle rages loud and long, And the stormy winds do blow.

Britannia needs no bulwarks, No towers along the steep; Her march is o'er the mountain-wave, Her home is on the deep.

With thunders from her native oak She quells the floods below, As they roar on the shore When the stormy winds do blow— When the battle rages loud and long, And the stormy winds do blow.

The meteor flag of England Shall yet terrific burn, Till danger's troubled night depart, And the star of peace return. Then, then, ye ocean-warriors! Our song and feast shall flow To the fame of your name, When the storm has ceased to blow,— When the fiery fight is heard no more, And the storm has ceased to blow.

Thomas Campbell.

The Knight's Tomb

Where is the grave of Sir Arthur O'Kellyn? Where may the grave of that good man be?— By the side of a spring, on the breast of Helvellyn, Under the twigs of a young birch tree!

The oak that in summer was sweet to hear, And rustled its leaves in the fall of the year, And whistled and roared in the winter alone, Is gone,—and the birch in its stead is grown.— The knight's bones are dust, And his good sword rust;— His soul is with the saints, I trust.

Samuel Taylor Coleridge.

How Sleep the Brave!

How sleep the Brave who sink to rest By all their country's wishes blest! When Spring, with dewy fingers cold, Returns to deck their hallowed mould, She there shall dress a sweeter sod Than Fancy's feet have ever trod.

By fairy hands their knell is rung; By forms unseen their dirge is sung; There Honor comes, a pilgrim gray, To bless the turf that wraps their clay; And Freedom shall awhile repair, To dwell a weeping hermit there!

William Collins.

Dirge
For One Who Fell in Battle.

Room for a soldier! lay him in the clover; He loved the fields, and they shall be his cover; Make his mound with hers who called him once her lover: Where the rain may rain upon it, Where the sun may shine upon it, Where the lamb hath lain upon it, And the bee will dine upon it.

Bear him to no dismal tomb under city churches; Take him to the fragrant fields, by the silver birches, Where the whip-poor-will shall mourn, where the oriole perches: Make his mound with sunshine on it, Where the bee will dine upon it, Where the lamb hath lain upon it, And the rain will rain upon it.

Busy as the bee was he, and his rest should be the clover; Gentle as the lamb was he, and the fern should be his cover; Fern and rosemary shall grow my soldier's pillow over: Where the rain may rain upon it, Where the sun may shine upon it, Where the lamb hath lain upon it, And the bee will dine upon it.

Sunshine in his heart, the rain would come full often Out of those tender eyes which evermore did soften: He never could look cold till we saw him in his coffin. Make his mound with sunshine on it. Plant the lordly pine upon it, Where the moon may stream upon it, And memory shall dream upon it.

"Captain or Colonel,"—whatever invocation Suit our hymn the best, no matter for thy station,— On thy grave the rain shall fall from the eyes of a mighty nation! Long as the sun doth shine upon it, Shall glow the goodly pine upon it, Long as the stars do gleam upon it, Shall memory come to dream upon it.

Thomas William Parsons.

The Burial of Sir John Moore

Not a drum was heard, not a funeral-note, As his corse to the rampart we hurried; Not a soldier discharged his farewell shot O'er the grave where our hero we buried.

We buried him darkly at dead of night, The sods with our bayonets turning, By the struggling moonbeam's misty light, And the lantern dimly burning.

No useless coffin enclosed his breast, Not in sheet or in shroud we wound him; But he lay like a warrior taking his rest, With his martial cloak around him.

Few and short were the prayers we said, And we spoke not a word of sorrow; But we steadfastly gazed on the face that was dead, And we bitterly thought of the morrow.

We thought as we hollow'd his narrow bed, And smooth'd down his lonely pillow, That the foe and the stranger would tread o'er his head, And we far away on the billow!

Lightly they'll talk of the spirit that's gone, And o'er his cold ashes upbraid him— But little he'll reck, if they let him sleep on In the grave where a Briton has laid him.

But half of our heavy task was done, When the clock struck the hour for retiring; And we heard the distant and random gun That the foe was sullenly firing.

Slowly and sadly we laid him down, From the field of his fame fresh and gory; We carved not a line, and we raised not a stone— But we left him alone in his glory.

Charles Wolfe.

Soldier, Rest!

Soldier, rest! thy warfare o'er, Sleep the sleep that knows not breaking: Dream of battle-fields no more, Days of danger, nights of waking. In our isle's enchanted hall, Hands unseen thy couch are strewing; Fairy strains of music fall, Every sense in slumber dewing. Soldier, rest! thy warfare o'er, Dream of fighting fields no more: Sleep the sleep that knows not breaking, Morn of toil, nor night of waking.

No rude sound shall reach thine ear, Armor's clang, or war-steed's champing; Trump nor pibroch summon here, Mustering clan, or squadron tramping. Yet the lark's shrill fife may come, At the day-break, from the fallow, And the bittern sound his drum, Booming from the sedgy shallow. Ruder sounds shall none be near, Guards nor warders challenge here, Here's no war-steed's neigh and champing, Shouting clans, or squadrons stamping.

Sir Walter Scott.

From "The Lady of the Lake."

Recessional

God of our fathers, known of old— Lord of our far-flung battle-line— Beneath Whose awful Hand we hold Dominion over palm and pine— Lord God of Hosts, be with us yet, Lest we forget—lest we forget!

The tumult and the shouting dies— The captains and the kings depart— Still stands Thine ancient Sacrifice, An humble and a contrite heart. Lord God of Hosts, be with us yet, Lest we forget—lest we forget!

Far-called our navies melt away— On dune and headland sinks the fire— Lo, all our pomp of yesterday Is one with Nineveh and Tyre! Judge of the Nations, spare us yet, Lest we forget—lest we forget!

If, drunk with sight of power, we loose Wild tongues that have not Thee in awe— Such boasting as the Gentiles use Or lesser breeds without the Law— Lord God of Hosts, be with us yet, Lest we forget—lest we forget!

For heathen heart that puts her trust In reeking tube and iron shard— All valiant dust that builds on dust, And guarding calls not Thee to guard— For frantic boast and foolish word, Thy Mercy on Thy People, Lord! Amen.

Rudyard Kipling.

The Fatherland

Where is the true man's fatherland? Is it where he by chance is born? Doth not the yearning spirit scorn In such scant borders to be spanned? Oh yes! his fatherland must be As the blue heaven wide and free!

Is it alone where freedom is, Where God is God and man is man? Doth he not claim a broader span For the soul's love of home than this? Oh yes! his fatherland must be As the blue heaven wide and free!

Where'er a human heart doth wear Joy's myrtle-wreath or sorrow's gyves, Where'er a human spirit strives After a life more true and fair, There is the true man's birthplace grand, His is a world-wide fatherland!

Where'er a single slave doth pine, Where'er one man may help another,— Thank God for such a birthright, brother,— That spot of earth is thine and mine! There is the true man's birthplace grand, His is a world-wide fatherland!

James Russell Lowell.

INTERLEAVES
New World and Old Glory

The verse in this division gives a poetic picture of America, dear land of all our love, from the very beginning of her world-life. It sings her story from the time when Columbus,

"Before him not the ghost of shores, Before him only shoreless seas,"

sailed toward the mysterious continent that lay hidden in the West; sings it from the thrilling moment when the weary sailors sighted the new land, up to the twentieth century, when Old Glory waves

"Wherever the sails of peace are seen And wherever the war-wind blows."

Heroic figures, familiar to us from childhood, appear in these metrical versions of episodes in our national history. Here is the red man whose hour, alas! was struck when first the pale-face looked upon his happy hunting-grounds; here are Pocahontas and her Captain; the Pilgrim Fathers; Washington, the soldier-statesman; the embattled farmers who fired at Concord the shot heard round the world; the Continentals in their ragged regimentals, and Old Ironsides with its memories of . Then, when "westward the Star of Empire takes its way," come the Argonauts of ', crossing the plains in their white-sailed prairie schooners in search, like Jason, of the Golden Fleece.

The years move on, and Abraham Lincoln, the Great Commoner, dear benefactor of the race, appears, and, kneeling at his feet, the dusky slave whose bonds he loosened. Gallant Phil Sheridan and Barbara Frietchie are here too; indeed, you will find that the number of poems inspired by the Civil War is very great; but the patriot host, above, below, knows now no North nor South; and Lincoln's "dear majestic ghost" looks down upon, as Old Glory floats over, a united commonwealth.

XI
NEW WORLD AND OLD GLORY
Dear Land of All My Love

Long as thine art shall love true love, Long as thy science truth shall know, Long as thine eagle harms no dove, Long as thy law by law shall grow, Long as thy God is God above, Thy brother every man below, So long, dear land of all my love, Thy name shall shine, thy fame shall glow.

Sidney Lanier.

From "The Centennial Ode" ().

From "Poems of Sidney Lanier," copyright , and published by Charles Scribner's Sons.

Columbus

Behind him lay the gray Azores, Behind the gates of Hercules; Before him not the ghost of shores, Before him only shoreless seas. The good mate said: "Now must we pray, For, lo! the very stars are gone. Brave Adm'r'l, speak; what shall I say?" "Why, say: 'Sail on, sail on! and on!'"

"My men grow mutinous day by day; My men grow ghastly wan and weak." The stout mate thought of home; a spray Of salt wave washed his swarthy cheek. "What shall I say, brave Adm'r'l, say, If we sight not but seas at dawn?" "Why, you shall say, at break of day: 'Sail on! sail on! sail on! and on!'"

They sailed and sailed as winds might blow, Until at last the blanched mate said: "Why, now not even God would know Should I and all my men fall dead. These very winds forget the way, For God from these dread seas is gone. Now speak, brave Adm'r'l, speak and say—" He said: "Sail on! sail on! and on!"

They sailed. They sailed. Then spake the mate: "This mad sea shows his teeth to-night; He curls his lip, he lies in wait, With lifted teeth, as if to bite: Brave Adm'r'l, say but one good word; What shall we do when hope is gone?" The words leapt as a leaping sword: "Sail on! sail on! sail on! and on!"

Then, pale and worn, he kept his deck And peered through darkness. Ah, that night Of all dark nights! And then a speck— A light! a light! a light! a light! It grew, a starlit flag unfurled! It grew to be Time's burst of dawn. He gained a world; he gave that world Its greatest lesson: "On! sail on!"

Joaquin Miller.

From "The Complete Poetical Works of Joaquin Miller" (copyrighted). By permission of the publishers, The Whitaker-Ray Company, San Francisco.

Pocahontas

Wearied arm and broken sword Wage in vain the desperate fight; Round him press a countless horde, He is but a single knight. Hark! a cry of triumph shrill Through the wilderness resounds, As, with twenty bleeding wounds, Sinks the warrior, fighting still.

Now they heap the funeral pyre, And the torch of death they light; Ah! 'tis hard to die by fire! Who will shield the captive knight? Round the stake with fiendish cry Wheel and dance the savage crowd, Cold the victim's mien and proud, And his breast is bared to die.

Who will shield the fearless heart? Who avert the murderous blade? From the throng with sudden start See, there springs an Indian maid. Quick she stands before the knight: "Loose the chain, unbind the ring! I am daughter of the king. And I claim the Indian right!"

Dauntlessly aside she flings Lifted axe and thirsty knife, Fondly to his heart she clings, And her bosom guards his life! In the woods of Powhattan, Still 'tis told by Indian fires How a daughter of their sires Saved a captive Englishman.

William Makepeace Thackeray.

Landing of the Pilgrim Fathers

The breaking waves dashed high On a stern and rock-bound coast, And the woods against a stormy sky Their giant branches tossed; And the heavy night hung dark The hills and waters o'er, When a band of exiles moored their bark On the wild New England shore.

Not as the conqueror comes, They, the true-hearted, came; Not with the roll of the stirring drums, And the trumpet that sings of fame: Not as the flying come, In silence and in fear: They shook the depths of the desert's gloom With their hymns of lofty cheer.

Amidst the storm they sang; And the stars heard, and the sea; And the sounding aisles of the dim woods rang To the Anthem of the Free. The ocean eagle soared From his nest by the white wave's foam; And the rocking pines of the forest roared,— This was their welcome home!

There were men with hoary hair Amidst that pilgrim band: Why had they come to wither there, Away from their childhood's land? There was woman's fearless eye, Lit by her deep love's truth; There was manhood's brow, serenely high, And the fiery heart of youth.

What sought they thus afar? Bright jewels of the mine? The wealth of seas, the spoils of war?— They sought a faith's pure shrine! Ay, call it holy ground, The soil where first they trod;— They have left unstained what there they found— Freedom to worship God.

Felicia Hemans.

The Twenty-second of December

Wild was the day; the wintry sea Moaned sadly on New England's strand, When first the thoughtful and the free, Our fathers, trod the desert land.

They little thought how pure a light, With years, should gather round that day; How love should keep their memories bright, How wide a realm their sons should sway.

Green are their bays; but greener still Shall round their spreading fame be wreathed, And regions, now untrod, shall thrill With reverence when their names are breathed,

Till where the sun, with softer fires, Looks on the vast Pacific's sleep, The children of the Pilgrim sires This hallowed day like us shall keep.

William Cullen Bryant.

By courtesy of D. Appleton & Co., publishers of Bryant's Complete Poetical Works.

Washington

Soldier and statesman, rarest unison; High-poised example of great duties done Simply as breathing, a world's honors worn As life's indifferent gifts to all men born; Dumb for himself, unless it were to God, But for his barefoot soldiers eloquent, Tramping the snow to coral where they trod, Held by his awe in hollow-eyed content; Modest, yet firm as Nature's self; unblamed Save by the men his nobler temper shamed; Never seduced through show of present good By other than unsetting lights to steer New-trimmed in Heaven, nor than his steadfast mood More steadfast, far from rashness as from fear; Rigid, but with himself first, grasping still In swerveless poise the wave-beat helm of will; Not honored then or now because he wooed The popular voice, but that he still withstood; Broad-minded, higher-souled, there is but one Who was all this and ours, and all men's,—Washington.

James Russell Lowell.

From "Under the Old Elm."

Warren's Address

Stand! the ground's your own, my braves! Will ye give it up to slaves? Will ye look for greener graves? Hope ye mercy still? What's the mercy despots feel? Hear it in that battle peal! Read it on yon bristling steel! Ask it,—ye who will!

Fear ye foes who kill for hire? Will ye to your homes retire? Look behind you! they're afire, And, before you, see Who have done it!—From the vale On they come!—and will ye quail?— Leaden rain and leaden hail Let their welcome be!

In the God of battles trust! Die we may,—and die we must; But oh, where can dust to dust Be consigned so well, As where Heaven its dews shall shed On the martyred patriot's bed, And the rocks shall raise their head Of his deeds to tell!

John Pierpont.

Carmen Bellicosum

In their ragged regimentals Stood the old Continentals, Yielding not, When the grenadiers were lunging, And like hail fell the plunging Cannon shot; When the files Of the isles, From their smoky night encampment, bore the banner of the rampant Unicorn, And grummer, grummer, grummer, roll'd the roll of the drummer, Through the morn!

Then with eyes to the front all, And guns horizontal, Stood our sires; And the balls whistled deadly, And in streams flashing redly Blazed the fires; As the roar On the shore, Swept the strong battle-breakers o'er the green sodded acres Of the plain; And louder, louder, louder, cracked the black gunpowder, Cracking amain!

Now like smiths at their forges Worked the red Saint George's Cannoniers, And the "villainous saltpetre" Rung a fierce, discordant metre 'Round their ears; As the swift Storm-drift, With hot, sweeping anger, came the Horse Guards' clangor On our flanks; And higher, higher, higher, burned the old-fashioned fire Through the ranks!

Then the old-fashioned Colonel Galloped through the white infernal Powder cloud; His broad-sword was swinging, And his brazen throat was ringing Trumpet loud; Then the blue Bullets flew, And the trooper-jackets redden at the touch of the leaden Rifle-breath; And rounder, rounder, rounder, roared our iron six-pounder, Hurling death!

Guy Humphreys McMaster.

The American Flag

(Extract)

When Freedom from her mountain height Unfurled her standard to the air, She tore the azure robe of night, And set the stars of glory there. She mingled with its gorgeous dyes The milky baldric of the skies, And striped its pure, celestial white, With streakings of the morning light; Then from his mansion in the sun She called her eagle bearer down, And gave into his mighty hand The symbol of her chosen land.

*   *   *   *

71

Flag of the free heart's hope and home! By angel hands to valor given; Thy stars have lit the welkin dome, And all thy hues were born in heaven. Forever float that standard sheet! Where breathes the foe but falls before us, With Freedom's soil beneath our feet, And Freedom's banner streaming o'er us!

Joseph Rodman Drake.

Old Ironsides

(U. S. S. "Constitution.")

Ay, tear her tattered ensign down! Long has it waved on high, And many an eye has danced to see That banner in the sky; Beneath it rung the battle shout, And burst the cannon's roar;— The meteor of the ocean air Shall sweep the clouds no more.

Her deck, once red with heroes' blood, Where knelt the vanquished foe, When winds were hurrying o'er the flood, And waves were white below, No more shall feel the victor's tread, Or know the conquered knee; The harpies of the shore shall pluck The eagle of the sea!

Oh, better that her shattered hulk Should sink beneath the wave; Her thunders shook the mighty deep, And there should be her grave: Nail to the mast her holy flag, Set every threadbare sail, And give her to the god of storms, The lightning and the gale!

Oliver Wendell Holmes.

Indians

Alas! for them, their day is o'er, Their fires are out on hill and shore; No more for them the wild deer bounds, The plough is on their hunting grounds; The pale man's axe rings through their woods, The pale man's sail skims o'er their floods; Their pleasant springs are dry; Their children,—look, by power opprest, Beyond the mountains of the west, Their children go to die.

Charles Sprague.

Crossing the Plains

What great yoked brutes with briskets low; With wrinkled necks like buffalo, With round, brown, liquid, pleading eyes, That turned so slow and sad to you, That shone like love's eyes soft with tears, That seemed to plead, and make replies, The while they bowed their necks and drew The creaking load; and looked at you. Their sable briskets swept the ground, Their cloven feet kept solemn sound.

Two sullen bullocks led the line, Their great eyes shining bright like wine; Two sullen captive kings were they, That had in time held herds at bay, And even now they crushed the sod With stolid sense of majesty, And stately stepped and stately trod, As if 't were something still to be Kings even in captivity.

Joaquin Miller.

From "The Complete Poetical Works of Joaquin Miller" (copyrighted). By permission of the publishers. The Whitaker-Ray Company, San Francisco.

Concord Hymn

Sung at the completion of the Battle Monument, April , .

By the rude bridge that arched the flood, Their flag to April's breeze unfurled, Here once the embattled farmers stood, And fired the shot heard round the world.

The foe long since in silence slept; Alike the conqueror silent sleeps; And Time the ruined bridge has swept Down the dark stream which seaward creeps.

On the green bank, by this soft stream, We set to-day a votive stone; That memory may her dead redeem, When, like our sires, our sons are gone.

Spirit, that made those heroes dare To die, and leave their children free, Bid Time and Nature gently spare The shaft we raise to them and thee.

Ralph Waldo Emerson.

Ode

Sung in the Town Hall, Concord, July , .

O tenderly the haughty day Fills his blue urn with fire; One morn is in the mighty heaven, And one in our desire.

The cannon booms from town to town, Our pulses beat not less, The joy-bells chime their tidings down, Which children's voices bless.

For He that flung the broad blue fold O'er-mantling land and sea, One third part of the sky unrolled For the banner of the free.

The men are ripe of Saxon kind To build an equal state,— To take the statute from the mind And make of duty fate.

United States! the ages plead,— Present and Past in under-song,— Go put your creed into your deed, Nor speak with double tongue.

For sea and land don't understand, Nor skies without a frown See rights for which the one hand fights By the other cloven down.

Be just at home; then write your scroll Of honor o'er the sea, And bid the broad Atlantic roll, A ferry of the free.

And henceforth there shall be no chain, Save underneath the sea The wires shall murmur through the main Sweet songs of liberty.

The conscious stars accord above, The waters wild below, And under, through the cable wove, Her fiery errands go.

For He that worketh high and wise, Nor pauses in His plan, Will take the sun out of the skies, Ere freedom out of man.

Ralph Waldo Emerson.

Stanzas on Freedom

Is true Freedom but to break Fetters for our own dear sake, And, with leathern hearts, forget That we owe mankind a debt? No! true freedom is to share All the chains our brothers wear, And, with heart and hand, to be Earnest to make others free!

They are slaves who fear to speak For the fallen and the weak; They are slaves who will not choose Hatred, scoffing, and abuse, Rather than in silence shrink From the truth they needs must think; They are slaves who dare not be In the right with two or three.

James Russell Lowell.

Abraham Lincoln

This man whose homely face you look upon, Was one of nature's masterful, great men; Born with strong arms, that unfought battles won; Direct of speech, and cunning with the pen. Chosen for large designs, he had the art Of winning with his humor, and he went Straight to his mark, which was the human heart; Wise, too, for what he could not break he bent. Upon his back a more than Atlas-load, The burden of the Commonwealth, was laid; He stooped, and rose up to it, though the road Shot suddenly downwards, not a whit dismayed. Hold, warriors, councillors, kings! All now give place To this dear benefactor of the race.

Richard Henry Stoddard.

Lincoln the Great Commoner

When the Norn-Mother saw the Whirlwind Hour, Greatening and darkening as it hurried on, She bent the strenuous Heavens and came down, To make a man to meet the mortal need. She took the tried clay of the common road— Clay warm yet with the genial heat of earth, Dashed through it all a strain of prophecy; Then mixed a laughter with the serious stuff. It was a stuff to wear for centuries, A man that matched the mountains and compelled The stars to look our way and honor us.

The color of the ground was in him, the red Earth, The tang and odor of the primal things, The rectitude and patience of the rocks; The gladness of the wind that shakes the corn; The courage of the bird that dares the sea; The justice of the rain that loves all leaves; The pity of the snow that hides all scars; The loving kindness of the wayside well; The tolerance and equity of light That gives as freely to the shrinking weed As to the great oak flaring to the wind— To the grave's low hill as to the Matterhorn That shoulders out the sky.

And so he came, From prairie cabin to the Capitol, One fair ideal led our chieftain on, Forevermore he burned to do his deed With the fine stroke and gesture of a King. He built the rail pile as he built the State, Pouring his splendid strength through every blow, The conscience of him testing every stroke, To make his deed the measure of a man.

So came the Captain with the mighty heart; And when the step of earthquake shook the house, Wrenching the rafters from their ancient hold, He held the ridgepole up and spiked again The rafters of the Home. He held his place— Held the long purpose like a growing tree— Held on through blame and faltered not at praise, And when he fell in whirlwind, he went down As when a kingly cedar green with boughs Goes down with a great shout upon the hills.

Edwin Markham.

Abraham Lincoln

(Summer, .)

Dead is the roll of the drums, And the distant thunders die, They fade in the far-off sky; And a lovely summer comes, Like the smile of Him on high.

*   *   *   *

How the tall white daisies grow, Where the grim artillery rolled! (Was it only a moon ago? It seems a century old,)—

And the bee hums in the clover, As the pleasant June comes on; Aye, the wars are all over,— But our good Father is gone.

There was tumbling of traitor fort, Flaming of traitor fleet— Lighting of city and port, Clasping in square and street.

There was thunder of mine and gun, Cheering by mast and tent,— When—his dread work all done,— And his high fame full won— Died the Good President.

*   *   *   *

And our boys had fondly thought, To-day, in marching by, From the ground so dearly bought, And the fields so bravely fought, To have met their Father's eye.

But they may not see him in place Nor their ranks be seen of him; We look for the well-known face, And the splendor is strangely dim.

Perished?—who was it said Our Leader had passed away? Dead? Our President dead? He has not died for a day!

We mourn for a little breath Such as, late or soon, dust yields; But the Dark Flower of Death Blooms in the fadeless fields.

We looked on a cold, still brow, But Lincoln could yet survive; He never was more alive, Never nearer than now.

For the pleasant season found him, Guarded by faithful hands, In the fairest of Summer Lands; With his own brave Staff around him, There our President stands.

There they are all at his side, The noble hearts and true, That did all men might do— Then slept, with their swords, and died.

*   *   *   *

Henry Howard Brownell.

O Captain! My Captain!

O Captain! my Captain! our fearful trip is done, The ship has weather'd every rack, the prize we sought is won, The port is near, the bells I hear, the people all exulting, While follow eyes the steady keel, the vessel grim and daring;

But O heart! heart! heart! O the bleeding drops of red, Where on the deck my Captain lies, Fallen cold and dead.

O Captain! my Captain! rise up and hear the bells; Rise up—for you the flag is flung—for you the bugle trills, For you bouquets and ribbon'd wreaths—for you the shores a-crowding, For you they call, the swaying mass, their eager faces turning; Here, Captain! dear father! This arm beneath your head! It is some dream that on the deck, You've fallen cold and dead.

My Captain does not answer, his lips are pale and still, My father does not feel my arm, he has no pulse nor will, The ship is anchor'd safe and sound, its voyage closed and done, From fearful trip the victor ship comes in with object won;

Exult, O shores! and ring, O bells! But I with mournful tread, Walk the deck my Captain lies, Fallen cold and dead.

Walt Whitman.

The Flag Goes By

Hats off! Along the street there comes A blare of bugles, a ruffle of drums, A flash of color beneath the sky: Hats off! The flag is passing by!

Blue and crimson and white it shines, Over the steel-tipped, ordered lines. Hats off! The colors before us fly; But more than the flag is passing by.

Sea-fights and land-fights, grim and great, Fought to make and to save the State: Weary marches and sinking ships; Cheers of victory on dying lips;

Days of plenty and years of peace; March of a strong land's swift increase; Equal justice, right and law, Stately honor and reverend awe;

Sign of a nation, great and strong To ward her people from foreign wrong: Pride and glory and honor,—all Live in the colors to stand or fall.

Hats off! Along the street there comes A blare of bugles, a ruffle of drums; And loyal hearts are beating high: Hats off! The flag is passing by!

Henry Holcomb Bennett.

The Black Regiment

Dark as the clouds of even, Ranked in the western heaven, Waiting the breath that lifts All the dead mass, and drifts Tempest and falling brand Over a ruined land,— So still and orderly, Arm to arm, knee to knee, Waiting the great event, Stands the black regiment.

Down the long dusky line Teeth gleam, and eyeballs shine; And the bright bayonet, Bristling and firmly set, Flashed with a purpose grand, Long ere the sharp command Of the fierce rolling drum Told them their time had come, Told them what work was sent For the black regiment.

"Now!" the flag-sergeant cried, "Though death and hell betide, Let the whole nation see If we are fit to be Free in this land; or bound Down, like the whining hound,— Bound with red stripes of pain In our cold chains again!" Oh, what a shout there went From the black regiment!

"Charge!" trump and drum awoke; Onward the bondsmen broke; Bayonet and sabre-stroke Vainly opposed their rush. Through the wild battle's crush, With but one thought aflush, Driving their lords like chaff, In the gun's mouth they laugh; Or at the slippery brands, Leaping with open hands, Down they tear man and horse, Down in their awful course; Trampling with bloody heel Over the crushing steel,— All their eyes forward bent, Rushed the black regiment.

"Freedom!" their battle-cry,— "Freedom! or leave to die!" Ah, and they meant the word! Not as with us 'tis heard,— Not a mere party shout; They gave their spirits out, Trusting the end to God, And on the gory sod Rolled in triumphant blood.

Glad to strike one free blow, Whether for weal or woe; Glad to breathe one free breath, Though on the lips of death; Praying—alas, in vain!— That they might fall again, So they could once more see That burst to liberty! This was what "freedom" lent To the black regiment.

Hundreds on hundreds fell; But they are resting well; Scourges, and shackles strong, Never shall do them wrong. Oh, to the living few, Soldiers, be just and true! Hail them as comrades tried; Fight with them side by side; Never, in field or tent, Scorn the black regiment!

George Henry Boker.

Night Quarters

Tang! tang! went the gong's wild roar Through the hundred cells of our great Sea-Hive! Five seconds—it couldn't be more— And the whole Swarm was humming and alive— (We were on an enemy's shore.)

With savage haste, in the dark, (Our steerage hadn't a spark,) Into boot and hose they blundered— From for'ard came a strange, low roar, The dull and smothered racket Of lower rig and jacket Hurried on, by the hundred, How the berth deck buzzed and swore!

The third of minutes ten, And half a thousand men, From the dream-gulf, dead and deep, Of the seamen's measured sleep, In the taking of a lunar, In the serving of a ration, Every man at his station!— Three and a quarter, or sooner! Never a skulk to be seen— From the look-out aloft to the gunner Lurking in his black magazine. There they stand, still as death, And, (a trifle out of breath, It may be,) we of the Staff, All on the poop, to a minute, Wonder if there's anything in it— Doubting if to growl or laugh.

But, somehow, every hand Feels for hilt and brand, Tries if buckle and frog be tight,— So, in the chilly breeze, we stand, Peering through the dimness of the night— The men by twos and ones, Grim and silent at the guns, Ready, if a Foe heave in sight!

But, as we look aloft, There, all white and soft, Floated on the fleecy clouds, (Stray flocks in heaven's blue croft)— How they shone, the eternal stars, 'Mid the black masts and spars And the great maze of lifts and shrouds!

Henry Howard Brownell.

(Flag Ship "Hartford," May, .)

Battle-Hymn of the Republic

Mine eyes have seen the glory of the coming of the Lord; He is trampling out the vintage where the grapes of wrath are stored, He hath loosed the fateful lightning of His terrible swift sword; His truth is marching on.

I have seen Him in the watch-fires of a hundred circling camps; They have builded Him an altar in the evening dews and damps, I can read His righteous sentence by the dim and flaring lamps; His day is marching on.

I have read a fiery gospel, writ in burnished rows of steel; "As ye deal with My contemners, so with you My grace shall deal: Let the Hero, born of woman, crush the serpent with his heel, Since God is marching on."

He has sounded forth the trumpet that shall never call retreat; He is sifting out the hearts of men before His judgment-seat: Oh, be swift, my soul, to answer Him,—be jubilant, my feet! Our God is marching on.

In the beauty of the lilies Christ was born across the sea, With a glory in His bosom that transfigures you and me: As He died to make men holy, let us die to make men free, While God is marching on.

Julia Ward Howe.

Sheridan's Ride

October , .

Up from the South at break of day, Bringing to Winchester fresh dismay, The affrighted air with a shudder bore, Like a herald in haste, to the chieftain's door, The terrible grumble, and rumble, and roar, Telling the battle was on once more, And Sheridan twenty miles away.

And wider still those billows of war Thundered along the horizon's bar; And louder yet into Winchester rolled The roar of that red sea uncontrolled, Making the blood of the listener cold, As he thought of the stake in that fiery fray, And Sheridan twenty miles away.

But there is a road from Winchester town, A good broad highway leading down; And there, through the flash of the morning light, A steed as black as the steeds of night Was seen to pass as with eagle flight; As if he knew the terrible need, He stretched away with the utmost speed; Hills rose and fell—but his heart was gay, With Sheridan fifteen miles away.

Still sprung from those swift hoofs, thundering South, The dust, like smoke from the cannon's mouth; On the tail of a comet, sweeping faster and faster, Foreboding to traitors the doom of disaster. The heart of the steed and the heart of the master Were beating like prisoners assaulting their walls, Impatient to be where the battlefield calls; Every nerve of the charger was strained to full play, With Sheridan only ten miles away.

Under his spurning feet the road Like an arrowy Alpine river flowed, And the landscape flowed away behind, Like an ocean flying before the wind; And the steed, like a bark fed with furnace ire, Swept on with his wild eyes full of fire; But lo!

he is nearing his heart's desire, He is snuffing the smoke of the roaring fray, With Sheridan only five miles away.

The first that the General saw were the groups Of stragglers, and then the retreating troops. What was done? what to do? A glance told him both. Then, striking his spurs, with a terrible oath, He dashed down the line, 'mid a storm of huzzas, And the wave of retreat checked its course there, because The sight of the master compelled it to pause. With foam and with dust the black charger was gray; By the flash of his eye, and the red nostril's play, He seemed to the whole great army to say, "I have brought you Sheridan all the way From Winchester down to save the day!"

Hurrah! hurrah for Sheridan! Hurrah! hurrah for horse and man! And when their statues are placed on high, Under the dome of the Union sky, The American soldier's Temple of Fame,— There with the glorious General's name, Be it said, in letters both bold and bright, "Here is the steed that saved the day By carrying Sheridan into the fight, From Winchester, twenty miles away!"

Thomas Buchanan Read.

By courtesy of J. B. Lippincott & Co.

Song of the Negro Boatman

O, praise an' tanks! De Lord he come To set de people free; An' massa tink it day ob doom, An' we ob jubilee. De Lord dat heap de Red Sea waves He jus' 'trong as den; He say de word: we las' night slaves; To-day, de Lord's freemen. De yam will grow, de cotton blow, We'll hab de rice an' corn; O nebber you fear, if nebber you hear De driver blow his horn!

Ole massa on he trabbels gone; He leaf de land behind: De Lord's breff blow him furder on, Like corn-shuck in de wind. We own de hoe, we own de plough, We own de hands dat hold; We sell de pig, we sell de cow, But nebber chile be sold. De yam will grow, de cotton blow, We'll hab de rice an' corn; O nebber you fear, if nebber you hear De driver blow his horn!

We pray de Lord: he gib us signs Dat some day we be free; De norf-wind tell it to de pines, De wild-duck to de sea; We tink it when de church-bell ring, We dream it in de dream; De rice-bird mean it when he sing, De eagle when he scream. De yam will grow, de cotton blow, We'll hab de rice an' corn; O nebber you fear, if nebber you hear De driver blow his horn!

We know de promise nebber fail, An' nebber lie de word; So like de 'postles in de jail, We waited for de Lord: An' now he open ebery door, An' trow away de key; He tink we lub him so before, We lub him better free. De yam will grow, de cotton blow, He'll gib de rice an' corn; O nebber you fear, if nebber you hear De driver blow his horn!

John Greenleaf Whittier.

From "At Port Royal."

Barbara Frietchie

Up from the meadows rich with corn, Clear in the cool September morn,

The clustered spires of Frederick stand Green-walled by the hills of Maryland.

Round about them orchards sweep, Apple and peach tree fruited deep,

Fair as a garden of the Lord, To the eyes of the famished rebel horde,

On that pleasant morn of the early fall When Lee marched over the mountain wall,—

Over the mountains, winding down, Horse and foot into Frederick town.

Forty flags with their silver stars, Forty flags with their crimson bars,

Flapped in the morning wind; the sun Of noon looked down, and saw not one.

Up rose old Barbara Frietchie then, Bowed with her fourscore years and ten;

Bravest of all in Frederick town, She took up the flag the men hauled down;

In her attic-window the staff she set, To show that one heart was loyal yet.

Up the street came the rebel tread, Stonewall Jackson riding ahead.

Under his slouch hat left and right He glanced: the old flag met his sight.

"Halt!"—the dust-brown ranks stood fast; "Fire!"—out blazed the rifle-blast.

It shivered the window, pane and sash; It rent the banner with seam and gash.

Quick, as it fell, from the broken staff Dame Barbara snatched the silken scarf;

She leaned far out on the window-sill, And shook it forth with a royal will.

"Shoot, if you must, this old gray head, But spare your country's flag," she said.

A shade of sadness, a blush of shame, Over the face of the leader came;

The nobler nature within him stirred To life at that woman's deed and word:

"Who touches a hair of yon gray head Dies like a dog! March on!" he said.

All day long through Frederick street Sounded the tread of marching feet;

All day long that free flag tost Over the heads of the rebel host.

Ever its torn folds rose and fell On the loyal winds that loved it well;

And through the hill-gaps sunset light Shone over it with a warm good-night.

Barbara Frietchie's work is o'er, And the rebel rides on his raids no more.

Honor to her! and let a tear Fall, for her sake, on Stonewall's bier.

Over Barbara Frietchie's grave, Flag of freedom and union wave!

Peace and order and beauty draw Round thy symbol of light and law;

And ever the stars above look down On thy stars below in Frederick town.

John Greenleaf Whittier.

Two Veterans

The last sunbeam Lightly falls from the finished Sabbath, On the pavement here, and there beyond it is looking Down a new-made double grave.

Lo! the moon ascending, Up from the east the silvery round moon, Beautiful over the house-tops, ghastly, phantom moon, Immense and silent moon.

I see a sad procession, And I hear the sound of coming full-keyed bugles, All the channels of the city streets they're flooding, As with voices and with tears.

I hear the great drums pounding, And the small drums steady whirring, And every blow of the great convulsive drums Strikes me through and through.

For the son is brought with the father, (In the foremost ranks of the fierce assault they fell, Two veterans, son and father, dropt together, And the double grave awaits them).

Now nearer blow the bugles, And the drums strike more convulsive, And the daylight o'er the pavement quite has faded, And the strong dead-march enwraps me.

In the eastern sky up-buoying, The sorrowful vast phantom moves illumined, ('Tis some mother's large transparent face In heaven brighter growing).

O strong dead-march you please me! O moon immense with your silvery face you soothe me! O my soldiers twain! O my veterans passing to burial! What I have I also give you.

The moon gives you light, And the bugles and the drums give you music, And my heart, O my soldiers, my veterans, My heart gives you love.

Walt Whitman.

Stand by the Flag!

Stand by the Flag! Its stars, like meteors gleaming, Have lighted Arctic icebergs, southern seas, And shone responsive to the stormy beaming Of old Arcturus and the Pleiades.

Stand by the Flag! Its stripes have streamed in glory, To foes a fear, to friends a festal robe, And spread in rhythmic lines the sacred story Of Freedom's triumphs over all the globe.

Stand by the Flag! On land and ocean billow By it your fathers stood unmoved and true, Living, defended; dying, from their pillow, With their last blessing, passed it on to you.

Stand by the Flag! Immortal heroes bore it Through sulphurous smoke, deep moat and armed defence; And their imperial Shades still hover o'er it, A guard celestial from Omnipotence.

John Nichols Wilder.

At Gibraltar

I

England, I stand on thy imperial ground, Not all a stranger; as thy bugles blow, I feel within my blood old battles flow— The blood whose ancient founts in thee are found, Still surging dark against the Christian bound Wide Islam presses; well its people know Thy heights that watch them wandering below; I think how Lucknow heard their gathering sound.

I turn, and meet the cruel, turbaned face. England, 'tis sweet to be so much thy son! I feel the conqueror in my blood and race; Last night Trafalgar awed me, and to-day Gibraltar wakened; hark, thy evening gun Startles the desert over Africa!

George Edward Woodberry.

Taken from "North Shore Watch and Other Poems" (copyrighted). By courtesy of The Macmillan Company.

At Gibraltar

II

Thou art the rock of empire, set mid-seas Between the East and West, that God has built; Advance thy Roman borders where thou wilt, While run thy armies true with his decrees; Law, justice, liberty—great gifts are these; Watch that they spread where English blood is spilt, Lest, mixed and sullied with his country's guilt, The soldier's life-stream flow, and Heaven displease!

Two swords there are: one naked, apt to smite, Thy blade of war; and, battle-storied, one Rejoices in the sheath, and hides from light. American I am; would wars were done! Now westward, look, my country bids good-night— Peace to the world from ports without a gun!

George Edward Woodberry.

Faith and Freedom

We must be free or die, who speak the tongue That Shakespeare spake; the faith and morals hold Which Milton held....
William Wordsworth.

Our Mother Tongue

Beyond the vague Atlantic deep, Far as the farthest prairies sweep, Where forest-glooms the nerve appal, Where burns the radiant western fall, One duty lies on old and young,— With filial piety to guard, As on its greenest native sward, The glory of the English tongue. That ample speech! That subtle speech! Apt for the need of all and each: Strong to endure, yet prompt to bend Wherever human feelings tend. Preserve its force—expand its powers; And through the maze of civic life, In Letters, Commerce, even in Strife, Forget not it is yours and ours.

Lord Houghton.

(Richard Monckton Milnes.)

The English Language

Give me of every language, first my vigorous English Stored with imported wealth, rich in its natural mines— Grand in its rhythmical cadence, simple for household employment— Worthy the poet's song, fit for the speech of a man.

*　　*　　*　　*

Fitted for every use like a great majestical river, Blending thy various streams, stately thou flowest along, Bearing the white-winged ship of Poesy over thy bosom, Laden with spices that come out of the tropical isles, Fancy's pleasuring yacht with its bright and fluttering pennons, Logic's frigates of war and the toil-worn barges of trade.

How art thou freely obedient unto the poet or speaker When, in a happy hour, thought into speech he translates; Caught on the word's sharp angles flash the bright hues of his fancy— Grandly the thought rides the words, as a good horseman his steed.

*　　*　　*　　*

William Wetmore Story.

To America

On a Proposed Alliance Between Two Great Nations.

What is the voice I hear On the winds of the western sea? Sentinel, listen from out Cape Clear And say what the voice may be. 'Tis a proud free people calling loud to a people proud and free.

And it says to them: "Kinsmen, hail; We severed have been too long. Now let us have done with a worn-out tale— The tale of ancient wrong— And our friendship last long as our love doth and be stronger than death is strong."

Answer them, sons of the self-same race, And blood of the self-same clan; Let us speak with each other face to face And answer as man to man, And loyally love and trust each other as none but free men can.

Now fling them out the breeze, Shamrock, Thistle, and Rose, And the Star-Spangled Banner unfurl with these— A message to friends and foes Wherever the sails of peace are seen and wherever the war wind blows—

A message to bond and thrall to wake, For wherever we come, we twain, The throne of the tyrant shall rock and quake, And his menace be void and vain, For you are lords of a strong land and we are lords of the main.

Yes, this is the voice of the bluff March gale; We severed have been too long, But now we have done with a worn-out tale— The tale of an ancient wrong— And our friendship last long as love doth last and stronger than death is strong.

Alfred Austin.

The Name of Old Glory

Old Glory! say, who By the ships and the crew, And the long, blended ranks of the Gray and the Blue— Who gave you Old Glory, the name that you bear With such pride everywhere, As you cast yourself free to the rapturous air, And leap out full length, as we're wanting you to?—

Who gave you that name, with the ring of the same, And the honor and fame so becoming to you? Your stripes stroked in ripples of white and of red, With your stars at their glittering best overhead— By day or by night Their delightfulest light Laughing down from their little square heaven of blue! Who gave you the name of Old Glory—say, who— Who gave you the name of Old Glory?

The old banner lifted and faltering then In vague lisps and whispers fell silent again.

Old Glory: the story we're wanting to hear Is what the plain facts of your christening were,— For your name—just to hear it, Repeat it, and cheer it, 's a tang to the spirit As salt as a tear;— And seeing you fly, and the boys marching by, There's a shout in the throat and a blur in the eye, And an aching to live for you always—or die, If, dying, we still keep you waving on high. And so, by our love For you, floating above, And the scars of all wars and the sorrow thereof, Who gave you the name of Old Glory, and why Are we thrilled at the name of Old Glory?

Then the old banner leaped like a sail in the blast And fluttered an audible answer at last.

And it spake with a shake of the voice, and it said: By the driven snow-white and the living blood-red Of my bars and their heaven of stars overhead— By the symbol conjoined of them all, skyward cast, As I float from the steeple or flap at the mast, Or droop o'er the sod where the long grasses nod,— My name is as old as the glory of God. ... So I came by the name of Old Glory.

James Whitcomb Riley.
From "Home Folks."

INTERLEAVES
In Merry Mood

"Then cast away care, let sorrow cease, A fig for melancholy."

All rules are suspended, grave affairs of state are laid aside, and the Court Jester demands a hearing. Is it my fancy, or do young eyes brighten, rosy cheeks dimple, lips part a little when he approaches? Clad all in gay motley, swinging his bauble, his cap and bells making merry music, he bounds upon the stage and bids us listen to his quips and jokes. He is by turns Puck and Ariel, Harlequin, Punchinello, and Court Fool. "Touchstone" we well may call him, this man of mirth, for when he tests the world's metal the pure gold of laughter shines out from the alloy. Seeing us smile even before he opens his lips he assumes a solemn attitude and cries:

"Good people all, of every sort, Give ear unto my song; And if you find it wondrous short It will not hold you long."

Then hark how the "light-heeled numbers laughing go!" He tells us tales that smooth out the wrinkles of dull Care and provoke Laughter to hold both his sides, as well as others less jolly but full of wit and good cheer. A quaint, breezy moral, too, creeps in here and there, for the Court Fool, if you study him well, is sometimes a preacher; but whether frolicking or preaching or philosophizing, he brings with him, like Milton's nymph:

"Jest and youthful jollity, Quips and cranks, and wanton Wiles, Nods and Becks and Wreathéd Smiles, Such as hang on Hebe's cheek, And love to live in dimple sleek."

XII
IN MERRY MOOD
On a Favorite Cat, Drowned in a Tub of Goldfishes

'T was on a lofty vase's side Where China's gayest art had dyed, The azure flowers that blow, Demurest of the tabby kind, The pensive Selima, reclined, Gazed on the lake below.

Her conscious tail her joy declared: The fair, round face, the snowy beard, The velvet of her paws, Her coat that with the tortoise vies, Her ears of jet, and emerald eyes,— She saw, and purred applause.

Still had she gazed, but 'midst the tide Two angel forms were seen to glide, The Genii of the stream: Their scaly armor's Tyrian hue, Through richest purple, to the view Betrayed a golden gleam.

The hapless Nymph with wonder saw: A whisker first, and then a claw, With many an ardent wish, She stretched, in vain, to reach the prize,— What female heart can gold despise? What cat's averse to fish?

Presumptuous maid! with looks intent, Again she stretched, again she bent, Nor knew the gulf between,— Malignant Fate sat by and smiled,— The slippery verge her feet beguiled; She tumbled headlong in!

Eight times emerging from the flood, She mewed to every watery god Some speedy aid to send: No Dolphin came, no Nereid stirred, Nor cruel Tom nor Susan heard,— A favorite has no friend!

From hence, ye Beauties! undeceived, Know one false step is ne'er retrieved, And be with caution bold: Not all that tempts your wandering eyes And heedless hearts is lawful prize, Nor all that glitters gold!

Thomas Gray.

The Priest and the Mulberry Tree

Did you hear of the curate who mounted his mare, And merrily trotted along to the fair? Of creature more tractable none ever heard; In the height of her speed she would stop at a word; But again with a word, when the curate said, "Hey," She put forth her mettle and gallop'd away.

As near to the gates of the city he rode, While the sun of September all brilliantly glow'd, The good priest discover'd, with eyes of desire, A mulberry tree in a hedge of wild brier; On boughs long and lofty, in many a green shoot, Hung, large, black and glossy, the beautiful fruit.

The curate was hungry and thirsty to boot; He shrunk from the thorns, though he long'd for the fruit; With a word he arrested his courser's keen speed, And he stood up erect on the back of his steed; On the saddle he stood while the creature stood still, And he gather'd the fruit till he took his good fill.

"Sure never," he thought, "was a creature so rare, So docile, so true, as my excellent mare; Lo, here now I stand," and he gazed all around, "As safe and as steady as if on the ground; Yet how had it been, if some traveller this way, Had, dreaming

79

no mischief, but chanced to cry, 'Hey'?"

He stood with his head in the mulberry tree, And he spoke out aloud in his fond revery; At the sound of the word the good mare made a push, And down went the priest in the wild-brier bush. He remember'd too late, on his thorny green bed, Much that well may be thought cannot wisely be said.

Thomas Love Peacock.

The Council of Horses

Upon a time a neighing steed, Who graz'd among a numerous breed, With mutiny had fired the train, And spread dissension through the plain On matters that concern'd the state. The council met in grand debate. A colt whose eyeballs flamed with ire, Elate with strength and youthful fire, In haste stept forth before the rest, And thus the listening throng address'd. "Goodness, how abject is our race, Condemn'd to slavery and disgrace! Shall we our servitude retain, Because our sires have borne the chain? Consider, friends! your strength and might; 'Tis conquest to assert your right. How cumbrous is the gilded coach! The pride of man is our reproach. Were we design'd for daily toil, To drag the ploughshare through the soil, To sweat in harness through the road, To groan beneath the carrier's load? How feeble are the two-legg'd kind! What force is in our nerves combin'd! Shall then our nobler jaws submit To foam and champ the galling bit? Shall haughty man my back bestride? Shall the sharp spur provoke my side? Forbid it, heavens! reject the rein; Your shame, your infamy, disdain. Let him the lion first control, And still the tiger's famish'd growl. Let us, like them, our freedom claim, And make him tremble at our name." A general nod approv'd the cause, And all the circle neigh'd applause. When lo! with grave and solemn pace, A steed advanc'd before the race, With age and long experience wise; Around he cast his thoughtful eyes, And, to the murmurs of the train, Thus spoke the Nestor of the plain. "When I had health and strength like you The toils of servitude I knew; Now grateful man rewards my pains, And gives me all these wide domains. At will I crop the year's increase; My latter life is rest and peace. I grant, to man we lend our pains, And aid him to correct the plains; But doth not he divide the care, Through all the labours of the year? How many thousand structures rise, To fence us from inclement skies! For us he bears the sultry day, And stores up all our winter's hay. He sows, he reaps the harvest's gain; We share the toil and share the grain. Since every creature was decreed To aid each other's mutual need, Appease your discontented mind, And act the part by heaven assign'd." The tumult ceas'd, the colt submitted, And, like his ancestors, was bitted.

John Gay.

The Diverting History of John Gilpin
Showing How He Went Farther Than He Intended, and Came Safe Home Again.

John Gilpin was a citizen Of credit and renown, A train-band Captain eke was he Of famous London town.

John Gilpin's spouse said to her dear, "Though wedded we have been These twice ten tedious years, yet we No holiday have seen.

To-morrow is our wedding day, And we will then repair Unto the Bell at Edmonton, All in a chaise and pair.

My sister and my sister's child, Myself and children three, Will fill the chaise, so you must ride On horseback after we."

He soon replied,—"I do admire Of womankind but one, And you are she, my dearest dear, Therefore it shall be done.

I am a linen-draper bold, As all the world doth know, And my good friend the Calender Will lend his horse to go."

Quoth Mrs. Gilpin,—"That's well said, And for that wine is dear, We will be furnish'd with our own, Which is both bright and clear."

John Gilpin kiss'd his loving wife; O'erjoyed was he to find That though on pleasure she was bent, She had a frugal mind.

The morning came, the chaise was brought, But yet was not allow'd To drive up to the door, lest all Should say that she was proud.

So three doors off the chaise was stay'd, Where they did all get in; Six precious souls, and all agog To dash through thick and thin.

Smack went the whip, round went the wheels, Were never folk so glad, The stones did rattle underneath As if Cheapside were mad.

John Gilpin at his horse's side, Seized fast the flowing mane, And up he got, in haste to ride, But soon came down again; For saddle-tree scarce reach'd had he, His journey to begin, When, turning round his head, he saw Three customers come in.

So down he came; for loss of time, Although it grieved him sore, Yet loss of pence, full well he knew, Would trouble him much more.

'T was long before the customers Were suited to their mind, When Betty screaming, came downstairs, "The wine is left behind!"

"Good lack!" quoth he, "yet bring it me, My leathern belt likewise, In which I bear my trusty sword When I do exercise."

Now mistress Gilpin, careful soul! Had two stone bottles found, To hold the liquor that she loved, And keep it safe and sound.

Each bottle had a curling ear, Through which the belt he drew, And hung a bottle on each side, To make his balance true.

Then over all, that he might be Equipp'd from top to toe, His long red cloak, well brush'd and neat, He manfully did throw.

Now see him mounted once again Upon his nimble steed, Full slowly pacing o'er the stones With caution and good heed.

But, finding soon a smoother road Beneath his well-shod feet, The snorting beast began to trot, Which gall'd him in his seat,

So "Fair and softly," John he cried, But John he cried in vain; That trot became a gallop soon, In spite of curb and rein.

So stooping down, as needs he must Who cannot sit upright, He grasp'd the mane with both his hands, And eke with all his might.

His horse, who never in that sort Had handled been before, What thing upon his back had got Did wonder more and more.

Away went Gilpin, neck or nought, Away went hat and wig! He little dreamt when he set out Of running such a rig!

The wind did blow, the cloak did fly, Like streamer long and gay, Till, loop and button failing both, At last it flew away.

Then might all people well discern The bottles he had slung; A bottle swinging at each side, As hath been said or sung.

The dogs did bark, the children scream'd, Up flew the windows all, And ev'ry soul cried out, "Well done!" As loud as he could bawl.

Away went Gilpin—who but he? His fame soon spread around— "He carries weight!" "He rides a race!" "'T is for a thousand pound!"

And still, as fast as he drew near, 'T was wonderful to view, How in a trice the turnpike-men Their gates wide open threw.

And now, as he went bowing down His reeking head full low, The bottles twain behind his back Were shattered at a blow.

Down ran the wine into the road, Most piteous to be seen, Which made his horse's flanks to smoke As they had basted been.

But still he seem'd to carry weight, With leathern girdle braced, For all might see the bottle-necks Still dangling at his waist.

Thus all through merry Islington These gambols he did play, Until he came unto the Wash Of Edmonton so gay.

And there he threw the Wash about On both sides of the way, Just like unto a trundling mop, Or a wild-goose at play.

At Edmonton his loving wife From the balcony spied Her tender husband, wond'ring much To see how he did ride.

"Stop, stop, John Gilpin!—Here's the house!" They all at once did cry; "The dinner waits and we are tired:" Said Gilpin—"So am I!"

But yet his horse was not a whit Inclined to tarry there; For why?—his owner had a house Full ten miles off, at Ware, So like an arrow swift he flew, Shot by an archer strong; So did he fly—which brings me to The middle of my song.

Away went Gilpin, out of breath. And sore against his will, Till at his friend the Calender's His horse at last stood still.

The Calender, amazed to see His neighbour in such trim, Laid down his pipe, flew to the gate, And thus accosted him:—

"What news? what news? your tidings tell, Tell me you must and shall— Say why bare-headed you are come, Or why you come at all?"

Now Gilpin had a pleasant wit, And loved a timely joke, And thus unto the Calender In merry guise he spoke:—

"I came because your horse would come; And if I well forebode, My hat and wig will soon be here, They are upon the road."

The Calender, right glad to find His friend in merry pin, Returned him not a single word, But to the house went in;

Whence straight he came with hat and wig, A wig that flow'd behind, A hat not much the worse for wear, Each comely in its kind.

He held them up, and in his turn Thus show'd his ready wit:— "My head is twice as big as yours, They therefore needs must fit.

But let me scrape the dirt away That hangs upon your face; And stop and eat, for well you may Be in a hungry case."

Said John—"It is my wedding-day, And all the world would stare, If wife should dine at Edmonton, And I should dine at Ware."

So, turning to his horse, he said— "I am in haste to dine; 'T was for your pleasure you came here, You shall go back for mine."

Ah, luckless speech and bootless boast! For which he paid full dear; For, while he spake, a braying ass Did sing most loud and clear; Whereat his horse did snort, as he Had heard a lion roar, And gallop'd off with all his might, As he had done before.

Away went Gilpin, and away Went Gilpin's hat and wig! He lost them sooner than at first, For why?—they were too big!

Now Mistress Gilpin, when she saw Her husband posting down Into the country far away, She pull'd out half-a-crown;

And thus unto the youth she said That drove them to the Bell— "This shall be yours when you bring back My husband safe and well."

The youth did ride, and soon did meet John coming back amain; Whom in a trice he tried to stop, By catching at his rein;

But not performing what he meant, And gladly would have done, The frighted steed he frighted more, And made him faster run.

Away went Gilpin, and away Went post-boy at his heels!— The post-boy's horse right glad to miss The lumb'ring of the wheels.

Six gentlemen upon the road, Thus seeing Gilpin fly. With post-boy scamp'ring in the rear, They raised the hue and cry:—

"Stop thief! stop thief—a highwayman!" Not one of them was mute; And all and each that pass'd that way Did join in the pursuit.

And now the turnpike gates again Flew open in short space; The toll-men thinking, as before, That Gilpin rode a race.

And so he did, and won it too, For he got first to town; Nor stopp'd till where he had got up He did again get down.

Now let us sing, Long live the king, And Gilpin, long live he; And when he next doth ride abroad, May I be there to see!

William Cowper.

To a Child of Quality
Five Years Old, , the Author Then Forty.

Lords, knights, and squires, the numerous band That wear the fair Miss Mary's fetters, Were summoned by her high command To show their passion by their letters.

My pen amongst the rest I took, Lest those bright eyes, that cannot read, Should dart their kindling fires, and look The power they have to be obey'd.

Nor quality, nor reputation, Forbid me yet my flame to tell; Dear Five-years-old befriends my passion, And I may write till she can spell.

For, while she makes her silkworms beds With all the tender things I swear; Whilst all the house my passion reads, In papers round her baby's hair;

She may receive and own my flame; For, though the strictest prudes should know it, She'll pass for a most virtuous dame, And I for an unhappy poet.

Then too, alas! when she shall tear The rhymes some younger rival sends, She'll give me leave to write, I fear, And we shall still continue friends.

For, as our different ages move, 'Tis so ordained (would Fate but mend it!), That I shall be past making love When she begins to comprehend it.

Matthew Prior.

Charade
(Campbell.)
(Thomas Campbell, the Poet.)

Come from my First, ay, come! For the battle hour is nigh: And the screaming trump and thundering drum Are calling thee to die! Fight, as thy father fought! Fall, as thy father fell! Thy task is taught, thy shroud is wrought;— So—onward—and farewell.

Toll ye my Second, toll! Fling wide the flambeau's light, And sing the hymn for a parted soul Beneath the silent night. With the wreath upon his head, And the cross upon his breast, Let the prayer be said, and the tear be shed;— So—take him to his rest Call ye my Whole,—ay, call The lord of lute and lay! And let him greet the sable pall With a noble song to-day! Ay, call him by his name! Nor fitter hand may crave To light the flame of a soldier's fame On the turf of a soldier's grave.

Winthrop Mackworth Praed.

A Riddle
(A Book.)

I'm a strange contradiction; I'm new, and I'm old, I'm often in tatters, and oft decked with gold. Though I never could read, yet lettered I'm found; Though blind, I enlighten; though loose, I am bound, I'm always in black, and I'm always in white; I'm grave and I'm gay, I am heavy and light— In form too I differ,—I'm thick and I'm thin, I've no flesh and no bones, yet I'm covered with skin; I've more points than the compass, more stops than the flute; I sing without voice, without speaking confute. I'm English, I'm German, I'm French, and I'm Dutch; Some love me too fondly, some slight me too much; I often die soon, though I sometimes lives ages, And no monarch alive has so many pages.

Hannah More.

A Riddle
(The Vowels.)

We are little airy creatures, All of different voice and features; One of us in glass is set, One of us you'll find in jet. T'other you may see in tin, And the fourth a box within. If the fifth you should pursue, It can never fly from you.

Jonathan Swift.

A Riddle

(The Letter H.)

'Twas whispered in Heaven, 'twas muttered in hell, And echo caught faintly the sound as it fell; On the confines of earth 'twas permitted to rest, And the depths of the ocean its presence confess'd; 'Twill be found in the sphere when 'tis riven asunder, Be seen in the lightning and heard in the thunder; 'Twas allotted to man with his earliest breath, Attends him at birth and awaits him in death, Presides o'er his happiness, honor and health, Is the prop of his house, and the end of his wealth. In the heaps of the miser 'tis hoarded with care, But is sure to be lost on his prodigal heir; It begins every hope, every wish it must bound, With the husbandman toils, and with monarchs is crowned; Without it the soldier and seaman may roam, But woe to the wretch who expels it from home! In the whispers of conscience its voice will be found, Nor e'er in the whirlwind of passion be drowned; 'Twill soften the heart; but though deaf be the ear, It will make it acutely and instantly hear. Set in shade, let it rest like a delicate flower; Ah! breathe on it softly, it dies in an hour.

Catherine M. Fanshawe.

Feigned Courage

Horatio, of ideal courage vain, Was flourishing in air his father's cane, And, as the fumes of valour swell'd his pate, Now thought himself *this* hero, and now *that*: "And now," he cried, "I will Achilles be; My sword I brandish; see, the Trojans flee! Now I'll be Hector, when his angry blade A lane through heaps of slaughter'd Grecians made! And now my deeds, still braver I'll evince, I am no less than Edward the Black Prince. Give way, ye coward French!" As thus he spoke, And aim'd in fancy a sufficient stroke To fix the fate of Crecy or Poiotiers (The Muse relates the Hero's fate with tears), He struck his milk-white hand against a nail, Sees his own blood, and feels his courage fail. Ah! where is now that boasted valour flown, That in the tented field so late was shown? Achilles weeps, great Hector hangs his head, And the Black Prince goes whimpering to bed.

Charles and Mary Lamb.

Baucis and Philemon

In ancient times, as story tells, The saints would often leave their cells, And stroll about, but hide their quality, To try good people's hospitality.

It happened on a winter night, As authors of the legend write, Two brother hermits, saints by trade, Taking their tour in masquerade, Disguised in tattered garments went To a small village down in Kent; Where, in the stroller's canting strain, They begged from door to door in vain, Tried every tone might pity win; But not a soul would take them in.

Our wandering saints, in woeful state, Treated at this ungodly rate, Having through all the village passed, To a small cottage came at last Where dwelt a good old honest yeoman, Call'd in the neighborhood Philemon; Who kindly did these saints invite In his poor hut to pass the night; And then the hospitable sire Bid goody Baucis mend the fire; While he from out the chimney took A flitch of bacon off the hook, And freely from the fattest side Cut out large slices to be fried; Then stepped aside to fetch them drink, Filled a large jug up to the brink, And saw it fairly twice go round; Yet (what is wonderful!) they found 'Twas still replenished to the top, As if they ne'er had touched a drop. The good old couple were amazed, And often on each other gazed; For both were frightened to the heart, And just began to cry, "What art!" Then softly turned aside to view Whether the lights were burning blue.

"Good folks, you need not be afraid, We are but saints," the hermits said; "No hurt shall come to you or yours: But for that pack of churlish boors, Not fit to live on Christian ground, They and their houses shall be drowned; Whilst you shall see your cottage rise, And grow a church before your eyes."

They scarce had spoke, when fair and soft, The roof began to mount aloft, Aloft rose every beam and rafter, The heavy wall climbed slowly after; The chimney widened and grew higher, Became a steeple with a spire. The kettle to the top was hoist, And there stood fastened to a joist; Doomed ever in suspense to dwell, 'Tis now no kettle, but a bell. A wooden jack which had almost Lost by disuse the art to roast, A sudden alteration feels, Increased by new intestine wheels; The jack and chimney, near allied, Had never left each other's side: The chimney to a steeple grown, The jack would not be left alone; But up against the steeple reared, Became a clock, and still adhered. The groaning chair began to crawl, Like a huge snail along the wall; There stuck aloft in public view, And with small change a pulpit grew. The cottage, by such feats as these, Grown to a church by just degrees, The hermits then desired the host To ask for what he fancied most. Philemon, having paused awhile, Returned them thanks in homely style: "I'm old, and fain would live at ease; Make me the parson, if you please."

Thus happy in their change of life Were several years this man and wife. When on a day which proved their last, Discoursing on old stories past, They went by chance, amidst their talk, To the churchyard to take a walk; When Baucis hastily cried out, "My dear, I see your forehead sprout!" "But yes! Methinks I feel it true; And really yours is budding too. Nay,—now I cannot stir my foot; It feels as if 'twere taking root!" Description would but tire my muse; In short they both were turned to yews.

Jonathan Swift.

The Lion and the Cub

A lion cub, of sordid mind, Avoided all the lion kind; Fond of applause, he sought the feasts Of vulgar and ignoble beasts; With asses all his time he spent, Their club's perpetual president. He caught their manners, looks, and airs; An ass in everything but ears! If e'er his Highness meant a joke, They grinn'd applause before he spoke; But at each word what shouts of praise; "Goodness! how natural he brays!"

Elate with flattery and conceit, He seeks his royal sire's retreat; Forward and fond to show his parts, His Highness brays; the lion starts. "Puppy! that curs'd vociferation: Betrays thy life and conversation: Coxcombs, an ever-noisy race, Are trumpets of their own disgrace." "Why so severe?" the cub replies; "Our senate always held me wise!" "How weak is pride," returns the sire: "All fools are vain when fools admire! But know, what stupid asses prize, Lions and noble beasts despise."

John Gay.

Elegy on the Death of a Mad Dog

Good people all, of every sort, Give ear unto my song; And if you find it wondrous short— It cannot hold you long.

In Islington there was a Man, Of whom the world might say, That still a godly race he ran— Whene'er he went to pray.

A kind and gentle heart he had, To comfort friends and foes: The naked every day he clad,— When he put on his clothes.

And in that town a Dog was found, As many dogs there be, Both mongrel, puppy, whelp, and hound, And curs of low degree.

This Dog and Man at first were friends; But when a pique began, The Dog, to gain some private ends, Went mad, and bit the Man.

Around from all the neighbouring streets The wondering neighbours ran, And swore the Dog had lost his wits, To bite so good a Man!

The wound it seem'd both sore and sad To every Christian eye: And while they swore the Dog was mad, They swore the Man would die.

But soon a wonder came to light, That show'd the rogues they lied:— The Man recovered of the bite, The Dog it was that died!

Oliver Goldsmith.

The Walrus and the Carpenter

The sun was shining on the sea, Shining with all his might: He did his very best to make The billows smooth and bright— And this was odd, because it was The middle of the night.

The moon was shining sulkily, Because she thought the sun Had got no business to be there After the day was done— "It's very rude of him," she said, "To come and spoil the fun!"

The sea was wet as wet could be, The sands were dry as dry. You could not see a cloud, because No cloud was in the sky: No birds were flying overhead— There were no birds to fly.

The Walrus and the Carpenter Were walking close at hand: They wept like anything to see Such quantities of sand: "If this were only cleared away, They said, "it would be grand!"

"If seven maids with seven mops Swept it for half a year, Do you suppose," the Walrus said, "That they could get it clear?" "I doubt it," said the Carpenter, And shed a bitter tear.

"O Oysters, come and walk with us!" The Walrus did beseech. "A pleasant walk, a pleasant talk, Along the briny beach: We cannot do with more than four, To give a hand to each."

The eldest Oyster looked at him, But never a word he said: The eldest Oyster winked his eye, And shook his heavy head— Meaning to say he did not choose To leave the oyster-bed.

But four young Oysters hurried up, All eager for the treat: Their coats were brushed, their faces washed, Their shoes were clean and neat— And this was odd, because, you know, They hadn't any feet.

Four other Oysters followed them, And yet another four; And thick and fast they came at last, And more, and more, and more— All hopping through the frothy waves, And scrambling to the shore.

The Walrus and the Carpenter Walked on a mile or so, And then they rested on a rock Conveniently low: And all the little Oysters stood And waited in a row.

"The time has come," the Walrus said, "To talk of many things: Of shoes—and ships—and sealing-wax— Of cabbages— and kings— And why the sea is boiling hot— And whether pigs have wings."

"But wait a bit," the Oysters cried, "Before we have our chat; For some of us are out of breath, And all of us are fat!" "No hurry!" said the Carpenter. They thanked him much for that.

"A loaf of bread," the Walrus said, "Is what we chiefly need: Pepper and vinegar besides Are very good indeed— Now, if you're ready, Oysters dear, We can begin to feed."

"But not on us!" the Oysters cried, Turning a little blue. "After such kindness, that would be A dismal thing to do!" "The night is fine," the Walrus said. "Do you admire the view?

"It was so kind of you to come! And you are very nice!" The Carpenter said nothing but "Cut us another slice. I wish you were not quite so deaf— I've had to ask you twice!"

"It seems a shame," the Walrus said, "To play them such a trick. After we've brought them out so far, And made them trot so quick!" The Carpenter said nothing but "The butter's spread too thick!"

"I weep for you," the Walrus said: "I deeply sympathize." With sobs and tears he sorted out Those of the largest size, Holding his pocket-handkerchief Before his streaming eyes.

"O Oysters," said the Carpenter, "You've had a pleasant run! Shall we be trotting home again?" But answer came there none— And this was scarcely odd, because They'd eaten every one.

Lewis Carroll.

Song of the Turtle and Flamingo

A lively young turtle lived down by the banks Of a dark rolling stream called the Jingo, And one summer day, as he went out to play, Fell in love with a charming flamingo— An enormously genteel flamingo! An expansively crimson flamingo! A beautiful, bouncing flamingo!

Spake the turtle in tones like a delicate wheeze: "To the water I've oft seen you in go, And your form has impressed itself deep on my shell, You perfectly modeled flamingo! You tremendously 'A' flamingo! You inex-pres-*si*-ble flamingo!

To be sure I'm a turtle, and you are a belle, And *my* language is not your fine lingo; But smile on me, tall one, and be my bright flame, You miraculous, wondrous flamingo! You blazingly beauteous flamingo! You turtle-absorbing flamingo! You inflammably gorgeous flamingo!"

Then the proud bird blushed redder than ever before, And that was quite un-nec-ces-sa-ry, And she stood on one leg and looked out of one eye, The position of things for to vary,— This aquatical, musing flamingo! This dreamy, uncertain flamingo! This embarrassing, harassing flamingo!

Then she cried to the quadruped, greatly amazed: "Why your passion toward *me* do you hurtle? I'm an ornithological wonder of grace, And you're an illogical turtle,— A waddling, impossible turtle! A low-minded, grass-eating turtle! A highly improbable turtle!"

Then the turtle sneaked off with his nose to the ground, And never more looked at the lasses; And falling asleep, while indulging his grief, Was gobbled up whole by Agassiz,— The peripatetic Agassiz! The turtle-dissecting Agassiz! The illustrious, industrious Agassiz!

Go with me to Cambridge some cool, pleasant day, And the skeleton lover I'll show you: He's in a hard case, but he'll look in your face, Pretending (the rogue!) he don't know you! Oh, the deeply deceptive young turtle! The double-faced, glassy-cased turtle! The *green*, but a very *mock*-turtle!

James T. Fields.

Captain Reece

Of all the ships upon the blue, No ship contained a better crew Than that of worthy Captain Reece, Commanding of *The Mantelpiece.*

He was adored by all his men, For worthy Captain Reece, R. N., Did all that lay within him to Promote the comfort of his crew.

If ever they were dull or sad, Their captain danced to them like mad, Or told, to make the time pass by, Droll legends of his infancy.

A feather-bed had every man, Warm slippers and hot-water can, Brown Windsor from the captain's store, A valet, too, to every four.

Did they with thirst in summer burn, Lo, seltzogenes at every turn, And on all very sultry days Cream ices handed round on trays.

Then currant wine and ginger-pops Stood handily on all the "tops;" And also, with amusement rife, A "Zoetrope, or Wheel of Life."

New volumes came across the sea From Mister Mudie's libraree; The *Times* and *Saturday Review* Beguiled the leisure of the crew.

Kind-hearted Captain Reece, R. N., Was quite devoted to his men; In point of fact, good Captain Reece Beatified *The Mantelpiece.*

One summer eve, at half-past ten, He said (addressing all his men): "Come, tell me, please, what I can do To please and gratify my crew.

"By any reasonable plan I'll make you happy if I can; My own convenience count as *nil*: It is my duty, and I will."

Then up and answered William Lee (The kindly captain's coxswain he, A nervous, shy, low-spoken man), He cleared his throat and thus began:

"You have a daughter, Captain Reece, Ten female cousins and a niece, A ma, if what I'm told is true, Six sisters, and an aunt or two.

"Now, somehow, sir, it seems to me, More friendly like we all should be, If you united of 'em to Unmarried members of the crew.

"If you'd ameliorate our life, Let each select from them a wife; And as for nervous me, old pal, Give me your own enchanting gal!"

Good Captain Reece, that worthy man, Debated on his coxswain's plan: "I quite agree," he said, "O Bill; It is my duty, and I will.

"My daughter, that enchanting gurl, Has just been promised to an Earl, And all my other familee To peers of various degree.

"But what are dukes and viscounts to The happiness of all my crew? The word I gave you I'll fulfil; It is my duty, and I will.

"As you desire it shall befall, I'll settle thousands on you all, And I shall be, despite my hoard, The only bachelor on board."

The boatswain of *The Mantelpiece*, He blushed and spoke to Captain Reece: "I beg your honour's leave," he said; "If you would wish to go and wed,

"I have a widowed mother who Would be the very thing for you— She long has loved you from afar; She washes for you, Captain R."

The Captain saw the dame that day— Addressed her in his playful way— "And did it want a wedding ring? It was a tempting ickle sing!

"Well, well, the chaplain I will seek, We'll all be married this day week At yonder church upon the hill; It is my duty, and I will!"

The sisters, cousins, aunts, and niece, And widowed ma of Captain Reece, Attended there as they were bid; It was their duty, and they did.

William Schwenck Gilbert.

The Cataract of Lodore

"How does the Water Come down at Lodore?" My little boy ask'd me Thus, once on a time; And moreover he task'd me To tell him in rhyme. Anon at the word, There first came one daughter, And then came another, To second and third The request of their brother, And to hear how the Water Comes down at Lodore, With its rush and its roar, As many a time They had seen it before. So I told them in rhyme, For of rhymes I had store; And 'twas in my vocation For their recreation That so I should sing; Because I was Laureate To them and the King. From its sources which well In the Tarn on the fell; From its fountains In the mountains, Its rills and its gills; Through moss and through brake, It runs and it creeps For awhile, till it sleeps In its own little Lake. And thence at departing, Awakening and starting, It runs through the reeds, And away it proceeds, Through meadow and glade, In sun and in shade, And through the wood-shelter, Among crags in its flurry, Helter-skelter, Hurry-scurry. Here it comes sparkling, And there it lies darkling; Now smoking and frothing Its tumult and wrath in, Till in this rapid race On which it is bent, It reaches the place Of its steep descent.

The Cataract strong Then plunges along, Striking and raging As if a war waging Its caverns and rocks among; Rising and leaping, Sinking and creeping, Swelling and sweeping, Showering and springing, Flying and flinging, Writhing and ringing, Eddying and whisking, Spouting and frisking, Turning and twisting, Around and around With endless rebound: Smiting and fighting, A sight to delight in; Confounding, astounding, Dizzying and deafening the ear with its sound.

Collecting, projecting, Receding and speeding, And shocking and rocking, And darting and parting, And threading and spreading, And whizzing and hissing, And dripping and skipping, And hitting and splitting, And shining and twining, And rattling and battling, And shaking and quaking, And pouring and roaring, And waving and raving, And tossing and crossing, And flowing and going, And running and stunning, And foaming and roaming, And dinning and spinning, And dropping and hopping, And working and jerking, And guggling and struggling, And heaving and cleaving, And moaning and groaning; And glittering and frittering, And gathering and feathering, And whitening and brightening, And quivering and shivering, And hurrying and skurrying, And thundering and floundering;

Dividing and gliding and sliding, And falling and brawling and sprawling, And driving and riving and striving, And sprinkling and twinkling and wrinkling, And sounding and bounding and rounding, And bubbling and troubling and doubling, And grumbling and rumbling and tumbling, And clattering and battering and shattering;

Retreating and beating and meeting and sheeting, Delaying and straying and playing and spraying, Advancing and prancing and glancing and dancing, Recoiling, turmoiling and toiling and boiling, And gleaming and streaming and steaming and beaming, And rushing and flushing and brushing and gushing, And flapping and rapping and clapping and slapping, And curling and whirling and purling and twirling, And thumping and plumping and bumping and jumping, And dashing and flashing and splashing and clashing; And so never ending, but always descending, Sounds and motions forever and ever are blending, All at once and all o'er, with a mighty uproar, And this way the Water comes down at Lodore.

Robert Southey.

The Enchanted Shirt

The king was sick. His cheek was red, And his eye was clear and bright; He ate and drank with kingly zest, And peacefully snored at night.

But he said he was sick, and a king should know, And the doctors came by the score. They did not cure him. He cut off their heads, And sent to the schools for more.

At last two famous doctors came, And one was as poor as a rat,— He had passed his life in studious toil, And never found time to grow fat.

The other had never looked in a book; His patients gave him no trouble: If they recovered, they paid him well; If they died, their heirs paid double.

Together they looked at the royal tongue, As the king on his couch reclined; In succession they thumped his august chest, But no trace of disease could find.

The old Sage said, "You're as sound as a nut." "Hang him up," roared the king in a gale— In a ten-knot gale of royal rage; The other leech grew a shade pale;

But he pensively rubbed his sagacious nose, And thus his prescription ran— *The king will be well, if he sleeps one night In the shirt of a Happy Man.*

* * * *

Wide o'er the realm the couriers rode, And fast their horses ran, And many they saw, and to many they spoke, But they found no Happy Man.

They found poor men who would fain be rich, And rich who thought they were poor; And men who twisted their waists in stays, And women who short hose wore.

At last they came to a village gate, A beggar lay whistling there; He whistled, and sang, and laughed, and rolled On the grass, in the soft June air.

The weary couriers paused and looked At the scamp so blithe and gay; And one of them said, "Heaven save you, friend! You seem to be happy to-day."

"O yes, fair Sirs," the rascal laughed, And his voice rang free and glad; "An idle man has so much to do That he never has time to be sad."

"This is our man," the courier said; "Our luck has led us aright. I will give you a hundred ducats, friend, For the loan of your shirt to-night."

The merry blackguard lay back on the grass, And laughed till his face was black; "I would do it, God wot," and he roared with the fun, "But I haven't a shirt to my back."

* * * *

Each day to the king the reports came in Of his unsuccessful spies, And the sad panorama of human woes Passed daily under his eyes.

And he grew ashamed of his useless life, And his maladies hatched in gloom; He opened his windows and let the air Of the free heaven into his room.

And out he went in the world, and toiled In his own appointed way; And the people blessed him, the land was glad, And the king was well and gay.

John Hay.

Made in the Hot Weather

Fountains that frisk and sprinkle The moss they overspill; Pools that the breezes crinkle; The wheel beside the mill, With its wet, weedy frill; Wind-shadows in the wheat; A water-cart in the street; The fringe of foam that girds An islet's ferneries; A green sky's minor thirds— To live, I think of these!

Of ice and glass the tinkle, Pellucid, silver-shrill, Peaches without a wrinkle; Cherries and snow at will From china bowls that fill The senses with a sweet Incuriousness of heat; A melon's dripping sherds; Cream-clotted strawberries; Dusk dairies set with curds— To live, I think of these!

Vale-lily and periwinkle; Wet stone-crop on the sill; The look of leaves a-twinkle With windlets clear and still; The feel of a forest rill That wimples fresh and fleet About one's naked feet; The muzzles of drinking herds; Lush flags and bulrushes; The chirp of rain-bound birds— To live, I think of these!

ENVOY

Dark aisles, new packs of cards, Mermaidens' tails, cool swards, Dawn dews and starlit seas, White marbles, whiter words— To live, I think of these!

William Ernest Henley.

The Housekeeper

The frugal snail, with forecast of repose, Carries his house with him where'er he goes; Peeps out,—and if there comes a shower of rain, Retreats to his small domicile again. Touch but a tip of him, a horn—'tis well,— He curls up in his sanctuary shell. He's his own landlord, his own tenant; stay Long as he will, he dreads no Quarter Day. Himself he boards and lodges; both invites And feasts himself; sleeps with himself o' nights. He spares the upholsterer trouble to procure Chattels; himself is his own furniture, And his sole riches. Wheresoe'er he roam,— Knock when you will,—he's sure to be at home.

Charles Lamb.

The Monkey

Monkey, little merry fellow, Thou art Nature's Punchinello; Full of fun as Puck could be— Harlequin might learn of thee!
* * * *

In the very ark, no doubt, You went frolicking about; Never keeping in your mind Drowned monkeys left behind!

Have you no traditions—none, Of the court of Solomon? No memorial how you went With Prince Hiram's armament?

Look now at him! slyly peep; He pretends he is asleep! Fast asleep upon his bed, With his arm beneath his head.

Now that posture is not right, And he is not settled quite; There! that's better than before— And the knave pretends to snore!

Ha! he is not half asleep: See, he slyly takes a peep. Monkey, though your eyes were shut, You could see this little nut.

You shall have it, pigmy brother! What, another! and another! Nay, your cheeks are like a sack— Sit down, and begin to crack.

There the little ancient man Cracks as fast as crack he can! Now good-bye, you merry fellow, Nature's primest Punchinello.

Mary Howitt.

November

No sun—no moon! No morn—no noon— No dawn—no dusk—no proper time of day— No sky—no earthly view— No distance looking blue— No road—no street—no "t'other side the way"— No end to any Row— No indications where the crescents go— No top to any steeple— No recognitions of familiar people— No courtesies for showing 'em— No knowing 'em! No traveling at all—no locomotion— No inkling of the way—no notion— "No go"—by land or ocean— No mail—no post— No news from any foreign coast— No park—no ring—no afternoon gentility— No company—no nobility— No warmth, no cheerfulness, no healthful ease, No comfortable feel in any member— No shade, no shine, no butterflies, no bees, No fruits, no flowers, no leaves, no birds— November!

Thomas Hood.

Captain Sword

Captain Sword got up one day, Over the hills to march away, Over the hills and through the towns, They heard him coming across the downs, Stepping in music and thunder sweet, Which his drums sent before him into the street, And lo! 'twas a beautiful sight in the sun; For first came his foot, all marching like one, With tranquil faces, and bristling steel, And the flag full of honour as though it could feel, And the officers gentle, the sword that hold 'Gainst the shoulder, heavy with trembling gold, And the massy tread, that in passing is heard, Though the drums and the music say never a word. And then came his horse, a clustering sound, Of shapely potency forward bound. Glossy black steeds, and riders tall Rank after rank, each looking like all; 'Midst moving repose and a threatening calm, With mortal sharpness at each right arm, And hues that painters and ladies love, And ever the small flag blushed above.

And ever and anon the kettledrums beat, Hasty power 'midst order meet; And ever and anon the drums and fifes Came like motion's voice, and life's; Or into the golden grandeurs fell Of deeper instruments mingling well, Burdens of beauty for winds to bear; And the cymbals kissed in the shining air, And the trumpets their visible voices rear'd, Each looking forth with its tapestried beard, Bidding the heavens and earth make way For Captain Sword and his battle array.

He, nevertheless, rode, indifferent-eyed, As if pomp were a toy to his manly pride, Whilst the ladies loved him the more for his scorn, And thought him the noblest man ever was born, And tears came into the bravest eyes, And hearts swell'd after him double their size, And all that was weak, and all that was strong, Seem'd to think wrong's self in him could not be wrong, Such love, though with bosom about to be gored, Did sympathy get for brave Captain Sword.

So half that night, as he stopped in the town, 'Twas all one dance going merrily down, With lights in windows and love in eyes And a constant feeling of sweet surprise; But all the next morning 'twas tears and sighs, For the sound of his drums grew less and less, Walking like carelessness off from distress; And Captain Sword went whistling gay, "Over the hills and far away."

Leigh Hunt.

INTERLEAVES
Story Poems: Romance and Reality

When the King in Lowell's poem asked his three daughters what fairings he should bring them on his home-coming, the two elder ones demanded jewels and rings, silks that would stand alone, and golden combs for the hair. But the youngest Princess, she that was whiter than thistledown—somehow it is always the youngest princess who is beloved of the poets and romancers—asked as her fairing the Singing Leaves. The King could not buy them in Vanity Fair, but in the deep heart of the greenwood he found Walter, the little foot-page, who drew a thin packet from his bosom and said,

"Now give you this to the Princess Anne, The Singing Leaves are therein."

She took them when the King met her at the castle gate, the lovely little Princess with the golden crown shining dim in the blithesome gold of her hair; took them with a smile that

"Lighted her tears as the summer sun Transfigures the summer rain."

The poems we give you here, young princes and princesses of the twentieth century, are all Singing Leaves of one sort or another. There are leaves that sing tragedies, like those in "Earl Haldan's Daughter," "The High Tide," or "The Sands o' Dee"; there are leaves that sing fantasies, like "The Forsaken Merman," "The Pied Piper," or the enchanting "Lady of Shalott," weaving her magic web of colors gay. There are Singing Leaves that grew on the Tree of Reality; leaves that tell stories like Bret Harte's "Greyport Legend" or Browning's "Hervé Riel"; while in "Seven Times Two," the "Swan's Nest," "Lord Ullin," "Young Lochinvar," and "Jock o' Hazledean" you have pure romances, sweet and youthful, gay and daring.

XIII
STORY POEMS: ROMANCE AND REALITY
The Singing Leaves
I

"What fairings will ye that I bring?" Said the King to his daughters three; "For I to Vanity Fair am boun', Now say what shall they be?"

Then up and spake the eldest daughter, That lady tall and grand: "Oh, bring me pearls and diamonds great, And gold rings for my hand."

Thereafter spake the second daughter, That was both white and red: "For me bring silks that will stand alone, And a gold comb for my head."

Then came the turn of the least daughter, That was whiter than thistle-down, And among the gold of her blithesome hair Dim shone the golden crown.

"There came a bird this morning, And sang 'neath my bower eaves, Till I dreamed, as his music made me, 'Ask thou for the Singing Leaves.'"

Then the brow of the King swelled crimson With a flush of angry scorn: "Well have ye spoken, my two eldest, And chosen as ye were born;

"But she, like a thing of peasant race, That is happy binding the sheaves;" Then he saw her dead mother in her face, And said, "Thou shalt have thy leaves."

II

He mounted and rode three days and nights Till he came to Vanity Fair, And 't was easy to buy the gems and the silk, But no Singing Leaves were there.

Then deep in the greenwood rode he, And asked of every tree, "Oh, if you have ever a Singing Leaf, I pray you give it me!"

But the trees all kept their counsel, And never a word said they, Only there sighed from the pine-tops A music of seas far away.

Only the pattering aspen Made a sound of growing rain, That fell ever faster and faster, Then faltered to silence again.

"Oh, where shall I find a little foot-page That would win both hose and shoon, And will bring to me the Singing Leaves If they grow under the moon?"

Then lightly turned him Walter the page, By the stirrup as he ran: "Now pledge you me the truesome word Of a king and gentleman,

"That you will give me the first, first thing You meet at your castle-gate, And the Princess shall get the Singing Leaves, Or mine be a traitor's fate."

The King's head dropt upon his breast A moment, as it might be; 'T will be my dog, he thought, and said, "My faith I plight to thee."

Then Walter took from next his heart A packet small and thin, "Now give you this to the Princess Anne, The Singing Leaves are therein."

III

As the King rode in at his castle-gate, A maiden to meet him ran, And "Welcome, father!" she laughed and cried Together, the Princess Anne.

"Lo, here the Singing Leaves," quoth he, "And woe, but they cost me dear!" She took the packet, and the smile Deepened down beneath the tear.

It deepened down till it reached her heart, And then gushed up again, And lighted her tears as the sudden sun Transfigures the summer rain.

And the first Leaf, when it was opened, Sang: "I am Walter the page, And the songs I sing 'neath thy window Are my only heritage."

And the second Leaf sang: "But in the land That is neither on earth nor sea, My lute and I are lords of more Than thrice this kingdom's fee."

And the third Leaf sang, "Be mine! Be mine!" And ever it sang, "Be mine!" Then sweeter it sang and ever sweeter, And said, "I am thine, thine, thine!"

At the first Leaf she grew pale enough, At the second she turned aside, At the third, 't was as if a lily flushed With a rose's red heart's tide.

"Good counsel gave the bird," said she, "I have my hope thrice o'er, For they sing to my very heart," she said, "And it sings to them evermore."

She brought to him her beauty and truth, But and broad earldoms three, And he made her queen of the broader lands He held of his lute in fee.

James Russell Lowell.

Seven Times Two

You bells in the steeple, ring, ring out your changes, How many soever they be, And let the brown meadow-lark's note as he ranges Come over, come over to me!

Yet birds' clearest carol by fall or by swelling No magical sense conveys; And bells have forgotten their old art of telling The fortune of future days.

"Turn again, turn again!" once they rang cheerily, While a boy listened alone; Made his heart yearn again, musing so wearily All by himself on a stone.

Poor bells! I forgive you; your good days are over, And mine, they are yet to be; No listening, no longing, shall aught, aught discover; You leave the story to me.

The foxglove shoots out of the green matted heather, And hangeth her hoods of snow; She was idle, and slept till the sunshiny weather: Oh, children take long to grow!

I wish and I wish that the spring would go faster, Nor long summer bide so late; And I could grow on like the foxglove and aster, For some things are ill to wait.

I wait for the day when dear hearts shall discover, While dear hands are laid on my head, "The child is a woman—the book may close over, For all the lessons are said."

I wait for my story: the birds cannot sing it, Not one, as he sits on the tree; The bells cannot ring it, but long years, oh bring it! Such as I wish it to be.

Jean Ingelow.

The Long White Seam

As I came round the harbor buoy, The lights began to gleam, No wave the land-locked harbor stirred, The crags were white as cream; And I marked my love by candlelight Sewing her long white seam. It's aye sewing ashore, my dear, Watch and steer at sea, It's reef and furl, and haul the line, Set sail and think of thee.

I climbed to reach her cottage door; Oh sweetly my love sings! Like a shaft of light her voice breaks forth, My soul to meet it springs, As the shining water leaped of old When stirred by angel wings. Aye longing to list anew, Awake and in my dream, But never a song she sang like this, Sewing her long white seam.

Fair fall the lights, the harbor lights, That brought me in to thee, And peace drop down on that low roof, For the sight that I did see, And the voice, my dear, that rang so clear, All for the love of me. For O, for O, with brows bent low, By the flickering candle's gleam, Her wedding gown it was she wrought, Sewing the long white seam.

Jean Ingelow.

Hannah Binding Shoes

Poor lone Hannah, Sitting at the window, binding shoes! Faded, wrinkled, Sitting, stitching, in a mournful muse. Bright-eyed beauty once was she, When the bloom was on the tree;— Spring and winter, Hannah's at the window, binding shoes.

Not a neighbor Passing, nod or answer will refuse To her whisper, "Is there from the fishers any news?" Oh, her heart's adrift with one On an endless voyage gone;— Night and morning, Hannah's at the window, binding shoes.

Fair young Hannah, Ben, the sunburnt fisher, gaily wooes; Hale and clever, For a willing heart and hand he sues. May-day skies are all aglow, And the waves are laughing so! For her wedding Hannah leaves her window and her shoes.

May is passing; 'Mid the apple-boughs a pigeon cooes; Hannah shudders, For the mild south-wester mischief brews.

Round the rocks of Marblehead, Outward bound a schooner sped; Silent, lonesome, Hannah's at the window, binding shoes.

'Tis November: Now no tear her wasted cheek bedews, From Newfoundland Not a sail returning will she lose, Whispering hoarsely: "Fishermen, Have you, have you heard of Ben?" Old with watching, Hannah's at the window, binding shoes.

Twenty winters Bleak and drear the ragged shore she views, Twenty seasons! Never one has brought her any news, Still her dim eyes silently Chase the white sails o'er the sea;— Hopeless, faithful, Hannah's at the window, binding shoes.

Lucy Larcom.

Lord Ullin's Daughter

A Chieftain to the Highlands bound Cries "Boatman, do not tarry! And I'll give thee a silver pound To row us o'er the ferry!"

"Now who be ye, would cross Lochgyle This dark and stormy water?" "O I'm the chief of Ulva's isle, And this, Lord Ullin's daughter.

"And fast before her father's men Three days we've fled together, For should he find us in the glen, My blood would stain the heather.

"His horsemen hard behind us ride— Should they our steps discover, Then who will cheer my bonny bride When they have slain her lover!"

Out spoke the hardy Highland wight "I'll go, my chief, I'm ready; It is not for your silver bright, But for your winsome lady:—

"And by my word! the bonny bird In danger shall not tarry; So though the waves are raging white I'll row you o'er the ferry."

By this the storm grew loud apace, The water-wraith was shrieking; And in the scowl of heaven each face Grew dark as they were speaking.

But still as wilder blew the wind And as the night grew drearer, Adown the glen rode arméd men, Their trampling sounded nearer.

"O haste thee, haste!" the lady cries, "Though tempests round us gather; I'll meet the raging of the skies, But not an angry father."

The boat has left a stormy land, A stormy sea before her,— When, O! too strong for human hand The tempest gather'd o'er her.

And still they row'd amidst the roar Of waters fast prevailing: Lord Ullin reach'd that fatal shore,— His wrath was changed to wailing.

For, sore dismay'd, through storm and shade His child he did discover:— One lovely hand she stretch'd for aid, And one was round her lover.

"Come back! come back!" he cried in grief "Across this stormy water: And I'll forgive your Highland chief, My daughter!— O my daughter!"

'Twas vain: the loud waves lash'd the shore, Return or aid preventing: The waters wild went o'er his child, And he was left lamenting.

Thomas Campbell.

The King of Denmark's Ride

Word was brought to the Danish king, (Hurry!) That the love of his heart lay suffering, And pined for the comfort his voice would bring (Oh! ride as if you were flying!) Better he loves each golden curl On the brow of that Scandinavian girl Than his rich crown-jewels of ruby and pearl; And his Rose of the Isles is dying!

Thirty nobles saddled with speed; (Hurry!) Each one mounted a gallant steed Which he kept for battle and days of need; (Oh! ride as though you were flying!) Spurs were stuck in the foaming flank, Worn-out chargers staggered and sank; Bridles were slackened and girths were burst; But, ride as they would, the king rode first, For his Rose of the Isles lay dying.

His nobles are beaten, one by one; (Hurry!) They have fainted, and faltered, and homeward gone; His little fair page now follows alone, For strength and for courage trying. The king looked back at that faithful child, Wan was the face that answering smiled. They passed the drawbridge with clattering din, Then he dropped, and only the king rode in Where his Rose of the Isles lay dying.

The king blew a blast on his bugle-horn, (Silence!) No answer came, but faint and forlorn An echo returned on the cold gray morn, Like the breath of a spirit sighing; The castle portal stood grimly wide; None welcomed the king from that weary ride! For, dead in the light of the dawning day, The pale sweet form of the welcomer lay, Who had yearned for his voice while dying.

The panting steed with a drooping crest Stood weary; The king returned from the chamber of rest, The thick sobs choking in his breast, And that dumb companion eying, The tears gushed forth, which he strove to check; He bowed his head on his charger's neck,— "O steed that every nerve didst strain, Dear steed! our ride hath been in vain To the halls where my love lay dying."

Caroline Elizabeth Norton.

The Shepherd to His Love

Come live with me, and be my Love, And we will all the pleasures prove, That hills and valleys, dale and field, And all the craggy mountains yield.

There will we sit upon the rocks, And see the shepherds feed their flocks By shallow rivers, to whose falls Melodious birds sing madrigals.

There will I make thee beds of roses, And a thousand fragrant posies, A cap of flowers, and a kirtle, Embroider'd all with leaves of myrtle;

A gown made of the finest wool, Which from our pretty lambs we pull; Fair-linèd slippers for the cold, With buckles of the purest gold;

A belt of straw and ivy-buds, With coral clasps and amber studs: And if these pleasures may thee move, Come live with me, and be my Love.

Thy silver dishes for thy meat, As precious as the gods do eat, Shall, on an ivory table, be Prepared each day for thee and me.

The shepherd swains shall dance and sing For thy delight each May-morning: If these delights thy mind may move, Then live with me, and be my Love.

Christopher Marlowe.

Ballad

a.d.

It was Earl Haldan's daughter, She looked across the sea; She looked across the water, And long and loud laughed she: "The locks of six princesses Must be my marriage fee: So, hey, bonny boat, and ho, bonny boat, Who comes a-wooing me!"

It was Earl Haldan's daughter, She walked along the sand, When she was aware of a knight so fair, Came sailing to the land. His sails were all of velvet, His mast of beaten gold, And "Hey, bonny boat, and ho, bonny boat. Who saileth here so bold?"

"The locks of five princesses I won beyond the sea; I shore their golden tresses To fringe a cloak for thee. One handful yet is wanting, But one of all the tale; So, hey, bonny boat, and ho, bonny boat, Furl up thy velvet sail!"

He leapt into the water, That rover young and bold; He gript Earl Haldan's daughter, He shore her locks of gold: "Go weep, go weep, proud maiden, The tale is full to-day. Now, hey, bonny boat, and ho, bonny boat, Sail Westward ho, and away!"

Charles Kingsley.

Romance of the Swan's Nest

Little Ellie sits alone 'Mid the beeches of a meadow, By a stream-side on the grass; And the trees are showering down Doubles of their leaves in shadow On her shining hair and face.

She has thrown her bonnet by; And her feet she has been dipping In the shallow water's flow— Now she holds them nakedly In her hands, all sleek and dripping While she rocketh to and fro.

Little Ellie sits alone, And the smile she softly uses, Fills the silence like a speech; While she thinks what shall be done,— And the sweetest pleasure chooses, For her future within reach.

Little Ellie in her smile Chooseth ... "I will have a lover, Riding on a steed of steeds! He shall love me without guile; And to *him* I will discover That swan's nest among the reeds.

"And the steed shall be red-roan And the lover shall be noble. With an eye that takes the breath, And the lute he plays upon, Shall strike ladies into trouble, As his sword strikes men to death.

"And the steed it shall be shod All in silver, housed in azure, And the mane shall swim the wind: And the hoofs along the sod Shall flash onward and keep measure, Till the shepherds look behind.

"But my lover will not prize All the glory that he rides in, When he gazes in my face. He will say, 'O Love, thine eyes Build the shrine my soul abides in; And I kneel here for thy grace.'

"Then, ay, then—he shall kneel low With the red-roan steed anear him Which shall seem to understand— Till I answer, 'Rise and go! For the world must love and fear him Whom I gift with heart and hand.'

"Then he will arise so pale, I shall feel my own lips tremble With a *yes* I must not say— Nathless maiden-brave, 'Farewell,' I will utter and dissemble— 'Light to-morrow with to-day.'

"Then he'll ride among the hills To the wide world past the river, There to put away all wrong: To make straight distorted wills, And to empty the broad quiver Which the wicked bear along.

"Three times shall a young foot-page Swim the stream and climb the mountain And kneel down beside my feet— 'Lo! my master sends this gage, Lady, for thy pity's counting! What wilt thou exchange for it?'

"And the first time, I will send A white rosebud for a guerdon,— And the second time a glove: But the third time—I may bend From my pride, and answer—'Pardon— If he comes to take my love.'

"Then the young foot-page will run— Then my lover will ride faster, Till he kneeleth at my knee: 'I am a duke's eldest son! Thousand serfs do call me master,— But, O Love, I love but *thee*!'

"He will kiss me on the mouth Then; and lead me as a lover, Through the crowds that praise his deeds: And, when soul-tied by one troth, Unto him I will discover That swan's nest among the reeds."

Little Ellie, with her smile Not yet ended, rose up gayly, Tied the bonnet, donned the shoe— And went homeward, round a mile, Just to see, as she did daily, What more eggs were with the *two*.

Pushing through the elm-tree copse Winding by the stream, light-hearted, Where the osier pathway leads— Past the boughs she stoops—and stops! Lo! the wild swan had deserted— And a rat had gnawed the reeds.

Ellie went home sad and slow: If she found the lover ever, With his red-roan steed of steeds, Sooth I know not! but I know She could never show him—never, That swan's nest among the reeds!

Elizabeth Barrett Browning.

Lochinvar

Oh, young Lochinvar is come out of the west; Through all the wide Border his steed was the best; And save his good broad-sword he weapons had none; He rode all unarmed, and he rode all alone. So faithful in love, and so dauntless in war, There never was knight like the young Lochinvar.

He stayed not for brake, and he stopped not for stone; He swam the Eske river where ford there was none; But, ere he alighted at Netherby gate, The bride had consented, the gallant came late: For a laggard in love, and a dastard in war, Was to wed the fair Ellen of brave Lochinvar.

So boldly he entered the Netherby hall, 'Mong bridesmen and kinsmen, and brothers and all: Then spoke the bride's father, his hand on his sword (For the poor craven bridegroom said never a word), "Oh, come ye in peace here, or come ye in war, Or to dance at our bridal, young Lord Lochinvar?"

"I long wooed your daughter, my suit you denied— Love swells like the Solway, but ebbs like its tide; And now I am come, with this lost love of mine To lead but one measure, drink one cup of wine. There are maidens in Scotland more lovely by far That would gladly be bride to the young Lochinvar."

The bride kissed the goblet; the knight took it up: He quaffed off the wine, and he threw down the cup. She looked down to blush, and she looked up to sigh, With a smile on her lips and a tear in her eye. He took her soft hand ere her mother could bar,— "Now tread we a measure!" said young Lochinvar.

So stately his form, and so lovely her face, That never a hall such a galliard did grace; While her mother did fret, and her father did fume, And the bridegroom stood dangling his bonnet and plume; And the bride-maidens whispered, "'Twere better by far To have matched our fair cousin with young Lochinvar."

One touch to her hand, and one word in her ear, When they reached the hall door and the charger stood near; So light to the croupe the fair lady he swung, So light to the saddle before her he sprung! "She is won! we are gone, over bank, bush, and scaur! They'll have fleet steeds that follow!" quoth young Lochinvar.

There was mounting 'mong Græmes of the Netherby clan; Forsters, Fenwicks, and Musgraves, they rode and they ran; There was racing and chasing on Cannobie Lee; But the lost bride of Netherby ne'er did they see. So daring in love, and so dauntless in war, Have ye e'er heard of gallant like young Lochinvar?

Sir Walter Scott.

From "Marmion."

Jock of Hazeldean

"Why weep ye by the tide, ladie? Why weep ye by the tide? I'll wed ye to my youngest son, And ye sall be his bride; And ye sall be his bride, ladie, Sae comely to be seen"— But aye she loot the tears down fa' For Jock of Hazeldean.

"Now let this wilfu' grief be done, And dry that cheek so pale; Young Frank is chief of Errington, And lord of Langley-dale; His step is first in peaceful ha', His sword in battle keen"— But aye she loot the tears down fa' For Jock of Hazeldean.

"A chain of gold ye sall not lack, Nor braid to bind your hair; Nor mettled hound, nor managed hawk, Nor palfrey fresh and fair; And you, the foremost o' them a', Shall ride our forest queen"— But aye she loot the tears down fa' For Jock of Hazeldean.

The kirk was decked at morning-tide, The tapers glimmered fair; The priest and bridegroom wait the bride, And dame and knight are there. They sought her baith by bower and ha', The ladie was not seen! She's o'er the Border, and awa' Wi' Jock of Hazeldean.

Sir Walter Scott.

The Lady of Shalott
Part I

On either side the river lie Long fields of barley and of rye, That clothe the wold and meet the sky; And through the fields the road runs by To many-towered Camelot; And up and down the people go, Gazing where the lilies blow Round an island there below, The island of Shalott.

Willows whiten, aspens quiver, Little breezes dusk and shiver Through the wave that runs forever By the island in the river Flowing down to Camelot; Four gray walls, and four gray towers, Overlook a space of flowers, And the silent isle imbowers The Lady of Shalott.

By the margin, willow-veiled, Slide the heavy barges trailed By slow horses; and unhailed The shallop flitteth silken-sailed, Skimming down to Camelot: But who hath seen her wave her hand? Or at the casement seen her stand? Or is she known in all the land, The Lady of Shalott.

Only reapers, reaping early In among the bearded barley, Hear a song that echoes cheerly, From the river winding clearly, Down to towered Camelot: And by the moon the reaper weary, Piling sheaves in uplands airy, Listening, whispers "'Tis the fairy Lady of Shalott."

Part II

There she weaves by night and day A magic web with colors gay. She has heard a whisper say, A curse is on her if she stay To look down to Camelot. She knows not what the curse may be And so she weaveth steadily, And little other care hath she, The Lady of Shalott.

And moving thro' a mirror clear That hangs before her all the year, Shadows of the world appear. There she sees the highway near Winding down to Camelot; There the river eddy whirls, And there the surly village churls, And the red cloaks of market-girls, Pass onward from Shalott.

Sometimes a troop of damsels glad, An abbot on an ambling pad, Sometimes a curly shepherd lad, Or long-haired page in crimson clad, Goes by to towered Camelot; And sometimes thro' the mirror blue The knights come riding two and two: She hath no loyal knight and true, The Lady of Shalott.

But in her web she still delights To weave the mirror's magic sights, For often thro' the silent nights A funeral, with plumes and lights. And music, went to Camelot: Or when the moon was overhead, Came two young lovers lately wed; "I am half sick of shadows," said The Lady of Shalott.

Part III

A bow-shot from her bower-eaves, He rode between the barley-sheaves, The sun came dazzling through the leaves, And flamed upon the brazen greaves Of bold Sir Lancelot. A red-cross knight forever kneeled To a lady in his shield, That sparkled on the yellow field, Beside remote Shalott.

The gemmy bridle glittered free, Like to some branch of stars we see Hung in the golden Galaxy. The bridle-bells rang merrily. As he rode down to Camelot: And from his blazoned baldric slung A mighty silver bugle hung, And as he rode his armor rung, Beside remote Shalott.

All in the blue unclouded weather Thick-jewelled shone the saddle-leather, The helmet and the helmet-feather Burned like one burning flame together, As he rode down to Camelot. As often through the purple night, Below the starry clusters bright, Some bearded meteor, trailing light, Moves over still Shalott.

His broad clear brow in sunlight glowed; On burnished hooves his war-horse trode; From underneath his helmet flowed His coal-black curls as on he rode, As he rode down to Camelot. From the bank and from the river He flashed into the crystal mirror, "Tirra lirra," by the river Sang Sir Lancelot.

She left the web, she left the loom, She made three paces thro' the room, She saw the water lily bloom, She saw the helmet and the plume, She looked down to Camelot. Out flew the web and floated wide; The mirror cracked from side to side; "The curse is come upon me," cried The Lady of Shalott.

Part IV

In the stormy east-wind straining, The pale yellow woods were waning, The broad stream in his banks complaining, Heavily the low sky raining Over towered Camelot; Down she came and found a boat Beneath a willow left afloat, And round about the prow she wrote, *The Lady of Shalott.*

And down the river's dim expanse— Like some bold seër in a trance, Seeing all his own mischance— With a glassy countenance Did she look to Camelot. And at the closing of the day She loosed the chain, and down she lay; The broad stream bore her far away, The Lady of Shalott.

Lying, robed in snowy white That loosely flew to left and right— The leaves upon her falling light— Thro' the noises of the night She floated down to Camelot: And as the boat-head wound along The willowy hills and fields among, They heard her singing her last song, The Lady of Shalott.

Heard a carol, mournful, holy, Chanted loudly, chanted lowly, Till her blood was frozen slowly, And her eyes were darkened wholly, Turned to towered Camelot; For ere she reached upon the tide The first house by the water-side, Singing in her song she died, The Lady of Shalott.

Under tower and balcony, By garden wall and gallery, A gleaming shape she floated by, Dead-pale between the houses high, Silent into Camelot. Out upon the wharfs they came, Knight and burgher, lord and dame, And round the prow they read her name, *The Lady of Shalott.*

Who is this? and what is here, And in the lighted palace near Died the sound of royal cheer; And they crossed themselves for fear, All the knights at Camelot: But Lancelot mused a little space; He said, "She has a lovely face; God in his mercy lend her grace, The Lady of Shalott."

Alfred, Lord Tennyson.

The High Tide on the Coast of Lincolnshire

The old mayor climbed the belfry tower, The ringers ran by two, by three; "Pull, if ye never pulled before; Good ringers, pull your best," quoth he. "Play uppe, play uppe, O Boston bells! Play all your changes, all your swells, Play uppe 'The Brides of Enderby.'"

Men say it was a stolen tyde— The Lord that sent it, He knows all; But in myne ears doth still abide The message that the bells let fall: And there was nought of strange, beside The flights of mews and peewits pied By millions crouched on the old sea wall.

I sat and spun within the doore, My thread brake off, I raised myne eyes; The level sun, like ruddy ore, Lay sinking in the barren skies; And dark against day's golden death She moved where Lindis wandereth, My sonne's faire wife, Elizabeth.

"Cusha! Cusha! Cusha!" calling, Ere the early dews were falling, Farre away I heard her song. "Cusha! Cusha!" all along; Where the reedy Lindis floweth, Floweth, floweth, From the meads where melick groweth Faintly came her milking song.—

"Cusha! Cusha! Cusha!" calling, "For the dews will soone be falling; Leave your meadow grasses mellow, Mellow, mellow; Quit your cowslips, cowslips yellow; Come uppe Whitefoot, come uppe Lightfoot, Quit the stalks of parsley hollow, Hollow, hollow; Come uppe Jetty, rise and follow, From the clovers lift your head; Come uppe Whitefoot, come uppe Lightfoot, Come uppe Jetty, rise and follow, Jetty, to the milking shed."

If it be long, aye, long ago, When I beginne to think howe long, Againe I hear the Lindis flow, Swift as an arrowe, sharpe and strong; And all the aire it seemeth mee Bin full of floating bells (sayth shee), That ring the tune of Enderby.

Alle fresh the level pasture lay, And not a shadowe mote be seene, Save where full fyve good miles away The steeple towered from out the greene; And lo! the great bell farre and wide Was heard in all the country side That Saturday at eventide.

The swannerds where their sedges are Moved on in sunset's golden breath, The shepherde lads I heard afarre, And my sonne's wife, Elizabeth; Till floating o'er the grassy sea Came downe that kyndly message free, The "Brides of Mavis Enderby."

Then some looked uppe into the sky, And all along where Lindis flows To where the goodly vessels lie, And where the lordly steeple shows. They sayde, "And why should this thing be, What danger lowers by land or sea? They ring the tune of Enderby!

"For evil news from Mablethorpe, Of pyrate galleys warping down; For shippes ashore beyond the scorpe, They have not spared to wake the towne: But while the west bin red to see, And storms be none, and pyrates flee, Why ring 'The Brides of Enderby'?"

I looked without, and lo! my sonne Came riding downe with might and main: He raised a shout as he drew on, Till all the welkin rang again, "Elizabeth! Elizabeth!" (A sweeter woman ne'er drew breath Than my sonne's wife, Elizabeth.)

"The olde sea wall (he cried) is downe, The rising tide comes on apace, And boats adrift in yonder towne Go sailing uppe the market-place." He shook as one that looks on death: "God save you, mother!" straight he saith; "Where is my wife, Elizabeth?"

"Good sonne, where Lindis winds away With her two bairns I marked her long; And ere yon bells beganne to play Afar I heard her milking song." He looked across the grassy sea, To right, to left, "Ho Enderby!" They rang "The Brides of Enderby!"

With that he cried and beat his breast; For lo! along the river's bed A mighty eygre reared his crest, And uppe the Lindis raging sped. It swept with thunderous noises loud; Shaped like a curling snow-white cloud, Or like a demon in a shroud.

And rearing Lindis backward pressed, Shook all her trembling bankes amaine; Then madly at the eygre's breast Flung uppe her weltering walls again. Then bankes came downe with ruin and rout— Then beaten foam flew round about— Then all the mighty floods were out.

So farre, so fast the eygre drave, The heart had hardly time to beat, Before a shallow seething wave Sobbed in the grasses at oure feet: The feet had hardly time to flee Before it brake against the knee, And all the world was in the sea.

Upon the roofe we sate that night, The noise of bells went sweeping by: I marked the lofty beacon light Stream from the church tower, red and high— A lurid mark and dread to see; And awsome bells they were to mee, That in the dark rang "Enderby."

95

They rang the sailor lads to guide From roofe to roofe who fearless rowed; And I—my sonne was at my side. And yet the ruddy beacon glowed; And yet he moaned beneath his breath, "O come in life, or come in death! O lost! my love, Elizabeth."

And didst thou visit him no more? Thou didst, thou didst my daughter deare; The waters laid thee at his doore, Ere yet the early dawn was clear. Thy pretty bairns in fast embrace, The lifted sun shone on thy face, Downe drifted to thy dwelling-place.

That flow strewed wrecks about the grass, That ebbe swept out the flocks to sea; A fatal ebbe and flow, alas! To manye more than myne and me: But each will mourn his own (she saith) And sweeter woman ne'er drew breath Than my sonne's wife, Elizabeth.

I shall never hear her more By the reedy Lindis shore, "Cusha, Cusha, Cusha!" calling, Ere the early dews be falling; I shall never hear her song, "Cusha, Cusha!" all along, Where the sunny Lindis floweth, Goeth, floweth; From the meads where melick groweth. When the water winding down, Onward floweth to the town.

I shall never see her more Where the reeds and rushes quiver. Shiver, quiver; Stand beside the sobbing river, Sobbing, throbbing, in its falling, To the sandy lonesome shore; I shall never hear her calling, "Leave your meadow grasses mellow, Mellow, mellow;

Quit your cowslips, cowslips yellow; Come uppe Whitefoot, come uppe Lightfoot; Quit your pipes of parsley hollow, Hollow, hollow; Come uppe Lightfoot, rise and follow; Lightfoot, Whitefoot, From your clovers lift the head; Come uppe Jetty, follow, follow, Jetty, to the milking shed."

Jean Ingelow.

The Forsaken Merman

Come, dear children, let us away; Down and away below. Now my brothers call from the bay; Now the great winds shoreward blow; Now the salt tides seaward flow; Now the wild white horses play, Champ and chafe and toss in the spray. Children dear, let us away, This way, this way!

Call her once before you go. Call once yet, In a voice that she will know: "Margaret! Margaret!" Children's voices should be dear (Call once more) to a mother's ear: Children's voices wild with pain. Surely she will come again. Call her once, and come away. This way, this way! "Mother dear, we cannot stay." The wild white horses foam and fret, Margaret! Margaret!

Come, dear children, come away down. Call no more. One last look at the white-walled town, And the little gray church on the windy shore, Then come down. She will not come though you call all day. Come away, come away.

Children dear, was it yesterday We heard the sweet bells over the bay? In the caverns where we lay, Through the surf and through the swell, The far-off sound of a silver bell? Sand-strewn caverns cool and deep, Where the winds are all asleep; Where the spent lights quiver and gleam; Where the salt weed sways in the stream; Where the sea-beasts rang'd all round Feed in the ooze of their pasture ground; Where the sea-snakes coil and twine, Dry their mail and bask in the brine; Where great whales come sailing by, Sail and sail, with unshut eye, Round the world forever and aye? When did music come this way? Children dear, was it yesterday?

Children dear, was it yesterday (Call yet once) that she went away? Once she sat with you and me, On a red-gold throne in the heart of the sea. And the youngest sat on her knee. She comb'd its bright hair, and she tended it well, When down swung the sound of the far-off bell, She sigh'd, she look'd up through the clear green sea, She said, "I must go, for my kinsfolk pray In the little gray church on the shore to-day.

'Twill be Easter-time in the world—ah me! And I lose my poor soul, Merman, here with thee." I said, "Go up, dear heart, through the waves: Say thy prayer, and come back to the kind sea-caves." She smiled, she went up through the surf in the bay. Children dear, was it yesterday?

Children dear, were we long alone? The sea grows stormy, the little ones moan; "Long prayers," I said, "in the world they say." "Come," I said, and we rose through the surf in the bay. We went up the beach in the sandy down Where the sea-stocks bloom, to the white-wall'd town, Through the narrow paved streets, where all was still, To the little gray church on the windy hill. From the church came a murmur of folk at their prayers, But we stood without in the cold blowing airs. We climb'd on the graves, on the stones worn with rains, And we gazed up the aisle through the small leaded panes. She sate by the pillar; we saw her clear; "Margaret, hist! come quick, we are here. Dear heart," I said, "we are here alone. The sea grows stormy, the little ones moan." But, ah, she gave me never a look, For her eyes were seal'd to the holy book. Loud prays the priest; shut stands the door. Come away, children, call no more, Come away, come down, call no more.

Down, down, down, Down to the depths of the sea, She sits at her wheel in the humming town, Singing most joyfully. Hark what she sings: "O joy, O joy, For the humming street, and the child with its toy, For the priest and the bell, and the holy well, For the wheel where I spun, And the blessèd light of the sun." And so she sings her fill, Singing most joyfully, Till the shuttle falls from her hand, And the whizzing wheel stands still. She steals to the window and looks at the sand; And over the sand at the sea; And her eyes are set in a stare; And anon there breaks a sigh, And anon there drops a tear, From a sorrow clouded eye, And a heart sorrow laden, A long, long sigh, For the cold strange eyes of a little Mermaiden, And the gleam of her golden hair.

Come away, away, children, Come children, come down. The hoarse wind blows colder; Lights shine in the town. She will start from her slumber When gusts shake the door; She will hear the winds howling, Will hear the waves roar. We shall see, while above us The waves roar and whirl, A ceiling of amber, A pavement of pearl. Singing, "Here came a mortal, But faithless was she, And alone dwell forever The kings of the sea."

But, children, at midnight, When soft the winds blow, When clear falls the moonlight, When spring-tides are low; When sweet airs come seaward From heaths starr'd with broom; And high rocks throw mildly On the blanch'd sands a gloom: Up the still, glistening beaches, Up the creeks we will hie; Over banks of bright seaweed The ebb-tide leaves dry. We will gaze from the sand-hills At the white sleeping town; At the church on the hillside— And then come back, down. Singing, "There dwells a loved one, But cruel is she: She left lonely forever The kings of the sea."

Matthew Arnold.

The Sands of Dee

I

"O Mary, go and call the cattle home, And call the cattle home, And call the cattle home Across the sands of Dee;" The western wind was wild and dank wi' foam, And all alone went she.

II

The western tide crept up along the sand, And o'er and o'er the sand, And round and round the sand, As far as eye could see. The rolling mist came down and hid the land— And never home came she.

III

"Oh! is it weed, or fish, or floating hair— A tress o' golden hair, A drownèd maiden's hair Above the nets at sea? Was never salmon yet that shone so fair Among the stakes on Dee."

IV

They rowed her in across the rolling foam, The cruel crawling foam, The cruel hungry foam, To her grave beside the sea: But still the boatmen hear her call the cattle home Across the sands of Dee!

Charles Kingsley.

The "Gray Swan"

"Oh, tell me, sailor, tell me true, Is my little lad, my Elihu, A-sailing with your ship?" The sailor's eyes were dim with dew. "Your little lad, your Elihu?" He said with trembling lip,— "What little lad? what ship?"

"What little lad? as if there could be Another such a one as he! What little lad, do you say? Why Elihu, that took to the sea The moment I put him off my knee! It was just the other day The 'Gray Swan' sailed away."

"The other day?" The sailor's eyes Stood open with a great surprise: "The other day? the 'Swan'?" His heart began in his throat to rise. "Ay, ay, sir, here in the cupboard lies The jacket he had on." "And so your lad is gone?"

"Gone with the 'Swan'?"—"And did she stand With her anchor clutching hold of the sand For a month, and never stir?" "Why, to be sure! I've seen from the land, Like a lover kissing his lady's hand, The wild sea kissing her,— A sight to remember, sir!"

"But, my good mother, do you know All this was twenty years ago? I stood on the 'Gray Swan's' deck, And to that lad I saw you throw, Taking it off as it might be,—so!— The kerchief from your neck." "Ay, and he'll bring it back!"

"And did the little lawless lad, That has made you sick and made you sad, Sail with the 'Gray Swan's' crew?" "Lawless! The man is going mad! The best boy ever mother had!— Be sure he sailed with the crew! What would you have him do?"

"And has he never written line, Nor sent you word, nor made you sign, To say he was alive?" "Hold! If 'twas wrong, the wrong is mine; Besides, he may lie in the brine; And could he write from the grave? Tut, man! what would you have?"

"Gone twenty years,—a long, long cruise! 'Twas wicked thus your love to abuse! But if the lad still live, And come back home, think you you can Forgive him?" "Miserable man! You're mad as the sea, you rave! What have I to forgive?"

The sailor twitched his shirt so blue, And from within his bosom drew The kerchief. She was wild. "O God, my Father! is it true? My little lad, my Elihu! My blessed boy, my child! My dead, my living child!"

Alice Cary.

The Wreck of the Hesperus

It was the schooner Hesperus That sailed the wintry sea; And the skipper had taken his little daughtèr To bear him company.

Blue were her eyes as the fairy-flax, Her cheeks like the dawn of day, And her bosom white as the hawthorn buds, That ope in the month of May.

The skipper he stood beside the helm, His pipe was in his mouth, And he watched how the veering flaw did blow The smoke now West, now South.

97

Then up and spake an old Sailòr Had sailed to the Spanish main, "I pray thee put into yonder port, For I fear a hurricane.

"Last night the moon had a golden ring, And to-night no moon we see!" The skipper he blew a whiff from his pipe, And a scornful laugh laughed he.

Colder and colder blew the wind, A gale from the Northeast; The snow fell hissing in the brine, And the billows frothed like yeast.

Down came the storm, and smote amain The vessel in its strength; She shuddered and paused like a frighted steed, Then leaped her cable's length.

"Come hither! come hither! my little daughtèr, And do not tremble so; For I can weather the roughest gale That ever wind did blow."

He wrapped her warm in his seaman's coat Against the stinging blast; He cut a rope from a broken spar, And bound her to the mast.

"O father! I hear the church-bells ring; O say, what may it be?" "'Tis a fog-bell on a rock-bound coast!" And he steered for the open sea.

"O father! I hear the sound of guns; O say, what may it be?" "Some ship in distress, that cannot live In such an angry sea!"

"O father I see a gleaming light; O say, what may it be?" But the father answered never a word, A frozen corpse was he.

Lashed to the helm, all stiff and stark, With his face turned to the skies, The lantern gleamed through the gleaming snow On his fixed and glassy eyes.

Then the maiden clasped her hands and prayed That savèd she might be; And she thought of Christ, who stilled the wave On the Lake of Galilee.

And fast through the midnight dark and drear, Through the whistling sleet and snow, Like a sheeted ghost the vessel swept Towards the reef of Norman's Woe.

And ever the fitful gusts between A sound came from the land; It was the sound of the trampling surf On the rocks and the hard sea-sand.

The breakers were right beneath her bows, She drifted a dreary wreck, And a whooping billow swept the crew Like icicles from her deck.

She struck where the white and fleecy waves Looked soft as carded wool, But the cruel rocks they gored her side Like the horns of an angry bull.

Her rattling shrouds, all sheathed in ice, With the masts went by the board: Like a vessel of glass she stove and sank,— Ho! ho! the breakers roared!

At daybreak, on the bleak sea-beach A fisherman stood aghast To see the form of a maiden fair Lashed close to a drifting mast.

The salt sea was frozen on her breast, The salt tears in her eyes; And he saw her hair, like the brown sea-weed, On the billows fall and rise.

Such was the wreck of the Hesperus, In the midnight and the snow! Christ save us all from a death like this On the reef of Norman's Woe!

Henry Wadsworth Longfellow.

A Greyport Legend

They ran through the streets of the seaport town; They peered from the decks of the ships that lay: The cold sea-fog that comes whitening down Was never as cold or white as they. "Ho, Starbuck, and Pinckney, and Tenterden, Run for your shallops, gather your men, Scatter your boats on the lower bay!"

Good cause for fear! In the thick midday The hulk that lay by the rotting pier, Filled with the children in happy play, Parted its moorings and drifted clear; Drifted clear beyond reach or call,— Thirteen children they were in all,— All adrift in the lower bay!

Said a hard-faced skipper, "God help us all! She will not float till the turning tide!" Said his wife, "My darling will hear *my* call, Whether in sea or heaven she bide!" And she lifted a quavering voice and high, Wild and strange as a sea-bird's cry, Till they shuddered and wondered at her side.

The fog drove down on each laboring crew, Veiled each from each and the sky and shore; There was not a sound but the breath they drew, And the lap of water and creak of oar. And they felt the breath of the downs fresh blown O'er leagues of clover and cold gray stone, But not from the lips that had gone before.

They came no more. But they tell the tale That, when fogs are thick on the harbor reef, The mackerel-fishers shorten sail; For the signal they know will bring relief, For the voices of children, still at play In a phantom-hulk that drifts alway Through channels whose waters never fail.

It is but a foolish shipman's tale, A theme for a poet's idle page; But still, when the mists of doubt prevail, And we lie becalmed by the shores of age, We hear from the misty troubled shore The voice of the children gone before, Drawing the soul to its anchorage!

Bret Harte.

The Glove and the Lions

King Francis was a hearty king, and loved a royal sport, And one day as his lions fought, sat looking on the court; The nobles filled the benches, with the ladies in their pride, And 'mongst them sat the Count de Lorge, with one for whom he sighed: And truly 'twas a gallant thing to see that crowning show, Valour and love, and a king above, and the royal beasts below.

Ramp'd and roar'd the lions, with horrid laughing jaws; They bit, they glared, gave blows like beams, a wind went with their paws; With wallowing might and stifled roar they rolled on one another, Till all the pit with sand and mane was in a thunderous smother; The bloody foam above the bars came whisking through the air; Said Francis then, "Faith, gentlemen, we're better here than there."

De Lorge's love o'erheard the king,—a beauteous lively dame With smiling lips and sharp bright eyes, which always seem'd the same: She thought, "The Count, my lover, is brave as brave can be; He surely would do wondrous things to show his love of me; King, ladies, lovers, all look on; the occasion is divine; I'll drop my glove, to prove his love; great glory will be mine."

She dropp'd her glove, to prove his love, then look'd at him and smiled; He bowed, and in a moment leapt among the lions wild: His leap was quick, return was quick, he has regain'd his place, Then threw the glove, but not with love, right in the lady's face. "Well done!" cried Francis, "bravely done!" and he rose from where he sat: "No love," quoth he, "but vanity, sets love a task like that."

Leigh Hunt.

How's My Boy?

Ho, sailor of the sea! How's my boy—my boy? "What's your boy's name, good wife, And in what good ship sailed he?"

My boy John— He that went to sea— What care I for the ship, sailor? My boy's my boy to me.

You come back from sea And not know my John? I might as well have asked some landsman Yonder down in the town. There's not an ass in all the parish But he knows my John.

How's my boy—my boy? And unless you let me know I'll swear you are no sailor, Blue jacket or no, Brass button or no, sailor, Anchor and crown or no! Sure his ship was the *Jolly Briton*— "Speak low, woman, speak low!"

And why should I speak low, sailor, About my own boy John? If I was loud as I am proud I'd sing him over the town! Why should I speak low, sailor? "That good ship went down."

How's my boy—my boy? What care I for the ship, sailor, I never was aboard her. Be she afloat, or be she aground, Sinking or swimming, I'll be bound Her owners can afford her! I say, how's my John? "Every man on board went down, Every man aboard her."

How's my boy—my boy? What care I for the men, sailor? I'm not their mother— How's my boy—my boy? Tell me of him and no other! How's my boy—my boy?

Sydney Dobell.

The Child-Musician

He had played for his lordship's levee, He had played for her ladyship's whim, Till the poor little head was heavy, And the poor little brain would swim.

And the face grew peaked and eerie, And the large eyes strange and bright; And they said—too late—"He is weary! He shall rest, for at least to-night!"

But at dawn, when the birds were waking, As they watched in the silent room, With the sound of a strained cord breaking, A something snapped in the gloom.

'Twas the string of his violoncello, And they heard him stir in his bed:— "Make room for a tired little fellow, "Kind God!" was the last he said.

Austin Dobson.

How They Brought the Good News from Ghent to Aix

I sprang to the stirrup, and Joris and he: I galloped, Dirck galloped, we galloped all three; "Good speed!" cried the watch as the gate-bolts undrew, "Speed!" echoed the wall to us galloping through, Behind shut the postern, the lights sank to rest, And into the midnight we galloped abreast.

Not a word to each other; we kept the great pace— Neck by neck, stride by stride, never changing our place; I turned in my saddle and made its girths tight, Then shortened each stirrup and set the pique right, Rebuckled the check-strap, chained slacker the bit, Nor galloped less steadily Roland a whit.

'Twas a moonset at starting; but while we drew near Lokeren, the cocks crew and twilight dawned clear; At Boom a great yellow star came out to see; At Düffeld 'twas morning as plain as could be; And from Mecheln church-steeple we heard the half chime— So Joris broke silence with "Yet there is time!"

At Aerschot up leaped of a sudden the sun, And against him the cattle stood black every one, To stare through the mist at us galloping past; And I saw my stout galloper Roland at last, With resolute shoulders, each butting away The haze, as some bluff river headland its spray; And his low head and crest, just one sharp ear bent back For my voice, and the other pricked out on his track; And one eye's black intelligence,—ever that glance O'er its white edge at me, his own master, askance; And the thick heavy spume-flakes, which aye and anon His fierce lips shook upward in galloping on.

By Hasselt Dirck groaned; and cried Joris, "Stay spur! Your Roos galloped bravely, the fault's not in her; We'll remember at Aix"—for one heard the quick wheeze Of her chest, saw the stretched neck, and staggering knees, And sunk tail, and horrible heave of the flank, As down on her haunches she shuddered and sank.

So we were left galloping, Joris and I, Past Looz and past Tongres, no cloud in the sky; The broad sun above laughed a pitiless laugh; 'Neath our feet broke the brittle, bright stubble like chaff; Till over by Dalhem a dome-spire sprang white, And "Gallop," gasped Joris, "for Aix is in sight!"

"How they'll greet us!"—and all in a moment his roan Rolled neck and croup over, lay dead as a stone; And there was my Roland to bear the whole weight Of the news which alone could save Aix from her fate, With his nostrils like pits full of blood to the brim, And with circles of red for his eye-sockets' rim.

Then I cast loose my buff-coat, each holster let fall, Shook off both my jack-boots, let go belt and all, Stood up in the stirrups, leaned, patted his ear, Called my Roland his pet-name, my horse without peer— Clapped my hands, laughed and sung, any noise, bad or good, Till at length into Aix Roland galloped and stood.

And all I remember is friends flocking round, As I sate with his head 'twixt my knees on the ground; And no voice but was praising this Roland of mine, As I poured down his throat our last measure of wine, Which (the burgesses voted by common consent) Was no more than his due who brought good news from Ghent.

Robert Browning.

The Inchcape Rock

No stir in the air, no stir in the sea, The ship was still as she could be; Her sails from heaven received no motion; Her keel was steady in the ocean.

Without either sign or sound of their shock, The waves flow'd over the Inchcape Rock; So little they rose, so little they fell, They did not move the Inchcape Bell.

The Abbot of Aberbrothok Had placed that Bell on the Inchcape Rock; On a buoy in the storm it floated and swung, And over the waves its warning rung.

When the Rock was hid by the surge's swell, The mariners heard the warning Bell; And then they knew the perilous Rock, And blest the Abbot of Aberbrothok.

The Sun in heaven was shining gay; All things were joyful on that day; The sea-birds scream'd as they wheel'd round. And there was joyance in their sound.

The buoy of the Inchcape Bell was seen A darker speck on the ocean green; Sir Ralph the Rover walk'd his deck, And he fix'd his eye on the darker speck.

He felt the cheering power of spring; It made him whistle, it made him sing; His heart was mirthful to excess, But the Rover's mirth was wickedness.

His eye was on the Inchcape float; Quoth he, "My men, put out the boat, And row me to the Inchcape Rock, And I'll plague the Abbot of Aberbrothok."

The boat is lower'd, the boatmen row, And to the Inchcape Rock they go; Sir Ralph bent over from the boat, And he cut the Bell from the Inchcape float.

Down sunk the Bell with a gurgling sound; The bubbles rose and burst around; Quoth Sir Ralph, "The next who comes to the Rock Won't bless the Abbot of Aberbrothok."

Sir Ralph the Rover sail'd away; He scour'd the seas for many a day; And now, grown rich with plunder'd store, He steers his course for Scotland's shore.

So thick a haze o'erspreads the sky, They cannot see the Sun on high; The wind hath blown a gale all day; At evening it hath died away.

On the deck the Rover takes his stand; So dark it is they see no land. Quoth Sir Ralph, "It will be lighter soon, For there is the dawn of the rising Moon."

"Canst hear," said one, "the breakers roar? For methinks we should be near the shore." "Now where we are I cannot tell, But I wish I could hear the Inchcape Bell."

They hear no sound; the swell is strong; Though the wind hath fallen, they drift along, Till the vessel strikes with a shivering shock,— "Oh God! it is the Inchcape Rock!"

Sir Ralph the Rover tore his hair; He curs'd himself in his despair; The waves rush in on every side; The ship is sinking beneath the tide.

But, even in his dying fear, One dreadful sound could the Rover hear— A sound as if, with the Inchcape Bell, The fiends below were ringing his knell.

Robert Southey.

A Night With a Wolf

Little one, come to my knee! Hark, how the rain is pouring Over the roof, in the pitch-black night, And the wind in the woods a-roaring!

Hush, my darling, and listen, Then pay for the story with kisses; Father was lost in the pitch-black night, In just such a storm as this is!

High up on the lonely mountains, Where the wild men watched and waited; Wolves in the forest, and bears in the bush, And I on my path belated.

The rain and the night together Came down, and the wind came after, Bending the props of the pine-tree roof, And snapping many a rafter.

I crept along in the darkness, Stunned, and bruised, and blinded,— Crept to a fir with thick-set boughs, And a sheltering rock behind it.

There, from the blowing and raining, Crouching, I sought to hide me: Something rustled, two green eyes shone, And a wolf lay down beside me.

Little one, be not frightened; I and the wolf together, Side by side, through the long, long night Hid from the awful weather.

His wet fur pressed against me; Each of us warmed the other; Each of us felt, in the stormy dark, That beast and man was brother.

And when the falling forest No longer crashed in warning, Each of us went from our hiding-place Forth in the wild, wet morning.

Darling, kiss me in payment! Hark, how the wind is roaring; Father's house is a better place When the stormy rain is pouring!

Bayard Taylor.

The Dove of Dacca

The freed dove flew to the Rajah's tower— Fled from the slaughter of Moslem kings— And the thorns have covered the city of Gaur. Dove—dove—oh, homing dove! Little white traitor, with woe on thy wings!

The Rajah of Dacca rode under the wall; He set in his bosom a dove of flight— "If she return, be sure that I fall." Dove—dove—oh, homing dove! Pressed to his heart in the thick of the fight.

"Fire the palace, the fort, and the keep— Leave to the foeman no spoil at all. In the flame of the palace lie down and sleep If the dove, if the dove—if the homing dove Come and alone to the palace wall."

The Kings of the North they were scattered abroad— The Rajah of Dacca he slew them all. Hot from slaughter he stooped at the ford,— And the dove—the dove—oh, the homing dove! She thought of her cote on the palace wall.

She opened her wings and she flew away— Fluttered away beyond recall; She came to the palace at break of day. Dove—dove—oh, homing dove! Flying so fast for a kingdom's fall.

The Queens of Dacca they slept in flame— Slept in the flame of the palace old— To save their honour from Moslem shame. And the dove—the dove—oh, the homing dove! She cooed to her young where the smoke-cloud rolled.

The Rajah of Dacca rode far and fleet, Followed as fast as a horse could fly, He came and the palace was black at his feet; And the dove—the dove—oh, the homing dove! Circled alone in the stainless sky.

So the dove flew to the Rajah's tower— Fled from the slaughter of Moslem kings; So the thorns covered the city of Gaur, And Dacca was lost for a white dove's wings. Dove—dove—oh, homing dove! Dacca is lost from the roll of the kings!

Rudyard Kipling.

The Abbot of Inisfalen

I

The Abbot of Inisfalen Awoke ere dawn of day; Under the dewy green leaves Went he forth to pray.

The lake around his island Lay smooth and dark and deep, And, wrapt in a misty stillness, The mountains were all asleep.

Low kneel'd the Abbot Cormac, When the dawn was dim and gray; The prayers of his holy office He faithfully 'gan say.

Low kneel'd the Abbot Cormac, When the dawn was waxing red, And for his sins' forgiveness A solemn prayer he said.

Low kneel'd that holy Abbot When the dawn was waxing clear; And he pray'd with loving-kindness For his convent brethren dear.

Low kneel'd that blessed Abbot, When the dawn was waxing bright; He pray'd a great prayer for Ireland, He pray'd with all his might.

Low kneel'd that good old father, While the sun began to dart; He pray'd a prayer for all mankind, He pray'd it from his heart.

II
The Abbot of Inisfalen Arose upon his feet; He heard a small bird singing, And, oh, but it sung sweet!

He heard a white bird singing well Within a holly-tree; A song so sweet and happy Never before heard he.

It sung upon a hazel, It sung upon a thorn; He had never heard such music Since the hour that he was born.

It sung upon a sycamore, It sung upon a briar; To follow the song and hearken This Abbot could never tire.

Till at last he well bethought him He might no longer stay; So he bless'd the little white singing-bird, And gladly went his way.

III
But when he came to his Abbey walls, He found a wondrous change; He saw no friendly faces there, For every face was strange.

The strangers spoke unto him; And he heard from all and each The foreign tone of the Sassenach, Not wholesome Irish speech.

Then the oldest monk came forward, In Irish tongue spake he: "Thou wearest the holy Augustine's dress, And who hath given it to thee?"

"I wear the holy Augustine's dress, And Cormac is my name, The Abbot of this good Abbey By grace of God I am.

"I went forth to pray, at the dawn of day; And when my prayers were said, I hearkened awhile to a little bird That sung above my head."

The monks to him made answer, "Two hundred years have gone o'er, Since our Abbot Cormac went through the gate, And never was heard of more.

"Matthias now is our Abbot, And twenty have passed away. The stranger is lord of Ireland; We live in an evil day."

IV
"Now give me absolution; For my time is come," said he. And they gave him absolution As speedily as might be.

Then, close outside the window, The sweetest song they heard That ever yet since the world began Was uttered by any bird.

The monks looked out and saw the bird, Its feathers all white and clean; And there in a moment, beside it, Another white bird was seen.

Those two they sung together, Waved their white wings, and fled; Flew aloft, and vanished; But the good old man was dead.

They buried his blessed body Where lake and greensward meet; A carven cross above his head, A holly-bush at his feet; Where spreads the beautiful water To gay or cloudy skies, And the purple peaks of Killarney From ancient woods arise.

William Allingham.

The Cavalier's Escape
Trample! trample! went the roan, Trap! trap! went the gray; But pad! *pad!* pad! like a thing that was mad, My chestnut broke away. It was just five miles from Salisbury town, And but one hour to day.

Thud! thud! came on the heavy roan, Rap! rap! the mettled gray; But my chestnut mare was of blood so rare, That she showed them all the way. Spur on! spur on!—I doffed my hat, And wished them all good-day.

They splashed through miry rut and pool,— Splintered through fence and rail; But chestnut Kate switched over the gate,— I saw them droop and tail. To Salisbury town—but a mile of down, Once over this brook and rail.

Trap! trap! I heard their echoing hoofs Past the walls of mossy stone; The roan flew on at a staggering pace, But blood is better than bone. I patted old Kate, and gave her the spur, For I knew it was all my own.

But trample! trample! came their steeds, And I saw their wolf's eyes burn; I felt like a royal hart at bay, And made me ready to turn. I looked where highest grew the May, And deepest arched the fern.

I flew at the first knave's sallow throat; One blow, and he was down. The second rogue fired twice, and missed; I sliced the villain's crown,— Clove through the rest, and flogged brave Kate, *Fast, fast to Salisbury town!*

Pad! pad! they came on the level sward, Thud! thud! upon the sand,— With a gleam of swords and a burning match, And a shaking of flag and hand; But one long bound, and I passed the gate, Safe from the canting band.

Walter Thornbury.

The Pied Piper of Hamelin
I
Hamelin town's in Brunswick, By famous Hanover city; The River Weser, deep and wide, Washes its walls on the southern side; A pleasanter spot you never spied; But, when begins my ditty, Almost five hundred years ago, To see the townsfolk suffer so From vermin, was a pity.

II

Rats! They fought the dogs and killed the cats, And bit the babies in the cradles, And ate the cheeses out of the vats, And licked the soup from the cooks' own ladles, Split open the kegs of salted sprats, Made nests inside men's Sunday hats, And even spoiled the women's chats, By drowning their speaking With shrieking and squeaking In fifty different sharps and flats.

III

At last the people in a body To the Town Hall came flocking: "'Tis clear," cried they, "our Mayor's a noddy, "And as for our Corporation—shocking "To think we buy gowns lined with ermine "For dolts that can't or won't determine "What's best to rid us of our vermin! "You hope, because you're old and obese, "To find in the furry civic robe ease? "Rouse up, Sirs! Give your brains a racking "To find the remedy we're lacking, "Or, sure as fate, we'll send you packing!" At this the Mayor and Corporation Quaked with a mighty consternation.

IV

An hour they sate in Council; At length the Mayor broke silence: "For a guilder I'd my ermine gown sell; "I wish I were a mile hence! "It's easy to bid one rack one's brain— "I'm sure my poor head aches again, "I've scratched it so, and all in vain. "Oh, for a trap, a trap, a trap!" Just as he said this, what should hap At the chamber door, but a gentle tap? "Bless us!" cried the Mayor, "what's that?" (With the Corporation as he sat, Looking little though wondrous fat; Nor brighter was his eye, nor moister Than a too-long-opened oyster, Save when at noon his paunch grew mutinous For a plate of turtle green and glutinous.) "Only a scraping of shoes on the mat! "Anything like the sound of a rat "Makes my heart go pit-a-pat!"

V

"Come in!" the Mayor cried, looking bigger, And in did come the strangest figure! His queer long coat, from heel to head Was half of yellow and half of red; And he himself was tall and thin, With sharp blue eyes, each like a pin, And light loose hair, yet swarthy skin, No tuft on cheek nor beard on chin, But lips where smiles went out and in; There was no guessing his kith and kin; And nobody could enough admire The tall man and his quaint attire. Quoth one: "It's as if my great-grandsire, "Starting up at the trump of Doom's tone, "Had walked this way from his painted tombstone!"

VI

He advanced to the council table: And, "Please your honours," said he, "I'm able, "By means of a secret charm, to draw "All creatures living beneath the sun, "That creep, or swim, or fly, or run, "After me so as you never saw! "And I chiefly use my charm "On creatures that do people harm,— "The mole, the toad, the newt, the viper: "And people call me the Pied Piper." (And here they noticed round his neck A scarf of red and yellow stripe To match his coat of the self-same cheque; And at the scarf's end hung a pipe; And his fingers, they noticed, were ever straying As if impatient to be playing Upon his pipe, as low it dangled Over his vesture so old-fangled.) "Yet," said he, "poor piper as I am, "In Tartary I freed the Cham, "Last June, from his huge swarm of gnats; "I eased in Asia the Nizam "Of a monstrous brood of vampyre bats: "And as for what your brain bewilders, "If I can rid your town of rats "Will you give me a thousand guilders?" "One! fifty thousand!" was the exclamation Of the astonished Mayor and Corporation.

VII

Into the street the Piper stept, Smiling first a little smile, As if he knew what magic slept In his quiet pipe the while; Then, like a musical adept, To blow the pipe his lips he wrinkled, And green and blue his sharp eyes twinkled, Like a candle-flame where salt is sprinkled; And ere three shrill notes the pipe had uttered, You heard as if an army muttered; And the muttering grew to a grumbling; And the grumbling grew to a mighty rumbling; And out of the houses the rats came tumbling. Great rats, small rats, lean rats, brawny rats, Brown rats, black rats, grey rats, tawny rats, Grave old plodders, gay young friskers, Fathers, mothers, uncles, cousins, Cocking tails, and pricking whiskers, Families by tens and dozens, Brothers, sisters, husbands, wives— Followed the Piper for their lives. From street to street he piped, advancing, And step for step they followed dancing, Until they came to the River Weser, Wherein all plunged and perished! —Save one, who, stout as Julius Cæsar, Swam across and lived to carry (As he, the manuscript he cherished) To Rat-land home his commentary: Which was, "At the first shrill note of the pipe "I heard a sound as of scraping tripe, "And putting apples, wondrous ripe, "Into a cider-press's gripe: "And a moving away of pickle-tub boards, "And a leaving ajar of conserve-cupboards, "And a drawing the corks of train-oil-flasks, "And a breaking the hoops of butter-casks: "And it seemed as if a voice "(Sweeter far than by harp or by psaltery "Is breathed) called out, 'Oh, rats, rejoice! "The world is grown to one vast drysaltery! "So munch on, crunch on, take your nuncheon, "Breakfast, dinner, supper, luncheon!' "And just as a bulky sugar-puncheon, "All ready staved, like a great sun shone "Glorious, scarce an inch before me, "Just as methought it said, 'Come, bore me!' "—I found the Weser rolling o'er me."

VIII

You should have heard the Hamelin people Ringing the bells till they rocked the steeple. "Go," cried the Mayor, "and get long poles, "Poke out the nests, and block up the holes! "Consult with carpenters and builders, "And leave in our town not even a trace "Of the rats!" When suddenly, up the face Of the Piper perked in the market-place, With a, "First, if you please, my thousand guilders!"

IX

A thousand guilders! The Mayor looked blue; So did the Corporation, too. For council dinners made rare havoc With Claret, Moselle, Vin-de-Grave, Hock; And half the money would replenish Their cellar's biggest butt with Rhenish. To pay this sum to a wandering fellow, With a gypsy coat of red and yellow! "Beside," quoth the Mayor, with a knowing wink, "Our business was done at the river's brink; "We saw with our eyes the vermin sink, "And what's dead can't come to life, I think. "So friend, we're not the folks to shrink "From the duty of giving you something to drink, "And a matter of money to put in your poke; "But, as for the guilders, what we spoke "Of them, as you very well know, was in joke. "Beside, our losses have made us thrifty. "A thousand guilders! come, take fifty!"

X

The Piper's face fell, and he cried, "No trifling! I can't wait, beside! "I've promised to visit by dinner-time "Bagdad, and accept the prime "Of the Head-Cook's pottage, all he's rich in, "For having left, in the Caliph's kitchen, "Of a nest of scorpions no survivor. "With him I proved no bargain-driver; "With you, don't think I'll bate a stiver! "And folks who put me in a passion "May find me pipe after another fashion."

XI

"How!" cried the Mayor, "d'ye think I'll brook "Being worse treated than a Cook? "Insulted by a lazy ribald "With idle pipe and vesture piebald! "You threaten us, fellow! Do your worst; "Blow your pipe there till you burst!"

XII

Once more he stept into the street, And to his lips again Laid his long pipe of smooth, straight cane; And ere he blew three notes (such sweet Soft notes as yet musician's cunning Never gave the enraptured air) There was a rustling that seemed like a bustling Of merry crowds justling at pitching and hustling, Small feet were pattering, wooden shoes clattering, Little hands clapping and little tongues chattering, And, like fowls in a farmyard when barley is scattering, Out came the children running. And all the little boys and girls, With rosy cheeks and flaxen curls, And sparkling eyes and teeth like pearls, Tripping and skipping ran merrily after The wonderful music with shouting and laughter.

XIII

The Mayor was dumb, and the Council stood As if they were changed into blocks of wood, Unable to move a step, or cry To the children merrily skipping by, —Could only follow with the eye That joyous crowd at the Piper's back. And now the Mayor was on the rack, And the wretched Council's bosoms beat, As the piper turned from the High Street To where the Weser rolled its waters Right in the way of their sons and daughters! However he turned from South to West, And to Koppelberg Hill his steps addressed, And after him the children pressed; Great was the joy in every breast. "He never can cross that mighty top! "He's forced to let the piping drop, "And we shall see our children stop!" When, lo, as they reached the mountain side, A wondrous portal opened wide, As if a cavern was suddenly hollowed; And the Piper advanced, and the children followed, And when all were in to the very last, The door in the mountain-side shut fast. Did I say all? No! One was lame, And could not dance the whole of the way; And in after years, if you would blame His sadness, he was used to say,— "It's dull in our town since my playmates left! "I can't forget that I'm bereft "Of all the pleasant sights they see, "Which the Piper also promised me: "For he led us, he said, to a joyous land, "Joining the town and just at hand, "Where waters gushed and fruit trees grew, "And flowers put forth a fairer hue, "And everything was strange and new; "The sparrows were brighter than peacocks here, "And their dogs outran our fallow-deer, "And honey-bees had lost their stings, "And horses were born with eagles' wings: "And just as I became assured "My lame foot would be speedily cured, "The music stopped, and I stood still, "And found myself outside the hill, "Left alone against my will, "To go now limping as before, "And never hear of that country more!"

XIV

Alas, alas for Hamelin! There came into many a burgher's pate A text which says that Heaven's gate Opes to the rich at as easy rate As the needle's eye takes a camel in! The Mayor sent East, West, North, and South, To offer the Piper, by word of mouth, Wherever it was man's lot to find him, Silver and gold to his heart's content, If he'd only return the way he went, And bring the children behind him. But when they saw 'twas a lost endeavour, And Piper and dancers were gone for ever, They made a decree that lawyers never Should think their records dated duly If, after the day of the month and the year, These words did not as well appear, "And so long after what happened here "On the Twenty-second of July, "Thirteen hundred and seventy-six": And the better in memory to fix The place of the children's last retreat, They called it, the Pied Piper's Street— Where any one playing on pipe or tabor Was sure for the future to lose his labour. Nor suffered they hostelry or tavern To shock with mirth a street so solemn; But opposite the place of the cavern They wrote the story on a column, And on the great church-window painted The same, to make the world acquainted How their children were stolen away, And there it stands to this very day. And I must not omit to say That in Transylvania there's a tribe Of alien people that ascribe The outlandish ways and dress On which their neighbours lay such stress, To their fathers and mothers having risen Out of some subterraneous prison Into which they were trepanned Long ago in a mighty band Out of Hamelin town in Brunswick land, But how or why, they don't understand.

XV

So, Willy, let you and me be wipers Of scores out with all men,—especially pipers! And, whether they pipe us free from rats or from mice, If we've promised them aught, let us keep our promise!

Robert Browning.

Hervé Riel

On the sea and at the Hogue, sixteen hundred ninety-two, Did the English fight the French,—woe to France! And, the thirty-first of May, helter-skelter thro' the blue, Like a crowd of frightened porpoises a shoal of sharks pursue, Came crowding ship on ship to St. Malo on the Rance, With the English fleet in view.

'Twas the squadron that escaped, with the victor in full chase; First and foremost of the drove, in his great ship, Damfreville; Close on him fled, great and small, Twenty-two good ships in all; And they signalled to the place "Help the winners of a race! Get us guidance, give us harbour, take us quick—or, quicker still, Here's the English can and will!"

Then the pilots of the place put out brisk and leapt on board; "Why, what hope or chance have ships like these to pass?" laughed they: "Rocks to starboard, rocks to port, all the passage scarred and scored, Shall the *Formidable* here with her twelve and eighty guns Think to make the river-mouth by the single narrow way, Trust to enter where 'tis ticklish for a craft of twenty tons, And with flow at full beside? Now, 'tis slackest ebb of tide. Reach the mooring? Rather say, While rock stands or water runs, Not a ship will leave the bay!"

Then was called a council straight. Brief and bitter the debate: "Here's the English at our heels; would you have them take in tow All that's left us of the fleet, linked together stern and bow, For a prize to Plymouth Sound? Better run the ships aground!" (Ended Damfreville his speech.) Not a minute more to wait! "Let the Captains all and each Shove ashore, then blow up, burn the vessels on the beach! France must undergo her fate.

"Give the word!" But no such word Was ever spoke or heard; For up stood, for out stepped, for in struck amid all these — A Captain? A Lieutenant? A Mate—first, second, third? No such man of mark, and meet With his betters to compete! But a simple Breton sailor pressed by Tourville for the fleet, A poor coasting-pilot he, Hervé Riel the Croisickese. And, "What mockery or malice have we here?" cries Hervé Riel: "Are you mad, you Malouins? Are you cowards, fools, or rogues? Talk to me of rocks and shoals, me who took the soundings, tell On my fingers every bank, every shallow, every swell 'Twixt the offing here and Grève where the river disembogues? Are you bought by English gold? Is it love the lying's for? Morn and eve, night and day, Have I piloted your bay, Entered free and anchored fast at foot of Solidor.

"Burn the fleet and ruin France? That were worse than fitty Hogues! Sirs, they know I speak the truth! Sirs, believe me there's a way! Only let me lead the line, Have the biggest ship to steer, Get this *Formidable* clear, Make the others follow mine, And I lead them, most and least, by a passage I know well, Right to Solidor past Grève, And there lay them safe and sound; And if one ship misbehave, —Keel so much as grate the ground, Why, I've nothing but my life,—here's my head!" cries Hervé Riel.

Not a minute more to wait. "Steer us in, then, small and great! Take the helm, lead the line, save the squadron!" cried his chief. "Captains, give the sailor place! He is Admiral, in brief." Still the north-wind, by God's grace! See the noble fellow's face, As the big ship with a bound, Clears the entry like a hound, Keeps the passage as its inch of way were the wide seas profound! See, safe thro' shoal and rock, How they follow in a flock, Not a ship that misbehaves, not a keel that grates the ground, Not a spar that comes to grief! The peril, see, is past, All are harboured to the last, And just as Hervé Riel hollas "Anchor!"—sure as fate Up the English come, too late!

So, the storm subsides to calm: They see the green trees wave On the heights o'erlooking Grève. Hearts that bled are stanched with balm. "Just our rapture to enhance, Let the English rake the bay, Gnash their teeth and glare askance, As they cannonade away! 'Neath rampired Solidor pleasant riding on the Rance!" How hope succeeds despair on each Captain's countenance! Out burst all with one accord, "This is Paradise for Hell! Let France, let France's King Thank the man that did the thing!" What a shout, and all one word, "Hervé Riel!"

As he stepped in front once more, Not a symptom of surprise In the frank blue Breton eyes, Just the same man as before.

Then said Damfreville, "My friend, I must speak out at the end, Though I find the speaking hard. Praise is deeper than the lips: You have saved the King his ships, You must name your own reward. 'Faith our sun was near eclipse! Demand whate'er you will, France remains your debtor still. Ask to heart's content and have! or my name's not Damfreville."

Then a beam of fun outbroke On the bearded mouth that spoke, As the honest heart laughed through Those frank eyes of Breton blue: "Since I needs must say my say, Since on board the duty's done, And from Malo Roads to Croisic Point, what is it but a run?— Since 'tis ask and have, I may— Since the others go ashore— Come! A good whole holiday! Leave to go and see my wife, whom I call the Belle Aurore!" That he asked and that he got,—nothing more.

Name and deed alike are lost: Not a pillar nor a post In his Croisic keeps alive the feat as it befell; Not a head in white and black On a single fishing smack, In memory of the man but for whom had gone to wrack All that France saved from the fight whence England bore the bell. Go to Paris: rank on rank Search the heroes flung pell-mell On the Louvre, face and flank! You shall look long enough ere you come to Hervé Riel. So, for better and for worse, Hervé Riel, accept my verse! In my verse, Hervé Riel, do thou once more Save the squadron, honour France, love thy wife, the Belle Aurore!

Robert Browning.

Vision of Belshazzar.

The King was on his throne, The Satraps throng'd the hall: A thousand bright lamps shone O'er that high festival. A thousand cups of gold, In Judah deem'd divine— Jehovah's vessels hold The godless Heathen's wine.

In that same hour and hall, The fingers of a hand Came forth against the wall, And wrote as if on sand: The fingers of a man— A solitary hand Along the letters ran, And traced them like a wand.

The monarch saw, and shook, And bade no more rejoice; All bloodless wax'd his look, And tremulous his voice. "Let the men of lore appear, The wisest of the earth, And expound the words of fear, Which mar our royal mirth."

Chaldea's seers are good, But here they have no skill; And the unknown letters stood Untold and awful still. And Babel's men of age Are wise and deep in lore; But now they were not sage, They saw—but knew no more.

A captive in the land, A stranger and a youth, He heard the king's command, He saw that writing's truth. The lamps around were bright, The prophecy in view; He read it on that night— The morrow proved it true.

"Belshazzar's grave is made, His kingdom pass'd away, He, in the balance weigh'd, Is light and worthless clay; The shroud his robe of state, His canopy the stone; The Mede is at his gate! The Persian on his throne!"

George Gordon, Lord Byron.

Solomon and the Bees

When Solomon was reigning in his glory, Unto his throne the Queen of Sheba came— (So in the Talmud you may read the story)— Drawn by the magic of the monarch's fame, To see the splendors of his court, and bring Some fitting tribute to the mighty King.

Nor this alone: much had her highness heard What flowers of learning graced the royal speech; What gems of wisdom dropped with every word; What wholesome lessons he was wont to teach In pleasing proverbs; and she wished, in sooth, To know if Rumor spoke the simple truth.

Besides, the Queen had heard (which piqued her most) How through the deepest riddles he could spy; How all the curious arts that women boast Were quite transparent to his piercing eye; And so the Queen had come—a royal guest— To put the sage's cunning to the test.

And straight she held before the monarch's view, In either hand, a radiant wreath of flowers; The one bedecked with every charming hue, Was newly culled from Nature's choicest bowers; The other, no less fair in every part, Was the rare product of divinest Art.

"Which is the true, and which the false?" she said. Great Solomon was silent. All amazed, Each wondering courtier shook his puzzled head; While at the garlands long the monarch gazed, As one who sees a miracle, and fain For very rapture, ne'er would speak again.

"Which is the true?" once more the woman asked, Pleased at the fond amazement of the King; "So wise a head should not be hardly tasked, Most learned Liege, with such a trivial thing!" But still the sage was silent; it was plain A deepening doubt perplexed the royal brain.

While thus he pondered, presently he sees, Hard by the casement—so the story goes— A little band of busy bustling bees, Hunting for honey in a withered rose. The monarch smiled, and raised his royal head; "Open the window!"—that was all he said.

The window opened at the King's command; Within the rooms the eager insects flew, And sought the flowers in Sheba's dexter hand! And so the King and all the courtiers knew That wreath was Nature's; and the baffled Queen Returned to tell the wonders she had seen.

My story teaches (every tale should bear A fitting moral) that the wise may find In trifles light as atoms of the air Some useful lesson to enrich the mind— Some truth designed to profit or to please— As Israel's King learned wisdom from the bees.

John G. Saxe.

The Burial of Moses

"And He buried him in a valley in the land of Moab, over against Beth-peor: but no man knoweth of his sepulchre unto this day."—Deut. xxxiv. .

By Nebo's lonely mountain, On this side Jordan's wave, In a vale in the land of Moab There lies a lonely grave. And no man knows that sepulchre, And no man saw it e'er, For the angels of God upturn'd the sod, And laid the dead man there.

That was the grandest funeral That ever passed on earth; But no man heard the trampling, Or saw the train go forth—

Noiselessly as the daylight Comes back when night is done, And the crimson streak on ocean's cheek Grows into the great sun;

Noiselessly as the spring-time Her crown of verdure weaves, And all the trees on all the hills, Open their thousand leaves; So without sound of music, Or voice of them that wept, Silently down from the mountain's crown, The great procession swept.

Perchance the bald old eagle, On grey Beth-peor's height, Out of his lonely eyrie Look'd on the wondrous sight; Perchance the lion stalking, Still shuns that hallow'd spot, For beast and bird have seen and heard That which man knoweth not.

But when the warrior dieth, His comrades in the war, With arms reversed and muffled drum, Follow his funeral car; They show the banners taken, They tell his battles won, And after him lead his masterless steed While peals the minute gun.

Amid the noblest of the land We lay the sage to rest, And give the bard an honour'd place With costly marble drest, In the great minster transept Where lights like glories fall (And the organ rings, and the sweet choir sings) Along the emblazon'd wall.

This was the truest warrior That ever buckled sword; This the most gifted poet That ever breathed a word. And never earth's philosopher Traced with his golden pen On the deathless page truths half so sage As he wrote down for men.

And had he not high honour, The hill-side for a pall, To lie in state, while angels wait With stars for tapers tall, And the dark rock-pines, like tossing plumes, Over his bier to wave, And God's own hand in that lonely land To lay him in the grave.

In that strange grave without a name, Whence his uncoffin'd clay Shall break again, O wondrous thought! Before the Judgment Day, And stand with glory wrapt around On the hills he never trod, And speak of the strife, that won our life, With the Incarnate Son of God.

O lonely grave in Moab's land! O dark Beth-peor's hill! Speak to these curious hearts of ours, And teach them to be still. God hath his mysteries of grace, Ways that we cannot tell, He hides them deep, like the hidden sleep Of him he loved so well.

Cecil Frances Alexander.

INTERLEAVES
When Banners Are Waving

Here are poems of Valor, Fortitude, Fearlessness, Courage. Give yourself up to the martial swing of the verse, with its clang of armor, its champing of war-steed, its sound of pibroch, its blare of trumpet, fife, and drum, its dancing of plumes and glitter of helmets. Pray Heaven that the fighting be all in a good cause and that the tramp, tramp of soldierly feet be that of the armies of Right, for there is no resisting this spirit of daring and bearing when it is voiced so nobly.

"When cannon are roaring, And hot bullets flying, He that would honor win Must not fear dying."

Here are hymns in praise of famous battles that have changed the fate of nations; here, records of gallant deeds that make the blood leap in the veins. Into the Valley of Death rode the immortal Six Hundred, and into that same Valley plunged "furious Frank and fiery Hun," Scot, Turk, Greek, and the brave Huguenot charging at Ivry for the Golden Lilies of France. Here are the songs of triumph, the loud hurrahs when the red field is won; here tales of glorious defeats and no less splendid failures; here, too, the dirge for the storied Brave, who lie at rest by all their Country's wishes blest.

The banners that once beckoned on the arméd hosts are hanging to-day in dim cathedrals, tattered, faded, and torn; high-hung banners that with every "opened door seem the old wave of battle to remember." And as for the heroes who carried them, can we not say, as of Marco Bozzaris,

"For ye are Freedom's now, and Fame's, Among the few, th' immortal names That were not born to die."

XIV
WHEN BANNERS ARE WAVING
When Banners Are Waving

When banners are waving, And lances a-pushing; When captains are shouting, And war-horses rushing; When cannon are roaring, And hot bullets flying, He that would honour win, Must not fear dying.

Though shafts fly so thick That it seems to be snowing; Though streamlets with blood More than water are flowing; Though with sabre and bullet Our bravest are dying, We speak of revenge, but We ne'er speak of flying.

Come, stand to it, heroes! The heathen are coming; Horsemen are round the walls, Riding and running; Maidens and matrons all Arm! arm! are crying, From petards the wildfire's Flashing and flying.

The trumpets from turrets high Loudly are braying; The steeds for the onset Are snorting and neighing; As waves in the ocean, The dark plumes are dancing; As stars in the blue sky, The helmets are glancing.

Their ladders are planting, Their sabres are sweeping; Now swords from our sheaths By the thousand are leaping; Like the flash of the levin Ere men hearken thunder, Swords gleam, and the steel caps Are cloven asunder.

The shouting has ceased, And the flashing of cannon! I looked from the turret For crescent and pennon: As flax touched by fire, As hail in the river, They were smote, they were fallen, And had melted for ever.

Unknown.

Battle of the Baltic

Of Nelson and the north Sing the glorious day's renown, When to battle fierce came forth All the might of Denmark's crown, And her arms along the deep proudly shone; By each gun the lighted brand In a bold, determined hand, And the prince of all the land Led them on.

Like leviathans afloat Lay their bulwarks on the brine; While the sign of battle flew On the lofty British line— It was ten of April morn by the chime. As they drifted on their path There was silence deep as death; And the boldest held his breath For a time.

But the might of England flushed To anticipate the scene; And her van the fleeter rushed O'er the deadly space between. "Hearts of oak!" our captain cried; when each gun From its adamantine lips Spread a death-shade round the ships, Like the hurricane eclipse Of the sun.

Again! again! again! And the havoc did not slack, Till a feeble cheer the Dane To our cheering sent us back; Their shots along the deep slowly boom— Then ceased—and all is wail, As they strike the shattered sail, Or in conflagration pale, Light the gloom.

Out spoke the victor then, As he hailed them o'er the wave: "Ye are brothers! ye are men! And we conquer but to save; So peace instead of death let us bring; But yield, proud foe, thy fleet, With the crews, at England's feet, And make submission meet To our king."

Then Denmark blessed our chief, That he gave her wounds repose; And the sounds of joy and grief From her people wildly rose, As death withdrew his shades from the day. While the sun looked smiling bright O'er a wide and woeful sight, Where the fires of funeral light Died away.

Now joy, old England, raise! For the tidings of thy might, By the festal cities' blaze, Whilst the wine-cup shines in light; And yet, amidst that joy and uproar, Let us think of them that sleep Full many a fathom deep, By thy wild and stormy steep, Elsinore!

Brave hearts! to Britain's pride Once so faithful and so true, On the deck of fame that died, With the gallant, good Riou— Soft sigh the winds of heaven o'er their grave! While the billow mournful rolls, And the mermaid's song condoles, Singing glory to the souls Of the brave!

Thomas Campbell.

The Pipes at Lucknow

Pipes of the misty moorlands, Voice of the glens and hills; The droning of the torrents, The treble of the rills! Not the braes of broom and heather, Nor the mountains dark with rain, Nor maiden bower, nor border tower, Have heard your sweetest strain!

Dear to the Lowland reaper, And plaided mountaineer,— To the cottage and the castle The Scottish pipes are dear;— Sweet sounds the ancient pibroch O'er mountain, loch, and glade; But the sweetest of all music The pipes at Lucknow played.

Day by day the Indian tiger Louder yelled, and nearer crept; Round and round, the jungle-serpent Near and nearer circles swept. "Pray for rescue, wives and mothers,— Pray to-day!" the soldier said, "To-morrow, death's between us And the wrong and shame we dread."

Oh, they listened, looked, and waited, Till their hope became despair; And the sobs of low bewailing Filled the pauses of their prayer. Then up spake a Scottish maiden, With her ear unto the ground: "Dinna ye hear it?—dinna ye hear it? The pipes o' Havelock sound!"

Hushed the wounded man his groaning; Hushed the wife her little ones; Alone they heard the drum-roll And the roar of Sepoy guns. But to sounds of home and childhood The Highland ear was true;— As her mother's cradle crooning The mountain pipes she knew.

Like the march of soundless music Through the vision of the seer, More of feeling than of hearing, Of the heart than of the ear, She knew the droning pibroch, She knew the Campbell's call: "Hark! hear ye no' MacGregor's, The grandest o' them all!"

O, they listened, dumb and breathless, And they caught the sound at last; Faint and far beyond the Goomtee Rose and fell the piper's blast! Then a burst of wild thanksgiving Mingled woman's voice and man's; "God be praised!—the march of Havelock! The piping of the clans!"

Louder, nearer, fierce as vengeance, Sharp and shrill as swords at strife, Came the wild MacGregor's clan-call, Stinging all the air to life. But when the far-off dust cloud To plaided legions grew, Full tenderly and blithesomely The pipes of rescue blew!

Round the silver domes of Lucknow, Moslem mosque and Pagan shrine, Breathed the air to Britons dearest, The air of Auld Lang Syne. O'er the cruel roll of war drums Rose that sweet and homelike strain; And the tartan clove the turban As the Goomtee cleaves the plain.

Dear to the corn-land reaper And plaided mountaineer,— To the cottage and the castle The piper's song is dear. Sweet sounds the Gaelic pibroch O'er mountain, glen, and glade; But the sweetest of all music The pipes at Lucknow played!

John Greenleaf Whittier.

The Battle of Agincourt

Fair stood the wind for France, When we our sails advance, Nor now to prove our chance Longer will tarry; But putting to the main, At Caux, the mouth of Seine, With all his martial train, Landed King Harry.

And taking many a fort, Furnished in warlike sort, Marched towards Agincourt In happy hour— Skirmishing day by day With those that stopped his way, Where the French general lay With all his power.

Which in his height of pride, King Henry to deride, His ransom to provide To the king sending. Which he neglects the while, As from a nation vile, Yet with an angry smile Their fall portending.

And turning to his men, Quoth our brave Henry then, "Though they be one to ten, Be not amazèd; Yet have we well begun, Battles so bravely won Have ever to the sun By fame been raisèd.

"And for myself," quoth he, "This my full rest shall be, England ne'er mourn for me, Nor more esteem me. Victor I will remain, Or on this earth lie slain, Never shall she sustain Loss to redeem me."

Poitiers and Cressy tell, When most their pride did swell, Under our swords they fell; No less our skill is Than when our grandsire great, Claiming the regal seat, By many a warlike feat Lopped the French lilies.

The Duke of York so dread The eager vaward led; With the main Henry sped, Amongst his henchmen. Excester had the rear— A braver man not there: O Lord! how hot they were On the false Frenchmen!

They now to fight are gone; Armor on armor shone; Drum now to drum did groan— To hear was wonder; That with the cries they make The very earth did shake; Trumpet to trumpet spake, Thunder to thunder.

Well it thine age became, O noble Erpingham! Which did the signal aim To our hid forces; When, from a meadow by, Like a storm suddenly, The English archery Struck the French horses, With Spanish yew so strong, Arrows a cloth-yard long, That like to serpents stung, Piercing the weather; None from his fellow starts, But playing manly parts, And like true English hearts, Stuck close together.

When down their bows they threw, And forth their bilboes drew, And on the French they flew, Not one was tardy; Arms were from shoulders sent, Scalps to the teeth were rent, Down the French peasants went, Our men were hardy.

This while our noble King, His broad sword brandishing, Down the French host did ding, As to o'erwhelm it; And many a deep wound lent, His arms with blood besprent, And many a cruel dent Bruisèd his helmet.

Gloucester, that duke so good, Next of the royal blood, For famous England stood, With his brave brother, Clarence, in steel so bright, Though but a maiden knight, Yet in that furious fight Scarce such another.

Warwick in blood did wade; Oxford the foe invade, And cruel slaughter made, Still as they ran up. Suffolk his axe did ply; Beaumont and Willoughby Bare them right doughtily, Ferrers and Fanhope.

Upon Saint Crispin's Day Fought was this noble fray, Which fame did not delay To England to carry; Oh, when shall Englishmen With such acts fill a pen, Or England breed again Such a King Harry?

Michael Drayton.

The Battle of Blenheim

It was a summer's evening, Old Kaspar's work was done, And he before his cottage door Was sitting in the sun; And by him sported on the green His little grandchild Wilhelmine.

She saw her brother Peterkin Roll something large and round, Which he, beside the rivulet, In playing there, had found. He came to ask what he had found, That was so large, and smooth, and round.

Old Kaspar took it from the boy, Who stood expectant by; And then the old man shook his head, And, with a natural sigh, "'Tis some poor fellow's skull," said he, "Who fell in the great victory!"

"I find them in the garden, For there's many here about; And often when I go to plough, The ploughshare turns them out; For many thousand men," said he, "Were slain in that great victory!"

"Now tell us what 'twas all about," Young Peterkin he cries; And little Wilhelmine looks up With wonder-waiting eyes; "Now tell us all about the war, And what they kill each other for."

"It was the English," Kaspar cried, "Who put the French to rout; But what they killed each other for I could not well make out. But everybody said," quoth he, "That 'twas a famous victory!

"My father lived at Blenheim then, Yon little stream hard by: They burned his dwelling to the ground, And he was forced to fly; So with his wife and child he fled, Nor had he where to rest his head.

"With fire and sword the country round Was wasted far and wide; And many a childing mother then And new-born baby died. But things like that, you know, must be At every famous victory.

"They say it was a shocking sight After the field was won; For many thousand bodies here Lay rotting in the sun. But things like that, you know, must be After a famous victory.

"Great praise the Duke of Marlborough won, And our good Prince Eugene." "Why, 'twas a very wicked thing!" Said little Wilhelmine. "Nay, nay, my little girl," quoth he, "It was a famous victory!

"And everybody praised the Duke Who this great fight did win." "But what good came of it at last?" Quoth little Peterkin. "Why that I cannot tell," said he, "But 'twas a famous victory."

Robert Southey.

The Armada: A Fragment

Attend, all ye who list to hear our noble England's praise; I sing of the thrice famous deeds she wrought in ancient days, When that great fleet invincible against her bore, in vain The richest spoils of Mexico, the stoutest hearts in Spain. It was about the lovely close of a warm summer's day, There came a gallant merchant-ship full sail to Plymouth Bay; The crew had seen Castile's black fleet, beyond Aurigny's isle, At earliest twilight, on the waves lie heaving many a mile. At sunrise she escaped their van, by God's especial grace; And the tall Pinta, till the noon, had held her close in chase. Forthwith a guard at every gun was placed along the wall; The beacon blazed upon the roof of Edgecumbe's lofty hall; Many a light fishing-bark put out to pry along the coast; And with loose rein and bloody spur rode inland many a post.

With his white hair unbonneted, the stout old sheriff comes; Behind him march the halberdiers; before him sound the drums: The yeoman round the market cross make clear an ample space; For there behooves him to set up the standard of Her Grace: And haughtily the trumpets peal, and gaily dance the bells, As slow upon the laboring wind the royal blazon swells.

Look how the Lion of the sea lifts up his ancient crown, And underneath his deadly paw treads the gay lilies down. So stalked he when he turned to flight, on that famed Picard field, Bohemia's plume, and Genoa's bow, and Cæsar's eagle shield. So glared he when at Agincourt in wrath he turned to bay, And crushed and torn beneath his claws the princely hunters lay. Ho! strike the flagstaff deep, Sir Knight: ho! scatter flowers, fair maids: Ho! gunners, fire a loud salute: ho! gallants, draw your blades: Thou sun, shine on her joyously; ye breezes, waft her wide; Our glorious *Semper Eadem*, the banner of our pride.

The freshening breeze of eve unfurled that banner's massy fold; The parting gleam of sunshine kissed that haughty scroll of gold; Night sank upon the dusky beach, and on the purple sea, Such night in England ne'er had been, nor e'er again shall be. From Eddystone to Berwick bounds, from Lynn to Milford Bay, That time of slumber was as bright and busy as the day;

For swift to east and swift to west the ghastly war-flame spread, High on St. Michael's Mount it shone: it shone on Beachy Head. Far o'er the deep the Spaniard saw, along each southern shire, Cape beyond cape, in endless range those twinkling points of fire. The fisher left his skiff to rock on Tamar's glittering waves: The rugged miners poured to war from Mendip's sunless caves: O'er Longleat's towers, o'er Cranbourne's oaks, the fiery herald flew: He roused the shepherds of Stonehenge, the rangers of Beaulieu. Right sharp and quick the bells all night rang out from Bristol town, And ere the day three hundred horse had met on Clifton Down; The sentinel on Whitehall gate looked forth into the night, And saw o'erhanging Richmond Hill, that streak of blood-red light: Then bugle's note and cannon's roar the death-like silence broke, And with one start, and with one cry, the royal city woke. At once on all her stately gates arose the answering fires; At once the wild alarum clashed from all her reeling spires; From all the batteries of the Tower pealed loud the voice of fear; And all the thousand masts of Thames sent back a louder cheer: And from the furthest wards was heard the rush of hurrying feet, And the broad streams of pikes and flags rushed down each roaring street; And broader still became the blaze, and louder still the din, As fast from every village round the horse came spurring in; And eastward straight from wild Blackheath the warlike errand went, And roused in many an ancient hall the gallant squires of Kent: Southward from Surrey's pleasant hills flew those bright couriers forth; High on bleak Hampstead's swarthy moor they started for the north; And on, and on, without a pause, untired they bounded still; All night from tower to tower they sprang; they sprang from hill to hill; Till the proud Peak unfurled the flag o'er Darwin's rocky dales; Till like volcanoes flared to heaven the stormy hills of Wales; Till twelve fair counties saw the blaze on Malvern's lonely height; Till streamed in crimson on the wind the Wrekin's crest of light; Till broad and fierce the star came forth, on Ely's stately fane, And tower and hamlet rose in arms o'er all the boundless plain; Till Belvoir's lordly terraces the sign to Lincoln sent, And Lincoln sped the message on o'er the wide vale of Trent: Till Skiddaw saw the fire that burned on Gaunt's embattled pile, And the red glare on Skiddaw roused the burghers of Carlisle.

Thomas Babington, Lord Macauley.

Ivry

A Song of the Huguenots.

Now glory to the Lord of hosts, from whom all glories are! And glory to our Sovereign Liege, King Henry of Navarre! Now let there be the merry sound of music and of dance, Through thy corn-fields green, and sunny vines, oh pleasant land of France! And thou, Rochelle, our own Rochelle, proud city of the waters, Again let rapture light the eyes of all thy mourning daughters. As thou wert constant in our ills, be joyous in our joy, For cold, and stiff, and still are they who wrought thy walls annoy. Hurrah! Hurrah! a single field hath turned the chance of war, Hurrah! Hurrah! for Ivry, and Henry of Navarre.

Oh! how our hearts were beating, when at the dawn of day We saw the army of the League drawn out in long array; With all its priest-led citizens, and all its rebel peers, And Appenzel's stout infantry, and Egmont's Flemish spears. There rode the brood of false Lorraine, the curses of our land; And dark Mayenne was in the midst, a truncheon in his hand: And, as we looked on them, we thought of Seine's empurpled flood, And good Coligni's hoary hair all dabbled with his blood; And we cried unto the living God, who rules the fate of war, To fight for His own holy name, and Henry of Navarre.

The King is come to marshal us, in all his armor drest; And he has bound a snow-white plume upon his gallant crest. He looked upon his people, and a tear was in his eye; He looked upon the traitors, and his glance was stern and high. Right graciously he smiled on us, as rolled from wing to wing, Down all our line, a deafening shout, "God save our Lord the King!"

"And if my standard-bearer fall, as fall full well he may— For never saw I promise yet of such a bloody fray— Press where ye see my white plume shine, amidst the ranks of war, And be your oriflamme to-day the helmet of Navarre."

Hurrah! the foes are moving. Hark to the mingled din Of fife, and steed, and trump, and drum, and roaring culverin. The fiery Duke is pricking fast across Saint André's plain, With all the hireling chivalry of Guelders and Almayne. Now by the lips of those ye love, fair gentlemen of France, Charge for the Golden Lilies—upon them with the lance! A thousand spurs are striking deep, a thousand spears in rest, A thousand knights are pressing close behind the snow-white crest; And in they burst, and on they rushed, while, like a guiding star, Amidst the thickest carnage blazed the helmet of Navarre.

Now, God be praised, the day is ours! Mayenne hath turned his rein; D'Aumale hath cried for quarter; the Flemish Count is slain; Their ranks are breaking like thin clouds before a Biscay gale; The field is heaped with bleeding steeds, and flags, and cloven mail. And then, we thought on vengeance, and, all along our van, "Remember St. Bartholomew!" was passed from man to man; But out spake gentle Henry—"No Frenchman is my foe: Down, down with every foreigner, but let your brethren go." Oh! was there ever such a knight, in friendship or in war, As our Sovereign Lord King Henry, the soldier of Navarre!

Right well fought all the Frenchmen who fought for France to-day; And many a lordly banner God gave them for a prey. But we of the religion have borne us best in fight; And the good lord of Rosny hath ta'en the cornet white— Our own true Maximilian the cornet white hath ta'en, The cornet white with crosses black, the flag of false Lorraine. Up with it high; unfurl it wide—that all the host may know How God hath humbled the proud house which wrought His Church such woe. Then on the ground, while trumpets sound their loudest point of war, Fling the red shreds, a footcloth meet for Henry of Navarre.

Ho! maidens of Vienna; ho! matrons of Lucerne, Weep, weep, and rend your hair for those who never shall return. Ho! Philip, send, for charity, thy Mexican pistoles, That Antwerp monks may sing a mass for thy poor spearmen's souls. Ho! gallant nobles of the League, look that your arms be bright; Ho! burghers of Saint Genevieve, keep watch and ward to-night; For our God hath crushed the tyrant, our God hath raised the slave, And mocked the counsel of the wise, and the valor of the brave. Then glory to His holy name, from whom all glories are; And glory to our Sovereign Lord, King Henry of Navarre!

Thomas Babington, Lord Macaulay.

On the Loss of the Royal George
Written when the News Arrived, September, .

Toll for the brave! The brave that are no more! All sunk beneath the wave, Fast by their native shore!

Eight hundred of the brave, Whose courage well was tried, Had made the vessel heel, And laid her on her side.

A land breeze shook the shrouds, And she was overset; Down went the Royal George, With all her crew complete.

Toll for the brave! Brave Kempenfelt is gone; His last sea-fight is fought; His work of glory done.

It was not in the battle; No tempest gave the shock; She sprang no fatal leak; She ran upon no rock.

His sword was in its sheath; His fingers held the pen, When Kempenfelt went down, With twice four hundred men.

Weigh the vessel up, Once dreaded by our foes! And mingle with our cup The tear that England owes.

Her timbers yet are sound, And she may float again, Full charged with England's thunder, And plough the distant main.

But Kempenfelt is gone, His victories are o'er, And he and his eight hundred Must plough the waves no more.

William Cowper.

The Charge of the Light Brigade

Half a league, half a league, Half a league onward, All in the valley of Death, Rode the six hundred. "Forward, the Light Brigade! Charge for the guns!" he said: Into the valley of Death Rode the six hundred.

"Forward, the Light Brigade!" Was there a man dismayed? Not though the soldier knew Some one had blundered; Theirs not to make reply, Theirs not to reason why, Theirs but to do and die;— Into the valley of Death Rode the six hundred.

Cannon to right of them, Cannon to left of them, Cannon in front of them Volleyed and thundered; Stormed at with shot and shell, Boldly they rode and well; Into the jaws of Death, Into the mouth of Hell Rode the six hundred.

Flashed all their sabres bare, Flashed as they turned in air, Sabring the gunners there, Charging an army, while All the world wondered: Plunged in the battery smoke, Right through the line they broke; Cossack and Russian Reeled from the sabre-stroke Shattered and sundered. Then they rode back, but not— Not the six hundred.

Cannon to right of them, Cannon to left of them, Cannon behind them Volleyed and thundered. Stormed at with shot and shell, While horse and hero fell, Those that had fought so well Came through the jaws of Death, Back from the mouth of Hell, All that was left of them, Left of six hundred.

When can their glory fade? Oh, the wild charge they made! All the world wondered. Honor the charge they made! Honor the Light Brigade! Noble six hundred!

Alfred, Lord Tennyson.

Bannockburn

Robert Bruce's Address to his Army.

Scots, wha hae wi' Wallace bled, Scots, wham Bruce has aften led, Welcome to your gory bed Or to victorie!

Now's the day, and now's the hour; See the front o' battle lower; See approach proud Edward's power— Chains and slaverie!

Wha will be a traitor knave? Wha can fill a coward's grave? Wha sae base as be a slave? Let him turn and flee!

Wha for Scotland's king and law Freedom's sword will strongly draw, Freeman stand, or freeman fa', Let him follow me!

By oppression's woes and pains! By your sons in servile chains! We will drain our dearest veins, But they shall be free!

Lay the proud usurpers low! Tyrants fall in every foe! Liberty's in every blow!— Let us do or die!

Robert Burns.

The Night Before Waterloo

There was a sound of revelry by night. And Belgium's capital had gather'd then Her Beauty and her Chivalry, and bright The lamps shone o'er fair women and brave men; A thousand hearts beat happily; and when Music arose with its voluptuous swell, Soft eyes look'd love to eyes which spake again, And all went merry as a marriage bell; But hush! hark! a deep sound strikes like a rising knell!

Did ye not hear it?—No; 'twas but the wind, Or the car rattling o'er the stony street; On with the dance! let joy be unconfined; No sleep till morn, when Youth and Pleasure meet To chase the glowing Hours with flying feet. But hark! that heavy sound breaks in once more, As if the clouds its echo would repeat; And nearer, clearer, deadlier than before! Arm! arm! it is—it is—the cannon's opening roar!

*   *   *   *

Ah! then and there was hurrying to and fro, And gathering tears, and tremblings of distress, And cheeks all pale, which but an hour ago Blush'd at the praise of their own loveliness; And there were sudden partings, such as press The life from out young hearts, and choking sighs Which ne'er might be repeated: who could guess If ever more should meet those mutual eyes, Since upon night so sweet such awful morn could rise!

And there was mounting in hot haste: the steed, The mustering squadron, and the clattering car, Went pouring forward with impetuous speed, And swiftly forming in the ranks of war; And the deep thunder peal on peal afar; And near, the beat of the alarming drum Roused up the soldier ere the morning star; While throng'd the citizens with terror dumb, Or whispering with white lips—"The foe! They come! they come!" Last noon beheld them full of lusty life, Last eve in Beauty's circle proudly gay, The midnight brought the signal-sound of strife, The morn the marshalling in arms—the day Battle's magnificently stern array! The thunder-clouds close o'er it, which when rent The earth is cover'd thick with other clay, Which her own clay shall cover, heap'd and pent, Rider and horse—friend, foe,—in one red burial blent!

George Gordon, Lord Byron.

From "Childe Harold's Pilgrimage."

Hohenlinden

On Linden when the sun was low, All bloodless lay the untrodden snow, And dark as winter was the flow Of Iser, rolling rapidly.

But Linden saw another sight When the drum beat, at dead of night, Commanding fires of death to light The darkness of her scenery.

By torch and trumpet fast array'd Each horseman drew his battle-blade, And furious every charger neigh'd, To join the dreadful revelry.

Then shook the hills with thunder riven, Then rush'd the steed to battle driven, And louder than the bolts of heaven Far flash'd the red artillery.

But redder yet that light shall glow On Linden's hills of stainéd snow, And darker yet shall be the flow Of Iser, rolling rapidly.

'Tis morn, but scarce yon lurid sun Can pierce the war-clouds, rolling dun, Where furious Frank and fiery Hun Shout in their sulphurous canopy.

The combat deepens. On, ye Brave, Who rush to glory, or the grave! Wave, Munich, all thy banners wave! And charge with all thy chivalry!

Few, few, shall part where many meet! The snow shall be their winding-sheet, And every turf beneath their feet Shall be a soldier's sepulchre.

Thomas Campbell.

Incident of the French Camp

You know we French stormed Ratisbon: A mile or so away, On a little mound, Napoleon Stood on our storming day; With neck out-thrust, you fancy how, Legs wide, arms locked behind, As if to balance the prone brow Oppressive with its mind.

Just as perhaps he mused, "My plans That soar, to earth may fall Let once my army-leader Lannes Waver at yonder wall,"— Out 'twixt the battery-smokes there flew A rider, bound on bound Full-galloping; nor bridle drew Until he reached the mound.

Then off there flung in smiling joy, And held himself erect By just his horse's mane, a boy: You hardly could suspect— (So tight he kept his lips compressed, Scarce any blood came through,) You looked twice e'er you saw his breast, Was all but shot in two.

"Well," cried he, "Emperor, by God's grace We've got you Ratisbon! The marshal's in the market-place, And you'll be there anon To see your flag-bird flap his vans Where I, to heart's desire, Perched him." The chief's eye flashed; his plans Soared up again like fire.

The chief's eye flashed; but presently Softened itself, as sheathes A film the mother eagle's eye When her bruised eaglet breathes: "You're wounded!" "Nay," his soldier's pride Touched to the quick, he said; "I'm killed, sire!" And, his chief beside, Smiling, the boy fell dead.

Robert Browning.

Marco Bozzaris

At midnight, in his guarded tent, The Turk was dreaming of the hour When Greece, her knee in suppliance bent, Should tremble at his power; In dreams, through camp and court he bore The trophies of a conqueror; In dreams, his song of triumph heard; Then wore his monarch's signet-ring; Then press'd that monarch's throne—a king: As wild his thoughts, as gay of wing, As Eden's garden bird.

At midnight in the forest shades, Bozzaris ranged his Suliote band, True as the steel of their tried blades, Heroes in heart and hand. There had the Persian's thousands stood, There had the glad earth drunk their blood, On old Platæa's day; And now there breathed that haunted air The sons of sires who conquer'd there, With arm to strike, and soul to dare, As quick, as far, as they.

An hour pass'd on: the Turk awoke: That bright dream was his last. He woke to hear his sentries shriek, "To arms! they come! the Greek! the Greek!" He woke, to die 'midst flame and smoke, And shout, and groan, and sabre-stroke, And death-shots falling thick and fast As lightnings from the mountain cloud, And heard, with voice as trumpet loud, Bozzaris cheer his band: "Strike!—till the last arm'd foe expires; Strike!—for your altars and your fires; Strike!—for the green graves of your sires; God, and your native land!"

They fought like brave men, long and well; They piled that ground with Moslem slain; They conquer'd;—but Bozzaris fell, Bleeding at every vein. His few surviving comrades saw His smile when rang their loud hurrah, And the red field was won; Then saw in death his eyelids close, Calmly as to a night's repose,— Like flowers at set of sun.

*　　*　　*　　*

Bozzaris! with the storied brave Greece nurtured in her glory's time, Rest thee: there is no prouder grave, Even in her own proud clime. She wore no funeral weeds for thee, Nor bade the dark hearse wave its plume, Like torn branch from death's leafless tree, In sorrow's pomp and pageantry, The heartless luxury of the tomb; But she remembers thee as one Long loved, and for a season gone;

For thee her poet's lyre is wreathed; Her marble wrought, her music breathed; For thee she rings the birthday bells; Of thee her babes' first lisping tells; For thee her evening prayer is said At palace-couch and cottage-bed; Her soldier, closing with the foe, Gives for thy sake a deadlier blow; His plighted maiden, when she fears For him, the joy of her young years, Thinks of thy fate, and checks her tears; And she, the mother of thy boys, Though in her eye and faded cheek Is read the grief she will not speak, The memory of her buried joys,— And even she who gave thee birth Will, by their pilgrim-circled hearth, Talk of thy doom without a sigh; For thou art Freedom's now, and Fame's, One of the few, th' immortal names That were not born to die.

Fitz-Greene Halleck.

The Destruction of Sennacherib

The Assyrian came down like the wolf on the fold, And his cohorts were gleaming in purple and gold; And the sheen of their spears was like stars on the sea, When the blue wave rolls nightly on deep Galilee.

Like the leaves of the forest when Summer is green, That host with their banners at sunset were seen: Like the leaves of the forest when Autumn hath blown, That host on the morrow lay wither'd and strown.

For the Angel of Death spread his wings on the blast, And breathed in the face of the foe as he pass'd; And the eyes of the sleepers wax'd deadly and chill, And their hearts but once heaved, and forever grew still!

And there lay the steed with his nostril all wide, But through it there roll'd not the breath of his pride; And the foam of his gasping lay white on the turf, And cold as the spray of the rock-beating surf.

And there lay the rider distorted and pale, With the dew on his brow, and the rust on his mail; And the tents were all silent, the banners alone, The lances unlifted, the trumpet unblown.

And the widows of Ashur are loud in their wail, And the idols are broke in the temple of Baal! And the might of the Gentile, unsmote by the sword, Hath melted like snow in the glance of the Lord!

George Gordon, Lord Byron.

INTERLEAVES
Tales of the Olden Time

These ancient ballads have come down to us from the long ago, having been told, like the old nursery tales, from generation to generation, altered, abbreviated, patched, and added to, as they passed from mouth to mouth of poet, high harper, gleeman, wandering minstrel, ballad-monger, and camp-follower. Some of them were repeated by the humble stroller who paid for a corner in the chimney-nook by the practice of his rude art; others were sung by minstrels of the court; most of them were chanted to a tune which served for a score of similar songs, while the verses were frequently interrupted by refrains of one sort or another, as, for instance, in "Hynde Horn," which is sometimes printed as follows:

"Near the King's Court was a young child born *With a hey lillalu and a how lo lan;* And his name it was called Young Hynde Horn *And the birk and the broom blooms bonnie."*

Many of the ballads are gloomy and tragic stories, but told simply and with right feeling; others are gay tales of true love ending happily. Some, like "Sir Patrick Spens" and "Chevy Chace," are built upon historical foundations, and others, while not following history, have a real personage for hero or heroine. Lord Beichan, for instance, is supposed to be Gilbert Becket, father of the famous Saint Thomas of Canterbury, while Glenlogie is Sir George, one of the "gay Gordons," but whoever they are, wise abbots, jolly friars, or noble outlaws, they are always bold fellows, true lovers, and merry men.

Inconsequent, fascinating, high-handed, impossible, picturesque, these old ballads have come to us from the childhood of the world, and still speak to the child-heart in us all.

XV
TALES OF THE OLDEN TIME
Sir Patrick Spens

The king sits in Dunfermline town, Drinking the blude-red wine; "O whare will I get a skeely skipper, To sail this new ship o' mine!"

O up and spake an eldern knight, Sat at the king's right knee,— "Sir Patrick Spens is the best sailor, That ever sail'd the sea."

The king has written a braid letter, And seal'd it with his hand, And sent it to Sir Patrick Spens, Was walking on the strand.

"To Noroway, to Noroway, To Noroway o'er the faem; The king's daughter of Noroway, 'Tis thou maun bring her hame."

The first word that Sir Patrick read, Sae loud, loud laughèd he; The neist word that Sir Patrick read, The tear blinded his e'e.

"O wha is this has done this deed, And tauld the king o' me, To send us out, at this time of the year, To sail upon the sea?

Be it wind, be it weet, be it hail, be it sleet, Our ship must sail the faem; The king's daughter of Noroway, 'Tis we must fetch her hame."

They hoysed their sails on Monenday morn, Wi' a' the speed they may; They hae landed in Noroway, Upon a Wodensday.

They hadna been a week, a week, In Noroway, but twae, When that the lords o' Noroway Began aloud to say,—

"Ye Scottishmen spend a' our king's goud, And a' our queenis fee." "Ye lee, ye lee, ye liars loud! Fu' loud I hear ye lee.

"For I brought as much white monie, As gane my men and me, And I brought a half-fou o' gude red goud, Out o'er the sea wi' me.

"Mak' ready, mak' ready, my merry men a'! Our gude ship sails the morn." "Now, ever alake, my master dear, I fear a deadly storm!

"I saw the new moon, late yestreen, Wi' the auld moon in her arm; And, if we gang to sea, master, I fear we'll come to harm."

They had not sailed a league, a league, A league but barely three, When the lift grew dark, and the wind blew loud, And gurly grew the sea.

The ankers brak, and the topmasts lap, It was sic a deadly storm; And the waves cam o'er the broken ship, Till a' her sides were torn.

"O where will I get a gude sailor, To tak' my helm in hand, Till I get up to the tall top-mast, To see if I can spy land?"

"O here am I, a sailor gude, To take the helm in hand, Till you go up to the tall top-mast; But I fear you'll ne'er spy land."

He hadna gane a step, a step, A step but barely ane, When a bout flew out o' our goodly ship, And the salt sea it came in.

"Gae, fetch a web o' the silken claith, Anither o' the twine, And wap them into our ship's side, And letna the sea come in."

They fetched a web o' the silken claith, Anither of the twine, And wapped them round that gude ship's side, But still the sea cam' in.

O laith, laith were our gude Scots lords To weet their cork-heel'd shoon! But lang or a' the play was play'd, They wat their hats aboon.

And mony was the feather-bed, That floated o'er the faem; And mony was the gude lord's son, That never mair came hame.

The ladyes wrang their fingers white, The maidens tore their hair, A' for the sake of their true loves; For them they'll see na mair.

O lang, lang, may the ladyes sit, Wi' their fans into their hand, Before they see Sir Patrick Spens Come sailing to the strand!

And lang, lang, may the maidens sit, Wi' their goud kaims in their hair, A' waiting for their ain dear loves! For them they'll see na mair.

Half ower, half ower to Aberdour, It's fifty fathoms deep, And there lies gude Sir Patrick Spens, Wi' the Scots lords at his feet.

Old Ballad.

The Bailiff's Daughter of Islington

There was a youthe, and a well-beloved youthe, And he was a squire's son; He loved the bayliffe's daughter deare, That lived in Islington.

Yet she was coye, and would not believe That he did love her soe, Noe nor at any time would she Any countenance to him showe.

But when his friendes did understand His fond and foolish minde, They sent him up to faire London, An apprentice for to binde.

And when he had been seven long yeares, And never his love could see,— "Many a teare have I shed for her sake, When she little thought of mee."

Then all the maids of Islington Went forth to sport and playe, All but the bayliffe's daughter deare; She secretly stole awaye.

She pulled off her gowne of greene, And put on ragged attire, And to faire London she would go Her true love to enquire.

And as she went along the high road, The weather being hot and drye, She sat her downe upon a green bank, And her true love came riding bye.

She started up, with a colour soe redd, Catching hold of his bridle-reine; "One penny, one penny, kind sir," she sayd, "Will ease me of much paine."

"Before I give you one penny, sweet-heart, Praye tell me where you were borne." "At Islington, kind sir," sayd shee, "Where I have had many a scorne."

"I prythee, sweet-heart, then tell to mee, O tell me, whether you knowe The bayliffe's daughter of Islington." "She is dead, sir, long agoe."

"If she be dead, then take my horse, My saddle and bridle also; For I will into some farr countrye, Where noe man shall me knowe."

"O staye, O staye, thou goodlye youthe, She standeth by thy side; She is here alive, she is not dead, And readye to be thy bride."

"O farewell griefe, and welcome joye, Ten thousand times therefore; For nowe I have founde mine owne true love, Whom I thought I should never see more."

Old Ballad.

King John and the Abbot of Canterbury

An ancient story I'll tell you anon Of a notable prince, that was called King John; And he ruled England with main and with might, For he did great wrong and maintained little right.

And I'll tell you a story, a story so merry, Concerning the Abbot of Canterbury; How for his housekeeping and high renown, They rode post for him to fair London town.

An hundred men, the King did hear say, The Abbot kept in his house every day; And fifty gold chains, without any doubt, In velvet coats waited the Abbot about.

"How now, Father Abbot, I hear it of thee, Thou keepest a far better house than me; And for thy housekeeping and high renown, I fear thou work'st treason against my crown."

"My liege," quo' the Abbot, "I would it were knowne, I never spend nothing but what is my owne; And I trust your Grace will not put me in fear, For spending of my owne true-gotten gear."

"Yes, yes, Father Abbot, thy fault is highe, And now for the same thou needst must dye; For except thou canst answer me questions three, Thy head shall be smitten from thy bodìe.

"And first," quo' the King, "when I'm in this stead, With my crowne of golde so faire on my head, Among all my liege-men, so noble of birthe, Thou must tell to one penny what I am worthe.

"Secondlye, tell me, without any doubt, How soone I may ride the whole world about, And at the third question thou must not shrink, But tell me here truly what I do think."

"Oh, these are hard questions for my shallow witt, Nor I cannot answer your Grace as yet; But if you will give me but three weekes space, Ile do my endeavour to answer your Grace."

"Now three weeks' space to thee will I give, And that is the longest time thou hast to live; For if thou dost not answer my questions three, Thy land and thy livings are forfeit to me."

Away rode the Abbot all sad at that word, And he rode to Cambridge and Oxenford; But never a doctor there was so wise, That could with his learning an answer devise.

Then home rode the Abbot of comfort so cold, And he met his Shepherd a-going to fold: "How now, my Lord Abbot, you are welcome home; What news do you bring us from good King John?"

"Sad news, sad news, Shepherd, I must give, That I have but three days more to live; I must answer the King his questions three, Or my head will be smitten from my bodie.

"The first is to tell him, there in that stead, With his crown of gold so fair on his head, Among all his liegemen so noble of birth, To within one penny of what he is worth.

"The seconde, to tell him, without any doubt, How soone he may ride this whole world about: And at the third question I must not shrinke, But tell him there truly what he does thinke."

"Now cheare up, Sire Abbot, did you never hear yet, That a fool he may learne a wise man witt? Lend me horse, and serving-men, and your apparel, And I'll ride to London to answere your quarrel.

"Nay frowne not, if it hath bin told unto mee, I am like your Lordship, as ever may bee: And if you will but lend me your gowne, There is none shall knowe us in fair London towne."

"Now horses and serving-men thou shalt have, With sumptuous array most gallant and brave; With crozier, and mitre, and rochet, and cope, Fit to appear 'fore our Father the Pope."

"Now welcome, Sire Abbot," the king he did say, "'Tis well thou'rt come back to keepe thy day; For and if thou canst answer my questions three, Thy life and thy living both saved shall bee.

"And first, when thou seest me, here in this stead, With my crown of golde so fair on my head, Among all my liege-men so noble of birthe, Tell me to one penny what I am worth."

"For thirty pence our Saviour was sold Among the false Jewes, as I have bin told: And twenty-nine is the worth of thee, For I thinke, thou art one penny worse than he."

The King he laughed, and swore by St. Bittel, "I did not think I had been worth so little! Now secondly tell me, without any doubt, How soon I may ride this whole world about."

"You must rise with the sun, and ride with the same, Until the next morning he riseth again; And then your Grace need not make any doubt But in twenty-four hours you'll ride it about."

The King he laughed, and swore by St. Jone, "I did not think it could be gone so soon. Now from the third question thou must not shrink, But tell me here truly what do I think."

"Yea, that I shall do and make your Grace merry; You think I'm the Abbot of Canterbury; But I'm his poor shepherd, as plain you may see, That am come to beg pardon for him and for me."

The King he laughed, and swore by the mass, "I'll make thee Lord Abbot this day in his place!" "Nay, nay, my Liege, be not in such speed, For alack, I can neither write nor read."

"Four nobles a week, then, I will give thee, For this merry jest thou hast shown unto me; And tell the old Abbot, when thou gettest home, Thou hast brought him a pardon from good King John."

Old Ballad.

Lord Beichan and Susie Pye

Lord Beichan was a noble lord, A noble lord of high degree; But he was ta'en by a savage Moor, Who treated him right cruellie.

In ilka shoulder was put a bore, In ilka bore was put a tree; And heavy loads they made him draw, Till he was sick, and like to dee.

Then he was cast in a dungeon deep, Where he cou'd neither hear nor see; And seven long years they kept him there, Both cold and hunger sore to dree.

The Moor he had an only daughter, The damsel's name was Susie Pye; And ilka day as she took the air, Lord Beichan's prison she pass'd by.

Young Susie Pye had a tender heart, Tho' she was come of a cruel kin; And sore she sigh'd, she knew not why, For him who lay that dungeon in.

"Oh, were I but the prison keeper, As I'm a lady of high degree, I soon wou'd set this youth at large, And send him to his own countrie."

She gave the keeper a piece of gold, And many pieces of white monie, To unlock to her the prison doors, That she Lord Beichan might go see.

Lord Beichan he did marvel sore, The Moor's fair daughter there to see; But took her for some captive maid, Brought from some land in Christendie.

For when she saw his wretched plight, Her tears fell fast and bitterlie; And thus the Moor's fair daughter spake Unto Lord Beichan tenderlie:

"Oh, have ye any lands," she said, "Or castles in your own countrie, That ye cou'd give to a lady fair, From prison strong to set you free?"

"Oh, I have lands both fair and braid, And I have castles fair to see; But I wou'd give them all," he said, "From prison strong to be set free."

"Plight me the truth of your right hand, The truth of it here plight to me, That till seven years are past and gone, No lady ye will wed but me."

"For seven long years I do make a vow, And seven long years I'll keep it true, If you wed with no other man, No other lady I'll wed but you."

Then she has bribed the prison-keeper, With store of gold and white monie, To loose the chain that bound him so, And set Lord Beichan once more free.

A ring she from her finger broke, And half of it to him gave she,— "Keep it, to mind you of the maid Who out of prison set you free."

She had him put on good shipboard, That he might safely cross the main; Then said, "Adieu! my Christian lord, I fear we ne'er may meet again."

Lord Beichan turn'd him round about, And lowly, lowly bent his knee; "Ere seven years are come and gone, I'll take you to my own countrie."

But Susie Pye cou'd get no rest, Nor day nor night cou'd happy be; For something whisper'd in her breast, "Lord Beichan will prove false to thee."

So she set foot on good shipboard, Well mann'd and fitted gallantlie; She bade adieu to her father's towers, And left behind her own countrie.

Then she sailed west, and she sailed north, She sailed far o'er the salt sea faem; And after many weary days, Unto fair England's shore she came.

Then she went to Lord Beichan's gate, And she tirl'd gently at the pin, And ask'd—"Is this Lord Beichan's hall, And is that noble lord within?"

The porter ready answer made,— "Oh yes, this is Lord Beichan's hall; And he is also here within, With bride and guests assembled all."

"And has he betroth'd another love, And has he quite forgotten me, To whom he plighted his love and troth, When from prison I did him free?

"Bear to your lord, ye proud porter, This parted ring, the plighted token Of mutual love, and mutual vows, By him, alas! now falsely broken.

"And bid him send one bit of bread, And bid him send one cup of wine, Unto the maid he hath betray'd, Tho' she freed him from cruel pine."

The porter hasten'd to his lord, And fell down on his bended knee: "My lord, a lady stands at your gate, The fairest lady I e'er did see.

"On every finger she has a ring, And on her middle finger three; With as much gold above her brow As wou'd buy an

117

earldom to me."

It's out then spake the bride's mother, Both loud and angry out spake she,— "Ye might have excepted our bonnie bride, If not more of this companie."

"My dame, your daughter's fair enough, Her beauty's not denied by me; But were she ten times fairer still, With this lady ne'er compare cou'd she.

"My lord, she asks one bit of bread, And bids you send one cup of wine; And to remember the lady's love, Who freed you out of cruel pine."

Lord Beichan hied him down the stair,— Of fifteen steps he made but three, Until he came to Susie Pye, Whom he did kiss most tenderlie.

He's ta'en her by the lily hand, And led her to his noble hall, Where stood his sore-bewilder'd bride, And wedding guests assembled all.

Fair Susie blushing look'd around, Upon the lords and ladies gay; Then with the tear-drops in her eyes, Unto Lord Beichan she did say:

"Oh, have ye ta'en another bride, And broke your plighted vows to me? Then fare thee well, my Christian lord, I'll try to think no more on thee.

"But sadly I will wend my way, And sadly I will cross the sea, And sadly will with grief and shame Return unto my own countrie."

"Oh, never, never, Susie Pye, Oh, never more shall you leave me; This night you'll be my wedded wife, And lady of my lands so free."

Syne up then spake the bride's mother, She ne'er before did speak so free,— "You'll not forsake my dear daughter, For sake of her from Pagandie."

"Take home, take home your daughter dear, She's not a pin the worse of me; She came to me on horseback riding, But shall go back in a coach and three."

Lord Beichan got ready another wedding, And sang, with heart brimful of glee,— "Oh, I'll range no more in foreign lands, Since Susie Pye has cross'd the sea."

Old Ballad.

The Gay Gos-hawk

"O well is me, my gay gos-hawk, That you can speak and flee; For you can carry a love-letter To my true love frae me."

"O how can I carry a letter to her, Or how should I her know? I bear a tongue ne'er wi' her spak', And eyes that ne'er her saw."

"The white o' my love's skin is white As down o' dove or maw; The red o' my love's cheek is red As blood that's spilt on snaw.

"When ye come to the castle, Light on the tree of ash, And sit you there and sing our loves As she comes frae the mass.

"Four and twenty fair ladies Will to the mass repair; And weel may ye my lady ken, The fairest lady there."

When the gos-hawk flew to that castle, He lighted on the ash; And there he sat and sang their loves As she came frae the mass.

"Stay where ye be, my maidens a', And sip red wine anon, Till I go to my west window And hear a birdie's moan."

She's gane unto her west window, The bolt she fainly drew; And unto that lady's white, white neck The bird a letter threw.

"Ye're bidden to send your love a send, For he has sent you twa; And tell him where he may see you soon, Or he cannot live ava."

"I send him the ring from my finger, The garland off my hair, I send him the heart that's in my breast; What would my love have mair? And at the fourth kirk in fair Scotland, Ye'll bid him wait for me there."

She hied her to her father dear As fast as gang could she: "I'm sick at the heart, my father dear; An asking grant you me!" "Ask me na for that Scottish lord, For him ye'll never see!"

"An asking, an asking, dear father!" she says, "An asking grant you me; That if I die in fair England, In Scotland ye'll bury me.

"At the first kirk o' fair Scotland, You cause the bells be rung; At the second kirk o' fair Scotland, You cause the mass be sung;

"At the third kirk o' fair Scotland, You deal gold for my sake; At the fourth kirk o' fair Scotland, O there you'll bury me at!

"This is all my asking, father, I pray you grant it me!" "Your asking is but small," he said; "Weel granted it shall be. But why do ye talk o' suchlike things? For ye arena going to dee."

The lady's gane to her chamber, And a moanfu' woman was she, As gin she had ta'en a sudden brash, And were about to dee.

The lady's gane to her chamber As fast as she could fare; And she has drunk a sleepy draught, She mix'd it wi' mickle care.

She's fallen into a heavy trance, And pale and cold was she; She seemed to be as surely dead As ony corpse could be.

Out and spak' an auld witch-wife, At the fireside sat she: "Gin she has killed herself for love, I wot it weel may be:

"But drap the het lead on her cheek, And drap in on her chin, And rap it on her bosom white, And she'll maybe speak again. 'Tis much that a young lady will do To her true love to win."

They drapped the het lead on her cheek, They drapped it on her chin, They drapped it on her bosom white, But she spake none again.

Her brothers they went to a room, To make to her a bier; The boards were a' o' the cedar wood, The edges o' silver clear.

Her sisters they went to a room, To make to her a sark; The cloth was a' o' the satin fine, And the stitching silken-wark.

"Now well is me, my gay gos-hawk, That ye can speak and flee! Come show me any love-tokens That you have brought to me."

"She sends you the ring frae her white finger, The garland frae her hair; She sends you the heart within her breast; And what would you have mair? And at the fourth kirk o' fair Scotland, She bids you wait for her there."

"Come hither, all my merry young men! And drink the good red wine; For we must on towards fair England To free my love frae pine."

The funeral came into fair Scotland, And they gart the bells be rung; And when it came to the second kirk, They gart the mass be sung.

And when it came to the third kirk, They dealt gold for her sake; And when it came to the fourth kirk, Her love was waiting thereat.

At the fourth kirk in fair Scotland Stood spearmen in a row; And up and started her ain true love, The chieftain over them a'.

"Set down, set down the bier," he says, "Till I look upon the dead; The last time that I saw her face, Its color was warm and red."

He stripped the sheet from aff her face A little below the chin; The lady then she open'd her eyes, And lookèd full on him.

"O give me a shive o' your bread, love, O give me a cup o' your wine! Long have I fasted for your sake, And now I fain would dine.

"Gae hame, gae hame, my seven brothers, Gae hame and blaw the horn! And ye may say that ye sought my skaith, And that I hae gi'en you the scorn.

"I cam' na here to bonny Scotland To lie down in the clay; But I cam' here to bonny Scotland To wear the silks sae gay!

"I cam' na here to bonny Scotland Amang the dead to rest; But I cam' here to bonny Scotland To the man that I lo'e best!" Old Ballad.

Earl Mar's Daughter

It was intill a pleasant time, Upon a simmer's day, The noble Earl of Mar's daughter Went forth to sport and play.

And as she played and sported Below a green aik tree, There she saw a sprightly doo Set on a branch sae hie.

"O Coo-my-doo, my love sae true, If ye'll come doun to me, Ye'se hae a cage o' gude red goud Instead o' simple tree.

"I'll tak' ye hame and pet ye weel, Within my bower and ha'; I'll gar ye shine as fair a bird As ony o' them a'!"

And she had nae these words weel spoke, Nor yet these words weel said, Till Coo-my-doo flew frae the branch, And lighted on her head.

Then she has brought this pretty bird Hame to her bower and ha', And made him shine as fair a bird As ony o' them a'.

When day was gane, and night was come, About the evening-tide, This lady spied a bonny youth Stand straight up by her side.

"Now whence come ye, young man," she said, "To put me into fear? My door was bolted right secure, And what way cam' ye here?"

"O haud your tongue, my lady fair, Lat a' your folly be; Mind ye not o' your turtle-doo Ye coax'd from aff the tree?"

"O wha are ye, young man?" she said, "What country come ye frae?" "I flew across the sea," he said, "'Twas but this verra day.

"My mither is a queen," he says, Likewise of magic skill; 'Twas she that turned me in a doo, To fly where'er I will.

"And it was but this verra day That I cam' ower the sea: I loved you at a single look; With you I'll live and dee."

"O Coo-my-doo, my love sae true, Nae mair frae me ye'se gae." "That's never my intent, my love; As ye said, it shall be sae."

There he has lived in bower wi' her, For six lang years and ane; Till sax young sons to him she bare, And the seventh she's brought hame.

But aye, as soon's a child was born, He carried them away, And brought them to his mither's care, As fast as he could fly.

Thus he has stay'd in bower wi' her For seven lang years and mair; Till there cam' a lord o' hie renown To court that lady fair.

But still his proffer she refused, And a' his presents too; Says, "I'm content to live alane Wi' my bird Coo-my-doo!"

Her father sware an angry oath, He sware it wi' ill-will: "To-morrow, ere I eat or drink, That bird I'll surely kill."

The bird was sitting in his cage, And heard what he did say; He jumped upon the window-sill: "'Tis time I was away."

Then Coo-my-doo took flight and flew Beyond the raging sea, And lighted at his mither's castle, Upon a tower sae hie.

The Queen his mither was walking out, To see what she could see, And there she saw her darling son Set on the tower sae hie.

"Get dancers here to dance," she said, "And minstrels for to play; For here's my dear son Florentine Come back wi' me to stay."

"Get nae dancers to dance, mither, Nor minstrels for to play; For the mither o' my seven sons, The morn's her wedding day."

"Now tell me, dear son Florentine, O tell, and tell me true; Tell me this day, without delay, What sall I do for you?"

"Instead of dancers to dance, mither, Or minstrels for to play, Turn four-and-twenty well-wight men, Like storks, in feathers gray;

"My seven sons in seven swans, Aboon their heads to flee; And I myself a gay gos-hawk, A bird o' high degree."

Then, sighing, said the Queen to hersell, "That thing's too high for me!" But she applied to an auld woman, Who had mair skill than she.

Instead o' dancers to dance a dance, Or minstrels for to play, Were four-and-twenty well-wight men Turn'd birds o' feathers gray;

Her seven sons in seven swans, Aboon their heads to flee; And he himsell a gay gos-hawk, A bird o' high degree.

This flook o' birds took flight and flew Beyond the raging sea; They landed near the Earl Mar's castle, Took shelter in every tree.

They were a flock o' pretty birds, Right wondrous to be seen; The weddin'eers they looked at them Whilst walking on the green.

These birds flew up frae bush and tree, And, lighted on the ha'; And, when the wedding-train cam' forth, Flew down amang them a'.

The storks they seized the boldest men, That they could not fight or flee; The swans they bound the bridegroom fast Unto a green aik tree.

They flew around the bride-maidens, Around the bride's own head; And, wi' the twinkling o' an ee, The bride and they were fled.

There's ancient men at weddings been For eighty years or more; But siccan a curious wedding-day They never saw before.

For naething could the company do, Nor naething could they say; But they saw a flock o' pretty birds That took their bride away.

Old Ballad.

Chevy-Chace

God prosper long our noble king, Our lives and safeties all; A woful hunting once there did In Chevy-Chace befall.

To drive the deer with hound and horn Earl Percy took his way; The child may rue that is unborn The hunting of that day.

The stout Earl of Northumberland A vow to God did make, His pleasure in the Scottish woods Three summer days to take,—

The chiefest harts in Chevy-Chace To kill and bear away. These tidings to Earl Douglas came, In Scotland where he lay;

Who sent Earl Percy present word He would prevent his sport. The English earl, not fearing that, Did to the woods resort

With fifteen hundred bowmen bold, All chosen men of might, Who knew full well in time of need To aim their shafts aright.

The gallant greyhounds swiftly ran To chase the fallow deer; On Monday they began to hunt Ere daylight did appear;

And long before high noon they had A hundred fat bucks slain; Then having dined, the drovers went To rouse the deer again.

The bowmen mustered on the hills, Well able to endure; And all their rear, with special care, That day was guarded sure.

The hounds ran swiftly through the woods, The nimble deer to take, That with their cries the hills and dales An echo shrill did make.

Lord Percy to the quarry went, To view the slaughtered deer; Quoth he, "Earl Douglas promisèd This day to meet me here;

"But if I thought he would not come, No longer would I stay;" With that a brave young gentleman Thus to the Earl did say:

"Lo, yonder doth Earl Douglas come, His men in armor bright; Full twenty hundred Scottish spears All marching in our sight;

"All men of pleasant Teviotdale, Fast by the river Tweed;" "Then cease your sports," Earl Percy said, "And take your bows with speed;

"And now with me, my countrymen, Your courage forth advance; For never was there champion yet, In Scotland or in France,

"That ever did on horseback come, But if my hap it were, I durst encounter man for man, With him to break a spear."

Earl Douglas on his milk-white steed, Most like a baron bold, Rode foremost of his company, Whose armor shone like gold.

"Show me," said he, "whose men you be, That hunt so boldly here, That, without my consent, do chase And kill my fallow-deer."

The first man that did answer make, Was noble Percy he— Who said, "We list not to declare, Nor show whose men we be:

"Yet will we spend our dearest blood Thy chiefest harts to slay." Then Douglas swore a solemn oath, And thus in rage did say:

"Ere thus I will out-bravèd be, One of us two shall die; I know thee well, an earl thou art— Lord Percy, so am I.

"But trust me, Percy, pity it were, And great offence, to kill Any of these our guiltless men, For they have done no ill.

"Let thou and I the battle try, And set our men aside." "Accursed be he," Earl Percy said, "By whom this is denied."

Then stepped a gallant squire forth, Witherington was his name, Who said, "I would not have it told To Henry, our king, for shame,

"That e'er my captain fought on foot, And I stood looking on. You two be earls," said Witherington, "And I a squire alone;

"I'll do the best that do I may, While I have power to stand; While I have power to wield my sword, I'll fight with heart and hand."

Our English archers bent their bows— Their hearts were good and true; At the first flight of arrows sent, Full fourscore Scots they slew.

Yet stays Earl Douglas on the bent, As Chieftain stout and good; As valiant Captain, all unmoved, The shock he firmly stood.

His host he parted had in three, As leader ware and tried; And soon his spearmen on their foes Bore down on every side.

Throughout the English archery They dealt full many a wound; But still our valiant Englishmen All firmly kept their ground.

And throwing straight their bows away, They grasped their swords so bright; And now sharp blows, a heavy shower, On shields and helmets light.

They closed full fast on every side— No slackness there was found; And many a gallant gentleman Lay gasping on the ground.

In truth, it was a grief to see How each one chose his spear, And how the blood out of their breasts Did gush like water clear.

At last these two stout earls did meet; Like captains of great might, Like lions wode, they laid on lode, And made a cruel fight.

They fought until they both did sweat, With swords of tempered steel, Until the blood, like drops of rain, They trickling down did feel.

"Yield thee, Lord Percy," Douglas said; "In faith I will thee bring Where thou shalt high advancèd be By James, our Scottish king.

"Thy ransom I will freely give, And this report of thee, Thou art the most courageous knight That ever I did see."

"No, Douglas," saith Earl Percy then, "Thy proffer I do scorn; I will not yield to any Scot That ever yet was born."

With that there came an arrow keen Out of an English bow, Which struck Earl Douglas to the heart, A deep and deadly blow;

Who never spake more words than these: "Fight on, my merry men all; For why, my life is at an end; Lord Percy sees my fall."

Then leaving life, Earl Percy took The dead man by the hand; And said, "Earl Douglas, for thy life Would I had lost my land!

"In truth, my very heart doth bleed With sorrow for thy sake; For sure a more redoubted knight Mischance did never take."

A knight amongst the Scots there was Who saw Earl Douglas die, Who straight in wrath did vow revenge Upon the Earl Percy.

Sir Hugh Montgomery was he called, Who, with a spear full bright, Well mounted on a gallant steed, Ran fiercely through the fight;

And past the English archers all, Without a dread or fear; And through Earl Percy's body then He thrust his hateful spear;

With such vehement force and might He did his body gore, The staff ran through the other side A large cloth-yard and more.

So thus did both these nobles die, Whose courage none could stain. An English archer then perceived The noble Earl was slain.

He had a bow bent in his hand, Made of a trusty tree; An arrow of a cloth-yard long To the hard head haled he.

Against Sir Hugh Montgomery So right the shaft he set, The gray goose wing that was thereon In his heart's blood was wet.

This fight did last from break of day Till setting of the sun: For when they rung the evening-bell, The battle scarce was done.

With stout Earl Percy there was slain Sir John of Egerton, Sir Robert Ratcliff, and Sir John, Sir James, that bold baròn.

And with Sir George and stout Sir James, Both knights of good account, Good Sir Ralph Raby there was slain, Whose prowess did surmount.

For Witherington needs must I wail As one in doleful dumps; For when his legs were smitten off, He fought upon his stumps.

And with Earl Douglas there was slain Sir Hugh Montgomery, Sir Charles Murray, that from the field, One foot would never flee.

Sir Charles Murray of Ratcliff, too— His sister's son was he; Sir David Lamb, so well esteemed, But saved he could not be.

And the Lord Maxwell in like case Did with Earl Douglas die: Of twenty hundred Scottish spears, Scarce fifty-five did fly.

Of fifteen hundred Englishmen, Went home but fifty-three; The rest on Chevy-Chace were slain, Under the greenwood tree.

Next day did many widows come, Their husbands to bewail; They washed their wounds in brinish tears, But all would not prevail.

Their bodies, bathed in purple blood, They bore with them away; They kissed them dead a thousand times, Ere they were clad in clay.

The news was brought to Edinburgh, Where Scotland's king did reign, That brave Earl Douglas suddenly Was with an arrow slain:

"Oh heavy news," King James did say; "Scotland can witness be I have not any captain more Of such account as he."

Like tidings to King Henry came Within as short a space, That Percy of Northumberland Was slain in Chevy-Chace:

"Now God be with him," said our king, "Since 'twill no better be; I trust I have within my realm Five hundred as good as he:

"Yet shall not Scots or Scotland say But I will vengeance take: I'll be revenged on them all, For brave Earl Percy's sake."

This vow full well the king performed After at Humbledown; In one day fifty knights were slain, With lords of high renown;

And of the rest, of small account, Did many hundreds die: Thus endeth the hunting of Chevy-Chace, Made by the Earl Percy.

God save the king, and bless this land, With plenty, joy and peace; And grant, henceforth, that foul debate 'Twixt noblemen may cease!

Old Ballad.

Hynde Horn

"Oh, it's Hynde Horn fair, and it's Hynde Horn free; Oh, where were you born, and in what countrie?" "In a far distant countrie I was born; But of home and friends I am quite forlorn."

Oh, it's seven long years he served the king, But wages from him he ne'er got a thing: Oh, it's seven long years he served, I ween, And all for love of the king's daughter Jean.

Oh, he gave to his love a silver wand, Her sceptre of rule over fair Scotland; With three singing laverocks set thereon, For to mind her of him when he was gone.

And his love gave to him a gay gold ring, With three shining diamonds set therein; Oh, his love gave to him this gay gold ring, Of virtue and value above all thing; Saying—"While the diamonds do keep their hue, You will know that my love holds fast and true; But when the diamonds grow pale and wan, I'll be dead, or wed to another man."

Then the sails were spread, and away sail'd he; Oh, he sail'd away to a far countrie; And when he had been seven years to sea, Hynde Horn look'd to see how his ring might be.

But when Hynde Horn look'd the diamonds upon, Oh, he saw that they were both pale and wan; And at once he knew, from their alter'd hue, That his love was dead or had proved untrue.

Oh, the sails were spread, and away sail'd he Back over the sea to his own countrie; Then he left the ship when it came to land, And he met an auld beggar upon the strand.

"What news, thou auld beggar man?" said he; "For full seven years I've been over the sea." Then the auld man said—"The strangest of all Is the curious wedding in our king's hall.

"For there's a king's daughter, came frae the wast, Has been married to him these nine days past; But unto him a wife the bride winna be, For love of Hynde Horn, far over the sea."

"Now, auld man, give to me your begging weed, And I will give to thee my riding steed; And, auld man, give to me your staff of tree, And my scarlet cloak I will give to thee.

"And you must teach me the auld beggar's role, As he goes his rounds, and receives his dole." The auld man he did as young Hynde Horn said, And taught him the way to beg for his bread.

Then Hynde Horn bent him to his staff of tree, And to the king's palace away hobbled he; And when he arrived at the king's palace gate, To the porter he thus his petition did state:

"Good porter, I pray, for Saints Peter and Paul, And for sake of the Saviour who died for us all, For one cup of wine, and one bit of bread, To an auld man with travel and hunger bestead.

"And ask the fair bride, for the sake of Hynde Horn, To hand them to one so sadly forlorn." Then the porter for pity the message convey'd, And told the fair bride all the beggar man said.

And when she did hear it, she tripp'd down the stair, And in her fair hands did lovingly bear A cup of red wine, and a farle of cake, To give the old man, for loved Hynde Horn's sake.

And when she came to where Hynde Horn did stand, With joy he did take the cup from her hand; Then pledged the fair bride, the cup out did drain, Dropp'd in it the ring, and return'd it again.

"Oh, found you that ring by sea or on land, Or got you that ring off a dead man's hand?" "Oh, I found not that ring by sea or on land, But I got that ring from a fair lady's hand.

"As a pledge of true love she gave it to me, Full seven years ago, as I sail'd o'er the sea; But now that the diamonds are chang'd in their hue, I know that my love has to me proved untrue."

"Oh, I will cast off my gay costly gown, And follow thee on from town unto town, And I will take the gold combs from my hair, And follow my true love for ever mair."

"You need not cast off your gay costly gown, To follow me on from town unto town; You need not take the gold combs from your hair, For Hynde Horn has gold enough, and to spare."

He stood up erect, let his beggar weed fall, And shone there the foremost and noblest of all; Then the bridegrooms were chang'd, and the lady re-wed, To Hynde Horn thus come back, like one from the dead.

Old Ballad.

Glenlogie

There was monie a braw noble Came to our Queen's ha'; But the bonnie Glenlogie Was the flower of them a'. And the young Ladye Jeanie, Sae gude and sae fair, She fancied Glenlogie Aboon a' that were there.

She speired at his footman, That ran by his side, His name, and his sirname, And where he did bide. "He bides at Glenlogie, When he is at hame; He's of the gay Gordons, And George is his name."

She wrote to Glenlogie, To tell him her mind: "My love is laid on you, Oh, will you prove kind?" He turn'd about lightly, As the Gordons do a': "I thank you, fair Ladye, But I'm promis'd awa."

She call'd on her maidens Her jewels to take, And to lay her in bed, For her heart it did break. "Glenlogie! Glenlogie! "Glenlogie!" said she; "If I getna Glenlogie, I'm sure I will dee."

"Oh, hold your tongue, daughter, And weep na sae sair; For you'll get Drumfindlay, His father's young heir." "Oh, hold your tongue, father, And let me alane; If I getna Glenlogie, I'll never wed ane."

Then her father's old chaplain— A man of great skill— He wrote to Glenlogie, The cause of this ill; And her father, he sent off This letter with speed, By a trusty retainer, Who rode his best steed.

The first line that he read, A light laugh gave he; The next line that he read, The tear fill'd each e'e: "Oh, what a man am I, That a leal heart should break? Or that sic a fair maid Should die for my sake?

"Go, saddle my horse, Go, saddle him soon, Go, saddle the swiftest E'er rode frae the toun." But ere it was saddled, And brought to the door, Glenlogie was on the road Three miles or more.

When he came to her father's, Great grief there was there; There was weepin' and wailin', And sabbin' full sair. Oh, pale and wan was she When Glenlogie gaed in; But she grew red and rosy When Glenlogie gaed ben.

Then out spake her father, With tears in each e'e: "You're welcome, Glenlogie, You're welcome to me." And out spake her mother: "You're welcome," said she; "You're welcome, Glenlogie, Your Jeanie to see."

"Oh, turn, Ladye Jeanie, Turn round to this side, And I'll be the bridegroom, And you'll be the bride." Oh, it was a blythe wedding, As ever was seen; And bonnie Jeanie Melville Was scarcely sixteen.

Old Ballad.

INTERLEAVES
Life Lessons
"They also serve who only stand and wait."
Milton.

"Small service is true service while it lasts."
Wordsworth.
"Build thee more stately mansions, O my soul, As the swift seasons roll!"
Holmes.
"When Duty whispers low 'Thou must,' The youth replies, 'I can.'"
Emerson.
"Thou must be true thyself, If thou the truth wouldst teach."
Bonar.
"I am content with what I have, Little be it, or much."
Bunyan.
"As one lamp lights another, nor grows less, So nobleness enkindleth nobleness."
Lowell.
"Who sweeps a room as for Thy laws Makes that and th' action fine."
Herbert.
"This above all—to thine own self be true; And it must follow, as the night the day, Thou canst not then be false to any man."
Shakespeare.

XVI
LIFE LESSONS
Life
*   *   *   *

Lives of great men all remind us We can make our lives sublime, And, departing, leave behind us Footprints on the sands of time;—

Footprints, that perhaps another, Sailing o'er life's solemn main, A forlorn and shipwrecked brother, Seeing, shall take heart again.

Let us, then, be up and doing, With a heart for any fate; Still achieving, still pursuing, Learn to labor and to wait.
Henry Wadsworth Longfellow.
From the "Psalm of Life."

In a Child's Album
Small service is true service while it lasts; Of humblest friends, bright creature! scorn not one; The Daisy, by the shadow that it casts, Protects the lingering dew-drop from the sun.
William Wordsworth.

To-Day
So here hath been dawning Another blue day: Think, wilt thou let it Slip useless away.

Out of Eternity This new day was born; Into Eternity, At night, will return.

Behold it aforetime No eye ever did; So soon it for ever From all eyes is hid.

Here hath been dawning Another blue day: Think, wilt thou let it Slip useless away.
Thomas Carlyle.

The Noble Nature
It is not growing like a tree In bulk doth make Man better be; Or standing long an oak, three hundred year, To fall a log at last, dry, bald, and sere: A lily of a day Is fairer far in May, Although it fall and die that night,— It was the plant and flower of Light: In small proportions we just beauties see, And in short measures life may perfect be.
Ben Jonson.

Forbearance
Hast thou named all the birds without a gun? Loved the wood-rose, and left it on its stalk? At rich men's tables eaten bread and pulse? Unarmed, faced danger with a heart of trust? And loved so well a high behavior, In man or maid, that thou from speech refrained, Nobility more nobly to repay? O, be my friend, and teach me to be thine!
Ralph Waldo Emerson.

The Chambered Nautilus
This is the ship of pearl, which, poets feign, Sails the unshadowed main,— The venturous bark that flings On the sweet summer wind its purpled wings In gulfs enchanted, where the Siren sings, And coral reefs lie bare, Where the cold sea-maids rise to sun their streaming hair.

Its webs of living gauze no more unfurl; Wrecked is the ship of pearl! And every chambered cell, Where its dim dreaming life was wont to dwell, As the frail tenant shaped his growing shell, Before thee lies revealed,— Its irised ceiling rent, its sunless crypt unsealed!

Year after year beheld the silent toil That spread his lustrous coil; Still, as the spiral grew, He left the past year's dwelling for the new, Stole with soft step its shining archway through, Built up its idle door, Stretched in his last-found home, and knew the old no more.

Thanks for the heavenly message brought by thee, Child of the wandering sea, Cast from her lap, forlorn! From thy dead lips a clearer note is born Than ever Triton blew from wreathèd horn! While on mine ear it rings, Through the deep caves of thought I hear a voice that sings:—

Build thee more stately mansions, O my soul, As the swift seasons roll! Leave thy low-vaulted past! Let each new temple, nobler than the last, Shut thee from heaven with a dome more vast, Till thou at length art free, Leaving thine outgrown shell by life's unresting sea!

Oliver Wendell Holmes.

Duty

So nigh is grandeur to our dust, So near is God to man; When Duty whispers low "Thou must," The youth replies, "I can."

Ralph Waldo Emerson.

On His Blindness

When I consider how my light is spent Ere half my days, in this dark world and wide, And that one Talent which is death to hide, Lodged with me useless, though my Soul more bent To serve therewith my Maker, and present My true account, lest he returning chide,— Doth God exact day-labor, light denied, I fondly ask:—But Patience, to prevent That murmur, soon replies, "God doth not need Either man's work or his own gifts; who best Bear his mild yoke, they serve Him best: His State Is Kingly; thousands at his bidding speed, And post o'er Land and Ocean without rest:— They also serve who only stand and wait."

John Milton.

Sir Launfal and the Leper

As Sir Launfal made morn through the darksome gate, He was ware of a leper, crouched by the same, Who begged with his hand and moaned as he sate; And a loathing over Sir Launfal came; The sunshine went out of his soul with a thrill, The flesh 'neath his armor did shrink and crawl, And midway its leap his heart stood still Like a frozen waterfall; For this man, so foul and bent of stature, Rasped harshly against his dainty nature, And seemed the one blot on the summer morn,— So he tossed him a piece of gold in scorn.

The leper raised not the gold from the dust: "Better to me the poor man's crust, Better the blessing of the poor, Though I turn me empty from his door; That is no true alms which the hand can hold; He gives nothing but worthless gold Who gives from a sense of duty; But he who gives a slender mite, And gives to that which is out of sight, That thread of the all-sustaining Beauty Which runs through all and doth all unite,— The hand cannot clasp the whole of his alms, The heart outstretches its eager palms, For a god goes with it and makes it store To the soul that was starving in darkness before."

James Russell Lowell.

From "The Vision of Sir Launfal."

Opportunity

This I beheld, or dreamed it in a dream:— There spread a cloud of dust along a plain; And underneath the cloud, or in it, raged A furious battle, and men yelled, and swords Shocked upon swords and shields. A prince's banner Wavered, then staggered backward, hemmed by foes. A craven hung along the battle's edge, And thought, "Had I a sword of keener steel— That blue blade that the king's son bears,—but this Blunt thing!" he snapt and flung it from his hand, And lowering crept away and left the field. Then came the king's son, wounded, sore bestead, And weaponless, and saw the broken sword, Hilt-buried in the dry and trodden sand, And ran and snatched it, and with battle-shout Lifted afresh he hewed his enemy down, And saved a great cause that heroic day.

Edward Rowland Sill.

Abou Ben Adhem and the Angel

Abou Ben Adhem (may his tribe increase!) Awoke one night from a deep dream of peace, And saw, within the moonlight in his room, Making it rich, and like a lily in bloom, An Angel writing in a book of gold:— Exceeding peace had made Ben Adhem bold, And to the Presence in the room he said, "What writest thou?"—The Vision raised its head, And with a look made of all sweet accord Answered, "The names of those who love the Lord." "And is mine one?" said Abou. "Nay, not so," Replied the Angel. Abou spoke more low, But cheerily still, and said, "I pray thee, then, Write me as one that loves his fellow men."

The Angel wrote and vanished. The next night It came again with a great wakening light, And showed the names whom love of God had blessed, And, lo! Ben Adhem's name led all the rest.

Leigh Hunt.

Be True

Thou must be true thyself, If thou the truth wouldst teach; Thy soul must overflow, if thou Another's soul wouldst reach! It needs the overflow of heart To give the lips full speech.

Think truly, and thy thoughts Shall the world's famine feed; Speak truly, and each word of thine Shall be a fruitful seed; Live truly, and thy life shall be A great and noble creed.

Horatio Bonar.

The Shepherd Boy Sings in the Valley of Humiliation

He that is down needs fear no fall, He that is low, no pride; He that is humble ever shall Have God to be his guide.

I am content with what I have, Little be it or much: And, Lord, contentment still I crave, Because Thou savest such.

Fullness to such a burden is That go on pilgrimage: Here little, and hereafter bliss, Is best from age to age.

John Bunyan.

A Turkish Legend

A certain pasha, dead five thousand years, Once from his harem fled in sudden tears,

And had this sentence on the city's gate Deeply engraven, "Only God is great."

So these four words above the city's noise Hung like the accents of an angel's voice.

And evermore from the high barbican, Saluted each returning caravan.

Lost is that city's glory. Every gust Lifts, with crisp leaves, the unknown pasha's dust,

And all is ruin, save one wrinkled gate Whereon is written, "Only God is great."

Thomas Bailey Aldrich.

Elegy written in a Country Churchyard

The curfew tolls the knell of parting day, The lowing herd winds slowly o'er the lea, The ploughman homeward plods his weary way, And leaves the world to darkness and to me.

Now fades the glimmering landscape on the sight, And all the air a solemn stillness holds, Save where the beetle wheels his droning flight, And drowsy tinklings lull the distant folds:

Save that from yonder ivy-mantled tow'r, The moping owl does to the moon complain Of such as, wand'ring near her secret bow'r, Molest her ancient solitary reign.

Beneath those rugged elms, that yew-tree's shade, Where heaves the turf in many a mould'ring heap, Each in his narrow cell for ever laid, The rude forefathers of the hamlet sleep.

The breezy call of incense-breathing morn, The swallow twitt'ring from the straw-built shed, The cock's shrill clarion, or the echoing horn, No more shall rouse them from their lowly bed.

For them no more the blazing hearth shall burn, Or busy housewife ply her evening care: No children run to lisp their sire's return, Or climb his knees the envied kiss to share.

Oft did the harvest to their sickle yield, Their furrow oft the stubborn glebe has broke: How jocund did they drive their team afield! How bow'd the woods beneath their sturdy stroke!

Let not Ambition mock their useful toil, Their homely joys, and destiny obscure; Nor Grandeur hear with a disdainful smile, The short and simple annals of the poor.

The boast of heraldry, the pomp of pow'r, And all that beauty, all that wealth e'er gave, Await alike th' inevitable hour— The paths of glory lead but to the grave.

Nor you, ye proud, impute to these the fault, If Mem'ry o'er their tomb no trophies raise, Where through the long-drawn aisle and fretted vault, The pealing anthem swells the note of praise.

Can storied urn or animated bust Back to its mansion call the fleeting breath? Can Honour's voice provoke the silent dust, Or Flatt'ry soothe the dull cold ear of death?

Perhaps in this neglected spot is laid Some heart once pregnant with celestial fire; Hands, that the rod of empire might have sway'd, Or wak'd to ecstasy the living lyre.

But Knowledge to their eyes her ample page, Rich with the spoils of time, did ne'er unroll; Chill Penury repress'd their noble rage, And froze the genial current of the soul.

Full many a gem of purest ray serene The dark unfathom'd caves of ocean bear: Full many a flower is born to blush unseen, And waste its sweetness on the desert air.

Some village Hampden, that with dauntless breast The little tyrant of his fields withstood, Some mute inglorious Milton here may rest, Some Cromwell guiltless of his country's blood.

Th' applause of list'ning senates to command, The threats of pain and ruin to despise, To scatter plenty o'er a smiling land, And read their hist'ry in a nation's eyes—

Their lot forbade: nor circumscribed alone Their growing virtues, but their crimes confined; Forbade to wade through slaughter to a throne, And shut the gates of mercy on mankind;

The struggling pangs of conscious truth to hide, To quench the blushes of ingenuous shame, Or heap the shrine of Luxury and Pride With incense kindled at the Muse's flame.

Far from the madding crowd's ignoble strife, Their sober wishes never learn'd to stray; Along the cool sequester'd vale of life They kept the noiseless tenor of their way.

Yet ev'n these bones from insult to protect Some frail memorial still erected nigh, With uncouth rhymes and shapeless sculpture deck'd, Implores the passing tribute of a sigh.

Their name, their years, spelt by th' unletter'd Muse, The place of fame and elegy supply: And many a holy text around she strews, That teach the rustic moralist to die.

For who, to dumb Forgetfulness a prey, This pleasing anxious being e'er resign'd, Left the warm precincts of the cheerful day, Nor cast one longing, ling'ring look behind?

On some fond breast the parting soul relies, Some pious drops the closing eye requires; E'en from the tomb the voice of Nature cries, E'en in our ashes live their wonted fires.

For thee, who, mindful of th' unhonour'd dead, Dost in these lines their artless tale relate; If chance, by lonely contemplation led, Some kindred spirit shall inquire thy fate,

Haply some hoary-headed swain may say, "Oft have we seen him at the peep of dawn Brushing with hasty steps the dews away, To meet the sun upon the upland lawn.

"There at the foot of yonder nodding beech, That wreathes its old fantastic roots so high, His listless length at noontide would he stretch, And pore upon the brook that babbles by.

"Hard by yon wood, now smiling as in scorn, Mutt'ring his wayward fancies he would rove: Now drooping, woful-wan, like one forlorn, Or craz'd with care, or cross'd in hopeless love.

"One morn I miss'd him on the custom'd hill, Along the heath, and near his fav'rite tree; Another came; nor yet beside the rill, Nor up the lawn, nor at the wood was he:

"The next, with dirges due in sad array, Slow through the church-way path we saw him borne.— Approach and read (for thou canst read) the lay Grav'd on the stone beneath yon agèd thorn."

THE EPITAPH

Here rests his head upon the lap of Earth A Youth, to Fortune and to Fame unknown; Fair Science frown'd not on his humble birth, And Melancholy mark'd him for her own.

Large was his bounty, and his soul sincere, Heav'n did a recompense as largely send: He gave to Mis'ry all he had, a tear, He gain'd from Heav'n ('t was all he wish'd) a friend.

No farther seek his merits to disclose, Or draw his frailties from their dread abode, (There they alike in trembling hope repose,) The bosom of his Father and his God.

Thomas Gray.

Polonius to Laertes

And these few precepts in thy memory Look thou character. Give thy thoughts no tongue Nor any unproportion'd thought his act. Be thou familiar, but by no means vulgar The friends thou hast, and their adoption tried, Grapple them to thy soul with hoops of steel; But do not dull thy palm with entertainment Of each new-hatch'd, unfledg'd comrade. Beware Of entrance to a quarrel; but, being in, Bear't, that th' opposer may beware of thee. Give every man thine ear, but few thy voice; Take each man's censure, but reserve thy judgment. Costly thy habit as thy purse can buy, But not express'd in fancy; rich, not gaudy: For the apparel oft proclaims the man; And they in France, of the best rank and station, Are of a most select and generous choice in that. Neither a borrower, nor a lender be; For loan oft loses both itself and friend, And borrowing dulls the edge of husbandry. This above all,—to thine own self be true; And it must follow, as the night the day, Thou canst not then be false to any man.

William Shakespeare.

From "Hamlet."

The Olive Tree

Said an ancient hermit, bending Half in prayer upon his knee, "Oil I need for midnight watching, I desire an olive tree."
Then he took a tender sapling, Planted it before his cave, Spread his trembling hands above it, As his benison he gave.

But he thought, the rain it needeth, That the root may drink and swell; "God! I pray Thee send Thy showers!" So a gentle shower fell.

"Lord, I ask for beams of summer, Cherishing this little child." Then the dripping clouds divided, And the sun looked down and smiled.

"Send it frost to brace its tissues, O my God!" the hermit cried. Then the plant was bright and hoary, But at evensong it died.

Went the hermit to a brother Sitting in his rocky cell: "Thou an olive tree possessest; How is this, my brother, tell?

"I have planted one, and prayed, Now for sunshine, now for rain; God hath granted each petition, Yet my olive tree hath slain!"

Said the other, "I entrusted To its God my little tree; He who made knew what it needed, Better than a man like me.

"Laid I on him no condition, Fixed no ways and means; so I Wonder not my olive thriveth, Whilst thy olive tree did die."

Sabine Baring-Gould.

Coronation

At the king's gate the subtle noon Wove filmy yellow nets of sun; Into the drowsy snare too soon The guards fell one by one.

Through the king's gate, unquestioned then, A beggar went, and laughed, "This brings Me chance, at last, to see if men Fare better, being kings."

The king sat bowed beneath his crown, Propping his face with listless hand; Watching the hour-glass sifting down Too slow its shining sand.

"Poor man, what wouldst thou have of me?" The beggar turned, and pitying, Replied, like one in dream, "Of thee, Nothing. I want the king."

Uprose the king, and from his head Shook off the crown, and threw it by. "O man! thou must have known," he said, "A greater king than I."

Through all the gates, unquestioned then, Went king and beggar hand in hand. Whispered the king, "Shall I know when Before *his* throne I stand?"

The beggar laughed. Free winds in haste Were wiping from the king's hot brow The crimson lines the crown had traced. "This is his presence now."

At the king's gate, the crafty noon Unwove its yellow nets of sun; Out of their sleep in terror soon The guards waked one by one.

"Ho there! Ho there! Has no man seen The king?" The cry ran to and fro; Beggar and king, they laughed, I ween, The laugh that free men know.

On the king's gate the moss grew gray; The king came not. They called him dead; And made his eldest son one day Slave in his father's stead.

H. H.

December

In a drear-nighted December, Too happy, happy tree, Thy branches ne'er remember Their green felicity: The north cannot undo them, With a sleety whistle through them; Nor frozen thawings glue them From budding at the prime.

In a drear-nighted December, Too happy, happy brook, Thy bubblings ne'er remember Apollo's summer look; But with a sweet forgetting, They stay their crystal fretting, Never, never petting About the frozen time.

Ah! would 'twere so with many A gentle girl and boy! But were there ever any Writhed not at passed joy? To know the change and feel it, When there is none to heal it, Nor numbed sense to steal it, Was never said in rhyme.

John Keats.

The End of the Play

The play is done; the curtain drops, Slow falling to the prompter's bell: A moment yet the actor stops, And looks around, to say farewell. It is an irksome word and task; And, when he's laughed and said his say, He shows, as he removes the mask, A face that's anything but gay.

One word, ere yet the evening ends, Let's close it with a parting rhyme, And pledge a hand to all young friends, As fits the merry Christmas time. On life's wide scenes you, too, have parts, That Fate ere long shall bid you play; Good-night! with honest gentle hearts A kindly greeting go alway!

*   *   *   *

Come wealth or want, come good or ill, Let young and old accept their part, And bow before the Awful Will, And bear it with ah honest heart. Who misses, or who wins the prize? Go, lose or conquer as you can: But if you fail, or if you rise, Be each, pray God, a gentleman.

A gentleman, or old or young! (Bear kindly with my humble lays;) The sacred chorus first was sung Upon the first of Christmas days: The shepherds heard it overhead— The joyful angels raised it then: Glory to Heaven on high, it said, And peace on earth to gentle men.

My song, save this, is little worth; I lay the weary pen aside, And wish you health, and love, and mirth, As fits the solemn Christmas-tide. As fits the holy Christmas birth, Be this, good friends, our carol still— Be peace on earth, be peace on earth, To men of gentle will.

William Makepeace Thackeray.

From "Dr. Birch and his Young Friends."
A Farewell
My fairest child, I have no song to give you; No lark could pipe to skies so dull and gray; Yet, ere we part, one lesson I can leave you For every day.

    *   *   *   *

Be good, sweet maid, and let who will be clever; Do noble things, not dream them, all day long: And so make life, death, and that vast forever One grand, sweet song.
    Charles Kingsley.

A Boy's Prayer
God who created me Nimble and light of limb, In three elements free, To run, to ride, to swim: Not when the sense is dim, But now from the heart of joy, I would remember Him: Take the thanks of a boy.

    *   *   *   *

    Henry Charles Beeching.

Chartless
I never saw a moor, I never saw the sea; Yet know I how the heather looks, And what a wave must be.
I never spoke with God, Nor visited in heaven; Yet certain am I of the spot As if the chart were given.
    Emily Dickinson.

Peace
My soul, there is a country, Afar beyond the stars, Where stands a wingèd sentry, All skilful in the wars. There, above noise and danger, Sweet Peace sits crowned with smiles, And One born in a manger Commands the beauteous files. He is thy gracious friend, And (O my soul, awake!) Did in pure love descend, To die here for thy sake.
If thou canst get but thither, There grows the flower of peace, The rose that cannot wither, Thy fortress, and thy ease. Leave then thy foolish ranges; For none can thee secure, But One who never changes, Thy God, thy Life, thy Cure.
    Henry Vaughan.

Consider
Consider The lilies of the field, whose bloom is brief— We are as they; Like them we fade away, As doth a leaf.
Consider The sparrows of the air, of small account: Our God doth view Whether they fall or mount— He guards us too.
Consider The lilies, that do neither spin nor toil, Yet are most fair— What profits all this care, And all this coil?
Consider The birds, that have no barn nor harvest-weeks; God gives them food— Much more our Father seeks To do us good.
    Christina G. Rossetti.

The Elixir
Teach me, my God and King, In all things Thee to see, And what I do in anything, To do it as for Thee.

    *   *   *   *

All may of Thee partake: Nothing can be so mean Which with this tincture (for Thy sake) Will not grow bright and clean.
A servant with this clause Makes drudgery divine: Who sweeps a room as for Thy laws, Makes that and th' action fine.
This is the famous stone That turneth all to gold; For that which God doth touch and own Cannot for less be told.
    George Herbert.

One by One
One by one the sands are flowing, One by one the moments fall; Some are coming, some are going; Do not strive to grasp them all.

One by one thy duties wait thee— Let thy whole strength go to each, Let no future dreams elate thee, Learn thou first what these can teach.

One by one (bright gifts from heaven) Joys are sent thee here below; Take them readily when given— Ready, too, to let them go.

One by one thy griefs shall meet thee; Do not fear an armèd band; One will fade as others greet thee— Shadows passing through the land.

Do not look at life's long sorrow; See how small each moment's pain; God will help thee for to-morrow, So each day begin again.

Every hour that fleets so slowly Has its task to do or bear; Luminous the crown, and holy, When each gem is set with care.

Do not linger with regretting, Or for passing hours despond; Nor, thy daily toil forgetting, Look too eagerly beyond.

Hours are golden links, God's token, Reaching heaven; but, one by one, Take them, lest the chain be broken Ere the pilgrimage be done.
    Adelaide Anne Procter.

The Commonwealth of the Bees

(Type of a Well-ordered State.)

For government, though high, and low, and lower, Put into parts, doth keep in one consent, Congreeing in a full and natural close, Like music. Therefore doth heaven divide The state of man in divers functions, Setting endeavor in continual motion; To which is fixed, as an aim or butt, Obedience; for so work the honey-bees, Creatures that, by a rule in nature, teach The art of order to a peopled kingdom: They have a king and officers of state, Where some, like magistrates, correct at home, Others, like merchants, venture trade abroad, Others, like soldiers, armed in their stings, Make boot upon the summer's velvet buds; Which pillage they with merry march bring home To the tent-royal of their emperor; Who, busied in his majesty, surveys The singing masons building roofs of gold, The civil citizens kneading up the honey, The poor mechanic porters crowding in Their heavy burdens at his narrow gate; The sad-eyed Justice, with his surly hum, Delivering o'er to executors pale The lazy, yawning drone.

William Shakespeare.

From "King Henry V."

The Pilgrim

Who would true valor see Let him come hither! One here will constant be, Come wind, come weather: There's no discouragement Shall make him once relent His first-avow'd intent To be a Pilgrim.

Whoso beset him round With dismal stories, Do but themselves confound; His strength the more is. No lion can him fright; He'll with a giant fight; But he will have a right To be a Pilgrim.

Nor enemy, nor fiend, Can daunt his spirit; He knows he at the end Shall Life inherit:— Then, fancies, fly away; He'll not fear what men say; He'll labor, night and day, To be a Pilgrim.

John Bunyan.

Be Useful

Be useful where thou livest, that they may Both want and wish thy pleasing presence still. ——Find out men's wants and will, And meet them there. All worldly joys go less To the one joy of doing kindnesses.

George Herbert.

INTERLEAVES
The Glad Evangel

When the Child of Nazareth was born, the sun, according to the Bosnian legend, "leaped in the heavens, and the stars around it danced. A peace came over mountain and forest. Even the rotten stump stood straight and healthy on the green hill-side. The grass was beflowered with open blossoms, incense sweet as myrrh pervaded upland and forest, birds sang on the mountain top, and all gave thanks to the great God."

It is naught but an old folk-tale, but it has truth hidden at its heart, for a strange, subtle force, a spirit of genial good-will, a new-born kindness, seem to animate child and man alike when the world pays its tribute to the "heaven-sent youngling," as the poet Drummond calls the infant Christ.

When the Three Wise Men rode from the East into the West on that "first, best Christmas night," they bore on their saddle-bows three caskets filled with gold and frankincense and myrrh, to be laid at the feet of the manger-cradled babe of Bethlehem. Beginning with this old, old journey, the spirit of giving crept into the world's heart. As the Magi came bearing gifts, so do we also; gifts that relieve want, gifts that are sweet and fragrant with friendship, gifts that breathe love, gifts that mean service, gifts inspired still by the star that shone over the City of David nearly two thousand years ago.

Then hang the green coronet of the Christmas-tree with glittering baubles and jewels of flame; heap offerings on its emerald branches; bring the Yule log to the firing; deck the house with holly and mistletoe,

"And all the bells on earth shall ring On Christmas day in the morning."

XVII
THE GLAD EVANGEL
A Christmas Carol

There's a song in the air! There's a star in the sky! There's a mother's deep prayer And a baby's low cry! And the star rains its fire while the Beautiful sing, For the manger of Bethlehem cradles a king.

There's a tumult of joy O'er the wonderful birth, For the virgin's sweet boy Is the Lord of the earth, Ay! the star rains its fire and the Beautiful sing, For the manger of Bethlehem cradles a king!

In the light of that star Lie the ages impearled; And that song from afar Has swept over the world. Every hearth is aflame, and the Beautiful sing In the homes of the nations that Jesus is king.

We rejoice in the light, And we echo the song That comes down through the night From the heavenly throng. Ay! we shout to the lovely evangel they bring, And we greet in his cradle our Saviour and King!

Josiah Gilbert Holland.

From "The Poetical Works of J. G. Holland." Copyright, , by Charles Scribner's Sons.

The Angels

Run, shepherds, run where Bethlehem blest appears. We bring the best of news; be not dismayed: A Saviour there is born more old than years, Amidst heaven's rolling height this earth who stayed. In a poor cottage inned, a virgin maid, A weakling did him bear, who all upbears; There is he poorly swaddled, in manger laid, To whom too narrow swaddlings are our spheres: Run, shepherds, run, and solemnize his birth. This is that night—no, day, grown great with bliss, In which the power of Satan broken is: In heaven be glory, peace unto the earth! Thus singing, through the air the angels swam, And cope of stars re-echoèd the same.

William Drummond.

"While Shepherds Watched Their Flocks by Night"

Like small curled feathers, white and soft, The little clouds went by, Across the moon, and past the stars, And down the western sky: In upland pastures, where the grass With frosted dew was white, Like snowy clouds the young sheep lay, That first, best Christmas night.

The shepherds slept; and, glimmering faint, With twist of thin, blue smoke, Only their fire's crackling flames The tender silence broke— Save when a young lamb raised his head, Or, when the night wind blew, A nesting bird would softly stir, Where dusky olives grew—

With finger on her solemn lip, Night hushed the shadowy earth, And only stars and angels saw The little Saviour's birth; Then came such flash of silver light Across the bending skies, The wondering shepherds woke, and hid Their frightened, dazzled eyes!

And all their gentle sleepy flock Looked up, then slept again, Nor knew the light that dimmed the stars Brought endless Peace to men— Nor even heard the gracious words That down the ages ring— "The Christ is born! the Lord has come, Good-will on earth to bring!"

Then o'er the moonlit, misty fields, Dumb with the world's great joy, The shepherds sought the white-walled town, Where lay the baby boy— And oh, the gladness of the world, The glory of the skies, Because the longed-for Christ looked up In Mary's happy eyes!

Margaret Deland.

The Star Song

Tell us, thou clear and heavenly tongue, Where is the Babe but lately sprung? Lies he the lily-banks among?

Or say, if this new Birth of ours Sleeps, laid within some ark of flowers, Spangled with dew-light; thou canst clear All doubts, and manifest the where.

Declare to us, bright star, if we shall seek Him in the morning's blushing cheek, Or search the beds of spices through, To find him out?

Star.—No, this ye need not do; But only come and see Him rest, A princely babe, in's mother's breast.

Robert Herrick.

Hymn for Christmas

Oh! lovely voices of the sky Which hymned the Saviour's birth, Are ye not singing still on high, Ye that sang, "Peace on earth"? To us yet speak the strains Wherewith, in time gone by, Ye blessed the Syrian swains, Oh! voices of the sky!

Oh! clear and shining light, whose beams That hour Heaven's glory shed, Around the palms, and o'er the streams, And on the shepherd's head. Be near, through life and death, As in that holiest night Of hope, and joy, and faith— Oh! clear and shining light!

*　　*　　*　　*

Felicia Hemans.

New Prince, New Pomp

Behold a simple, tender Babe, In freezing winter night, In homely manger trembling lies; Alas! a piteous sight.

The inns are full; no man will yield This little Pilgrim bed; But forced he is with silly beasts In crib to shroud his head.

Despise him not for lying there; First what he is inquire: An Orient pearl is often found In depth of dirty mire.

Weigh not his crib, his wooden dish, Nor beasts that by him feed; Weigh not his mother's poor attire, Nor Joseph's simple weed. This stable is a Prince's court, The crib his chair of state; The beasts are parcel of his pomp, The wooden dish his plate.

The persons in that poor attire His royal liveries wear; The Prince himself is come from heaven: This pomp is praisèd there.

With joy approach, O Christian wight! Do homage to thy King; And highly praise this humble pomp, Which he from heaven doth bring.

Robert Southwell.

The Three Kings

Three Kings came riding from far away, Melchior and Gaspar and Baltasar; Three Wise Men out of the East were they, And they travelled by night and they slept by day, For their guide was a beautiful, wonderful star.

The star was so beautiful, large and clear, That all the other stars of the sky Became a white mist in the atmosphere; And by this they knew that the coming was near Of the Prince foretold in the prophecy.

Three caskets they bore on their saddle-bows, Three caskets of gold with golden keys; Their robes were of crimson silk, with rows Of bells and pomegranates and furbelows, Their turbans like blossoming almond-trees.

And so the Three Kings rode into the West, Through the dusk of night over hills and dells, And sometimes they nodded with beard on breast, And sometimes talked, as they paused to rest, With the people they met at the wayside wells.

"Of the child that is born," said Baltasar, "Good people, I pray you, tell us the news; For we in the East have seen his star, And have ridden fast, and have ridden far, To find and worship the King of the Jews."

And the people answered, "You ask in vain; We know of no king but Herod the Great!" They thought the Wise Men were men insane, As they spurred their horses across the plain Like riders in haste who cannot wait.

And when they came to Jerusalem, Herod the Great, who had heard this thing, Sent for the Wise Men and questioned them; And said, "Go down unto Bethlehem, And bring me tidings of this new king."

So they rode away, and the star stood still, The only one in the gray of morn; Yes, it stopped, it stood still of its own free will, Right over Bethlehem on the hill, The city of David where Christ was born.

And the Three Kings rode through the gate and the guard, Through the silent street, till their horses turned And neighed as they entered the great inn-yard; But the windows were closed, and the doors were barred, And only a light in the stable burned.

And cradled there in the scented hay, In the air made sweet by the breath of kine, The little child in the manger lay, The Child that would be King one day Of a kingdom not human, but divine.

His mother, Mary of Nazareth, Sat watching beside his place of rest, Watching the even flow of his breath, For the joy of life and the terror of death Were mingled together in her breast.

They laid their offerings at his feet: The gold was their tribute to a King; The frankincense, with its odor sweet, Was for the Priest, the Paraclete; The myrrh for the body's burying.

And the mother wondered and bowed her head, And sat as still as a statue of stone; Her heart was troubled yet comforted, Remembering what the angel had said Of an endless reign and of David's throne.

Then the Kings rode out of the city gate, With a clatter of hoofs in proud array; But they went not back to Herod the Great, For they knew his malice and feared his hate, And returned to their homes by another way.

Henry Wadsworth Longfellow.

The Three Kings

From out Cologne there came three kings To worship Jesus Christ, their King; To him they sought fine herbs they brought And many a beauteous golden thing; They brought their gifts to Bethlehem town And in that manger set them down.

Then spake the first king, and he said: "O Child most heavenly, bright and fair, I bring this crown to Bethlehem town For Thee, and only Thee, to wear; So give a heavenly crown to me When I shall come at last to Thee."

The second then: "I bring thee here This royal robe, O Child!" he cried; "Of silk 'tis spun and such an one There is not in the world beside! So in the day of doom requite Me with a heavenly robe of white!"

The third king gave his gift, and quoth: "Spikenard and myrrh to Thee I bring, And with these twain would I most fain Anoint the body of my King. So may their incense some time rise To plead for me in yonder skies."

Thus spake the three kings of Cologne That gave their gifts and went their way; And now kneel I in prayer hard-by The cradle of the Child to-day; Nor crown, nor robe, nor spice I bring As offering unto Christ my King.

Yet have I brought a gift the Child May not despise, however small; For here I lay my heart to-day, And it is fun of love to all! Take Thou the poor, but loyal thing, My only tribute, Christ, my King.

Eugene Field.

From "With Trumpet and Drum" by Eugene Field Copyright, , by Charles Scribner's Sons.

A Christmas Hymn

It was the calm and silent night! Seven hundred years and fifty-three Had Rome been growing up to might, And now was queen of land and sea. No sound was heard of clashing wars— Peace brooded o'er the hushed domain: Apollo, Pallas, Jove and Mars Held undisturbed their ancient reign, In the solemn midnight, Centuries ago.

'Twas in the calm and silent night! The senator of haughty Rome, Impatient, urged his chariot's flight, From lordly revel rolling home; Triumphal arches, gleaming, swell His breast with thoughts of boundless sway; What recked the Roman what befell A paltry province far away, In the solemn midnight, Centuries ago?

Within that province far away Went plodding home a weary boor; A streak of light before him lay, Falling through a half-shut stable-door Across his path. He passed—for naught Told what was going on within; How keen the stars, his only thought— The air how calm, and cold, and thin, In the solemn midnight, Centuries ago!

Oh, strange indifference! low and high Drowsed over common joys and cares; The earth was still—but knew not why, The world was listening, unawares. How calm a moment may precede One that shall thrill the world for ever! To that still moment, none would heed, Man's doom was linked no more to sever— In the solemn midnight, Centuries ago!

It is the calm and solemn night! A thousand bells ring out, and throw Their joyous peals abroad, and smite The darkness—charmed and holy now! The night that erst no name had worn, To it a happy name is given; For in that stable lay, new-born, The peaceful prince of earth and heaven, In the solemn midnight, Centuries ago!
Alfred Dommett.

O Little Town of Bethlehem
O little town of Bethlehem, How still we see thee lie! Above thy deep and dreamless sleep The silent stars go by; Yet in thy dark streets shineth The everlasting Light; The hopes and fears of all the years Are met in thee to-night.

For Christ is born of Mary, And, gathered all above, While mortals sleep, the angels keep Their watch of wondering love. O morning stars, together Proclaim the holy birth! And praises sing to God the King, And peace to men on earth.

How silently, how silently, The wondrous gift is given! So God imparts to human hearts The blessings of His heaven. No ear may hear His coming, But in this world of sin, Where meek souls will receive Him still, The dear Christ enters in.

O holy Child of Bethlehem! Descend to us, we pray; Cast out our sin, and enter in, Be born in us to-day. We hear the Christmas angels The great glad tidings tell; Oh, come to us, abide with us, Our Lord Emmanuel!
Phillips Brooks.

While Shepherds Watched Their Flocks by Night
While shepherds watched their flocks by night, All seated on the ground, The angel of the Lord came down, And glory shone around.

"Fear not," said he, for mighty dread Had seized their troubled mind; "Glad tidings of great joy I bring To you and all mankind.

"To you, in David's town, this day Is born, of David's line, The Saviour, who is Christ the Lord, And this shall be the sign:
"The heavenly babe you there shall find To human view displayed, All meanly wrapped in swaddling bands, And in a manger laid."

Thus spake the seraph; and forthwith Appeared a shining throng Of angels, praising God, who thus Addressed their joyful song:

"All glory be to God on high, And to the earth be peace; Good will henceforth from Heaven to men Begin and never cease."
Nahum Tate.

Christmas Carol
As Joseph was a-walking, He heard an angel sing, "This night shall be the birthnight Of Christ our heavenly King.
"His birth-bed shall be neither In housen nor in hall, Nor in the place of paradise, But in the oxen's stall.
"He neither shall be rockèd In silver nor in gold, But in the wooden manger That lieth in the mould.
"He neither shall be washen With white wine nor with red, But with the fair spring water That on you shall be shed.
"He neither shall be clothèd In purple nor in pall, But in the fair, white linen That usen babies all."
As Joseph was a-walking, Thus did the angel sing, And Mary's son at midnight Was born to be our King.
Then be you glad, good people, At this time of the year; And light you up your candles, For His star it shineth clear.
Old English.

Old Christmas
Now he who knows old Christmas, He knows a carle of worth; For he is as good a fellow As any upon earth.

He comes warm cloaked and coated, And buttoned up to the chin, And soon as he comes a-nigh the door We open and let him in.

We know that he will not fail us, So we sweep the hearth up clean; We set him in the old arm-chair, And a cushion whereon to lean.

And with sprigs of holly and ivy We make the house look gay, Just out of an old regard to him, For it was his ancient way.

*   *   *   *

He must be a rich old fellow: What money he gives away! There is not a lord in England Could equal him any day.

Good luck unto old Christmas, And long life, let us sing, For he doth more good unto the poor Than many a crownèd king!
Mary Howitt.

God Rest Ye, Merry Gentlemen

God rest ye, merry gentlemen; let nothing you dismay, For Jesus Christ, our Saviour, was born on Christmas-day. The dawn rose red o'er Bethlehem, the stars shone through the gray, When Jesus Christ, our Saviour, was born on Christmas-day.

God rest ye, little children; let nothing you affright, For Jesus Christ, your Saviour, was born this happy night; Along the hills of Galilee the white flocks sleeping lay, When Christ, the child of Nazareth, was born on Christmas-day.

God rest ye, all good Christians; upon this blessed morn The Lord of all good Christians was of a woman born: Now all your sorrows He doth heal, your sins He takes away; For Jesus Christ, our Saviour, was born on Christmas-day.

Dinah Maria Mulock.

Minstrels and Maids

Outlanders, whence come ye last? *The snow in the street and the wind on the door.* Through what green seas and great have ye past? *Minstrels and maids, stand forth on the floor.*

From far away, O masters mine, *The snow in the street and the wind on the door.* We come to bear you goodly wine, *Minstrels and maids, stand forth on the floor.*

From far away we come to you, *The snow in the street and the wind on the door.* To tell of great tidings strange and true, *Minstrels and maids, stand forth on the floor.*

News, news of the Trinity, *The snow in the street and the wind on the door.* And Mary and Joseph from over the sea! *Minstrels and maids, stand forth on the floor.*

For as we wandered far and wide, *The snow in the street and the wind on the door.* What hap do you deem there should us betide! *Minstrels and maids, stand forth on the floor.*

Under a bent when the night was deep, *The snow in the street and the wind on the door.* There lay three shepherds tending their sheep. *Minstrels and maids, stand forth on the floor.*

"O ye shepherds, what have ye seen, *The snow in the street and the wind on the door.* To slay your sorrow, and heal your teen?" *Minstrels and maids, stand forth on the floor.*

"In an ox-stall this night we saw, *The snow in the street and the wind on the door.* A babe and a maid without a flaw. *Minstrels and maids, stand forth on the floor.*

"There was an old man there beside, *The snow in the street and the wind on the door.* His hair was white and his hood was wide. *Minstrels and maids, stand forth on the floor.*

"And as we gazed this thing upon, *The snow in the street and the wind on the door.* Those twain knelt down to the Little One, *Minstrels and maids, stand forth on the floor.*

"And a marvellous song we straight did hear, *The snow in the street and the wind on the door.* That slew our sorrow and healed our care." *Minstrels and maids, stand forth on the floor.*

News of a fair and marvellous thing, *The snow in the street and the wind on the door.* Nowell, nowell, nowell, we sing! *Minstrels and maids, stand forth on the floor.*

William Morris.

An Ode on the Birth of Our Saviour

In numbers, and but these few, I sing thy birth, O Jesu! Thou pretty baby, born here With sup'rabundant scorn here: Who for thy princely port here, Hadst for thy place Of birth, a base Out-stable for thy court here.

Instead of neat enclosures Of interwoven osiers, Instead of fragrant posies Of daffodils and roses, Thy cradle, kingly stranger, As gospel tells, Was nothing else But here a homely manger.

But we with silks, not crewels, With sundry precious jewels, And lily work will dress thee; And, as we dispossess thee Of clouts, we'll make a chamber, Sweet babe, for thee Of ivory, And plaster'd round with amber.

*   *   *   *

Robert Herrick.

Old Christmas Returned

All you that to feasting and mirth are inclined, Come here is good news for to pleasure your mind, Old Christmas is come for to keep open house, He scorns to be guilty of starving a mouse: Then come, boys, and welcome for diet the chief, Plum-pudding, goose, capon, minced pies, and roast beef.

The holly and ivy about the walls wind And show that we ought to our neighbors be kind, Inviting each other for pastime and sport, And where we best fare, there we most do resort; We fail not of victuals, and that of the chief, Plum-pudding, goose, capon, minced pies, and roast beef.

All travellers, as they do pass on their way, At gentlemen's halls are invited to stay, Themselves to refresh, and their horses to rest, Since that he must be Old Christmas's guest; Nay, the poor shall not want, but have for relief, Plum-pudding, goose, capon, minced pies, and roast beef.

Old Carol.

Ceremonies for Christmas

Come, bring with a noise, My merry, merry boys, The Christmas log to the firing, While my good dame, she Bids ye all be free, And drink to your heart's desiring.

With the last year's brand Light the new block, and For good success in his spending, On your psalteries play, That sweet luck may Come while the log is a-teending.

Drink now the strong beer, Cut the white loaf here, The while the meat is a-shredding; For the rare mince-pie, And the plums stand by, To fill the paste that's a-kneading.

Robert Herrick.

Christmas in England.

Heap on more wood!—the wind is chill; But let it whistle as it will, We'll keep our Christmas merry still; Each age has deem'd the new-born year The fittest time for festal cheer; Even, heathen yet, the savage Dane At Iol more deep the mead did drain; High on the beach his galleys drew, And feasted all his pirate crew.

*   *   *   *

On Christmas Eve the bells were rung; On Christmas Eve the mass was sung: That only night in all the year Saw the stoled priest the chalice rear. The damsel donned her kirtle sheen; The hall was dressed with holly green; Forth to the wood did merry-men go, To gather in the mistletoe; Then open'd wide the baron's hall To vassal, tenant, serf, and all. Power laid his rod of rule aside, And Ceremony doffed his pride. The heir, with roses in his shoes, That night might village partner choose; The Lord, underogating, share The vulgar game of "Post and pair." All hail'd with uncontroll'd delight And general voice the happy night, That to the cottage, as the crown, Brought tidings of salvation down.

*   *   *   *

"England was merry England when Old Christmas brought his sports again. 'Twas Christmas broach'd the mightiest ale; 'Twas Christmas told the merriest tale; A Christmas gambol oft could cheer The poor man's heart through half the year."

Sir Walter Scott.

From "Marmion."

The Gracious Time

Some say that ever 'gainst that season comes Wherein our Saviour's birth is celebrated, The bird of dawning singeth all night long: And then, they say, no spirit dares stir abroad; The nights are wholesome; then no planets strike, No fairy takes, nor witch hath power to charm, So hallow'd and so gracious is the time.

William Shakespeare.

From "Hamlet."

Brightest and Best of the Sons of the Morning

Brightest and best of the Sons of the morning! Dawn on our darkness and lend us thine aid! Star of the East, the horizon adorning, Guide where our Infant Redeemer is laid!

Cold on His cradle the dewdrops are shining, Low lies His head with the beasts of the stall; Angels adore Him in slumber reclining, Maker and Monarch and Saviour of all!

Say, shall we yield Him, in costly devotion, Odors of Edom and offerings divine? Gems of the mountain and pearls of the ocean, Myrrh from the forest, or gold from the mine?

Vainly we offer each ample oblation; Vainly with gifts would His favor secure: Richer by far is the heart's adoration; Dearer to God are the prayers of the poor.

Brightest and best of the Sons of the morning! Dawn on our darkness and lend us thine aid! Star of the East, the horizon adorning, Guide where our Infant Redeemer is laid!

Reginald Heber.

THE END

Made in United States
North Haven, CT
30 March 2022

17686508R00076